UNCHARTED

I0808194

UNCHARTED

The New Landscapes Of Tourism

Translation	Illustration	Endnote ref.	Paragraph
Author	Subtitle	Endnotes	Quote
Graphic	Localization	End	Excerpt

ACTAR

UNCHARTED CONTENT

1

PRESENTATION

ON HIS MAJESTY'S 198 SECRET SERVICE

190 David Goodman

Director of Undergraduate Studies in Architecture, IE University

As a state institution we have obligations to the State of Texas. As a professional school we have obligations to the architects of Texas. Our still primary obligations are to our students. For the present we shall confine our discussion to our student obligations, which are two:

1. To equip the student with the skills necessary for the practice of his profession; and

2. To enable him to develop his powers of selection by the process of his own judgment.

Colin Rowe. Comments of Harwell Hamilton Harris to the Faculty of the University of Texas School of Architecture, 1954.

1. THIS IS REALLY HAPPENING

Architectural practice is under attack. By implication, so is architectural education. That the previous two sentences are—the author imagines—unlikely to shock or prove terribly controversial, only confirms the accuracy of the sentiment. A provisional consensus seems to be emerging that the architectural profession will be transformed radically in the coming years, whether or not architects themselves accept this fact or are willing partners in the transformation. Observations like these are sometimes accompanied by the assertion that the new order of things will inevitably (and, perhaps, fortunately) imply a diminished role for the architect, and that the disciplinary tools of architecture—while noble and worth conserving, if only for sentimental reasons—are at best unrelated to the new environment and, at worst, somehow antagonistic to it.

An alternate response to the current crisis in practice has been to defend the previous (imagined?) status of the architect and of architecture itself, strengthening and indeed developing new disciplinary tools either to keep architecture alive until the storm subsides, or to detach it from broader economic and social forces, thus preserving a pure sample of autonomous architecture culture, uncontaminated by the demands of the market and of the present conditions. The first approach outlined above suggests that the discipline of architecture can most effectively remain alive and relevant by dissolving itself almost entirely into direct action and citizen empowerment. This mode of action is usually linked to an explicit political critique and tends to use architecture, or what remains of it, as a vehicle or substitute for political activity, generating happenings and episodes of architectural and civic activism. This work inverts Le Corbusier's exhortation in the final pages of *Vers une Architecture*, coming down squarely on the side of Revolution, and concluding that Architecture can be avoided.

The architect, to the degree that he or she is present in this sort of work, is often a facilitator for urges and desires initiated elsewhere. Though no doubt effective and inspiring, the results discount the value of the disciplinary tools of architecture in favor of direct action, and perhaps more problematically, this approach tends to institutionalize opposition and the critical posture. That is, it assumes that the architect always operates in a mode critical of the status quo and therefore very frequently on the margins of the forces that actually shape it. A critical posture is one of many available to architects and students of architecture, and it is most certainly intended to address, or at least to protest, some of the most flagrant injustices of the day. Yet it would be a mistake to conflate a broader understanding of architectural practice solely with "emancipatory" approaches, or with the protest mode of action. And it would similarly be a mistake to limit students' understanding of the range of professional outlets available to those in the critical mode. Quite simply: our students ought to be free to man the barricades, but not obliged to do so.

The second approach described at the outset of this piece is essentially a version of the Adornian argument for autonomy and disciplinary purity: by refusing to engage the market and the broader social forces that condition architectural production, the argument goes, architects can keep their discipline authentic and alive, although, once again, condemned to the margins of everyday life. Such a position frequently leads to rich exploration of disciplinary tools, but in trying to avoid contamination by outside forces, it can instead lead to a sterile exploration of forms or processes without references to the very real demands being posed to the architectural profession, broadly understood.

What, then, is an architect—or an architecture program—to do in the face of the current turbulence?

2. SYSTEMATIC TRANSGRESSIONS

What, then, is an architect—or an architecture program—to do in the face of the current turbulence? If the challenge seems acute for those searching for ways to define their own practices, it is even more daunting for those of us who are engaged in the education of future architects, as our obligations are manifold: to the student, to the profession, and to the society of which both are part. How, then, to educate the architect for an uncertain professional future? And what is the role of disciplinary tools in that future? These have been the central questions and the overriding missions guiding the Undergraduate Architecture program at IE University, and these lines of inquiry were central to the Thesis work you see in the current volume.

Our approach has been to teach architecture as design entrepreneurship, based on a focused exploration of disciplinary tools combined with a broad understanding of what constitutes the future of architectural practice. Put succinctly, our goal is the following: to use disciplinary architectural tools to transgress disciplinary boundaries, and to make this transgression itself a structural and institutionalized element in architectural pedagogy. We pursue this goal throughout the five-year program by combining rigorous design education (our students receive their professional licensure in Spain immediately upon graduating) with training in management and entrepreneurship, and a three-year sequence of professional internships in architecture and related disciplines. But the approach is, perhaps, most evident in the fifth-year course sequence, and in the structure of Thesis program itself. The first semester of our students' fifth and final year is dedicated exclusively to a sequence of "Alternative Practices" workshops. Each of these workshops, undertaken one-at-a-time in a series of 3-week long modules, deals with a "misapplication" of the disciplinary tools learned throughout the core sequence of design studios and workshops, here directed toward subjects like Image and Simulation, Landscape and Environment, The City, Management and Entrepreneurship, or Design and Cultural Entrepreneurship. Each workshop is conducted like a short design studio, with students engaged in design projects ranging from the design of urban planning guidelines, to construction toys, to video games.

Upon concluding this sequence of workshops, fifth-year students begin the Thesis project semester documented here. The Thesis project is intended at once to include a comprehensive building design and an entrepreneurial proposal; our students define program and site, and link their individual projects to a broader agenda for regional revitalization through tourism.

In order to avoid the master-apprentice dynamic between student and thesis tutor, we assembled a team of design critics, studio professors and invited guests to create an atmosphere of debate in which the student is forced to choose among several viewpoints in order to form a project that responds both to an agenda or brief imposed from without (in this case, tourism in the declining mining regions of Asturias and León), as well as to an individual agenda.

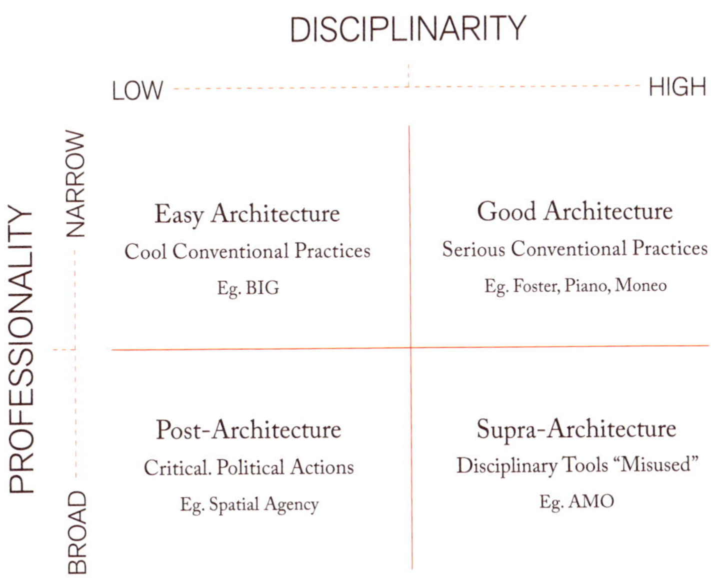

Figure 1: Professionality and Disciplinarity in Architecture Practices

3. SUPRA-ARCHITECTURE

In discussing the projects that appear in this volume, and in the IE University Undergraduate Architecture program in general, it may be productive to position the work within a matrix mapping the variables "disciplinarity" and "professionality" (Figure 1). For our purposes, disciplinarity refers to the degree to which the work is conceived and executed through the use of tools specific to the discipline of architecture, such as orthographic projection or mapping, while the term professionality will describe the breadth of professional outlets seen to be available to the architect.

A narrow definition of professionality, for example, might understand architectural practice to be limited primarily to the design of buildings and the built environment, while a broad definition might include design of a novel organizational structure, or the design of new modes of civic engagement, as well as the physical manifestations of this engagement.

Based on this matrix, we might classify (with only mild irony) as "Good Architecture," that work with a high degree of disciplinarity and a narrow definition of professionality. Here, we find the highly authorial work of the masters, catalogued in hardcover monographs, and recognized with international awards. The work of Foster, Piano, Moneo and Zumthor might well be located in this quadrant. Work of low disciplinarity and a narrow definition of professionality might be classified as "Easy Architecture," describing work such as that of the Bjarke Ingalls Group or Work AC, inhabiting the traditional limits of the architectural profession, but adopting something akin to the relaxed "projective" mode of production described by Robert Somol and Sarah Whiting in their 2002 essay "The Doppler Effect," rather than the labored and almost ostentatiously rigorous work of the "good" architect. The quadrant of low disciplinarity and professionality, which we might label "Post-Architecture," captures the critical, activist mode of production, wherein political efficacy is more important than authorship, form, language, or expression, and professional boundaries matter little. We might classify the work of Spatial Agency, EXZYT, or *Recetas Urbanas* within this quadrant.

Our obligation to serve the common good is no longer met if we solely train good architects.

I am most interested in the remaining quadrant. We could label as "Supra-Architecture" work of high disciplinarity and a broad conception of professionality. This work would apply the tools of the architect to problems not immediately or exclusively related to architecture. It would misuse architectural tools to maximum effect, and would ignore boundaries between professions. The work of OMA/AMO, in my opinion far more embedded in and dependent on disciplinary tools than is the work of its many offspring firms, might well be considered a Supra-Architecture firm, able to approach the design of a house, flag, or fashion show with the same disciplinary rigor and a profound disrespect of the boundaries between architecture and everything else. This is where one might classify the best of the work we see in this volume, and it is in this quadrant that I believe we ought to dedicate most of our efforts in architecture education.

4. HIS MAJESTY

The architectural degrees our students receive are not formally conferred by the Architecture degree program, nor by the University, nor the regional or Spanish governments, nor still the European Union. They are, in fact, granted to our students—a minority of whom are Spanish—by His Majesty the King of Spain. Officially, the work we do at this University is on his behalf, in the service of the common good. This essay began with an epigraph, ghost-written by Colin Rowe for Harwell Hamilton Harris, proclaiming the triple obligation of the architecture educator: to the state, to the profession, and to the student. In the current sociopolitical context, it is increasingly impossible to separate these obligations; an architect trained only to build is a burden on all three of these parties.

Our obligation to serve the common good is no longer met if we solely train good architects, though this is, officially, all that is asked of us. We must therefore work quietly, almost secretly, to expand the scope of these demands, without neglecting the most basic among them. We therefore focus intensely on our discipline, while assiduously ignoring the limits of our profession.

Today, Good Architecture is simply not good enough.

UNVEILING THE HIDDEN
WORK, FOLK, PLACE

2

METHOD

UTP IE: 140 DAYS AND 140 NIGHTS

Fernando Rodríguez, Pablo Oriol and Lina Toro
Directors of Undergraduate Thesis Projects IE University

TEACHING

"By osmosis." That was John Hejduk's response, in an interview at the beginning of the 1990s with his good friend the poet David Shapiro, when he was asked how he taught architecture. In his response, Hejduk added: "I bring out what the students have inside. I still feel like that's the only way to bring architects into society who really do work that can be considered architecture. [...] The process of teaching a student should be something more like in a laboratory. I mean, a process that, in working with reality, constantly dies and is reborn... understanding and accepting that there is no other truth than the possibility of learning from a mistake and not trying to hide it."[1]

UPDATING

At a time of necessary change, when architects are in the midst of a professional redefinition, it seems inevitable to question the methods and processes that have obscured the objective of the Undergraduate Thesis Project, which marks the endpoint of the university degree in architecture. As the profession is transformed and architects' battlegrounds multiply, there is no doubt that students' musculature needs to be built up at university with the aim of preparing them for future events.

We need to be suspicious of persistent teaching based on acquiring knowledge and learning about processes. Without a doubt, today it seems more useful and honest to promote individual criteria and freedoms; heightening abilities and passions that will allow future architects to surf with maximum agility through the height of surrealism that is reality.

PRODUCTION – PRODUCT

The IE Undergraduate Theses Project began in 2013 and was developed along the lines of the North American "studio culture" under the organization of three directors and a team of professors with a well-defined target. The organization is complex and multidirectional. The team includes diverse and contrasting professional profiles, intentionally chosen with the sole goal of reinforcing the criteria of future architects. This mixture always implies a certain risk factor but, as Hejduk said in his interview with Shapiro, "without this kind of challenges, you lose the chance nature of possibility, the element of doubt, the risk of failure" and of course, the success of moving forward.

INTENSITY

The greatest challenge of this UTP, however, has been conditioned as much by its multi-directionality as by the limited time allowed for its development and completion. The UTP is intended as high-intensity training, programmed for the short-term. During each of twenty weeks, marked by exercises with a particular objective according to the specificity of each project and each student, the program focuses on an architectural theme with the goal of producing a powerful document with high graphic quality and a detailed format. The goal is to construct a puzzle-project, structured through the accumulation and fitting together of the collection of pieces and specific architectural issues tested in each project. This non-linear method, adaptable to particular needs, allows students to tackle the project from different angles, establishing a protocol that is more like a lab experiment, where the project is strengthened by both necessary and inevitable successes and failures.

Those 140 days provide the opportunity for experimenting with essential content that reaches beyond the commitment of creating an architectural design.

It also involves the challenge of exploring the tangents that are vital to the project conception, such as organization, transmission and the communication of the idea: What kind of information is it that we really need? What types of documents are required for each specific project? Which documents and formats allow for providing information and transmitting our thoughts in different spheres?... These are all recurring questions in the current global university debate. That is why we commit to searching for the most direct, thrilling and powerful side of a design, to derive a carefully edited, specific manifesto from each one.

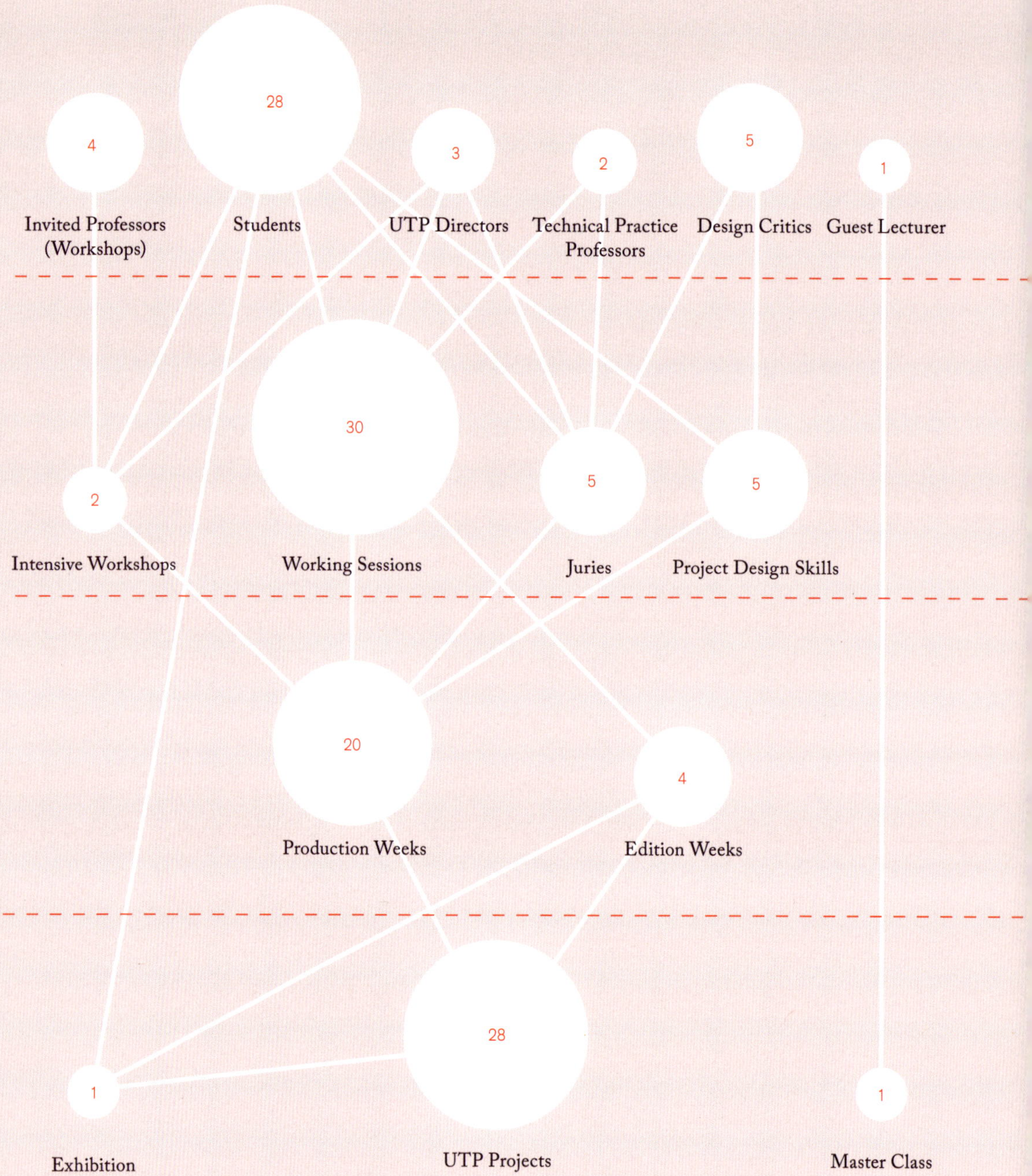
28
4
3
2
5
1
Invited Professors (Workshops)
Students
UTP Directors
Technical Practice Professors
Design Critics
Guest Lecturer
30
2
5
5
Intensive Workshops
Working Sessions
Juries
Project Design Skills
20
4
Production Weeks
Edition Weeks
28
1
1
Exhibition
UTP Projects
Master Class

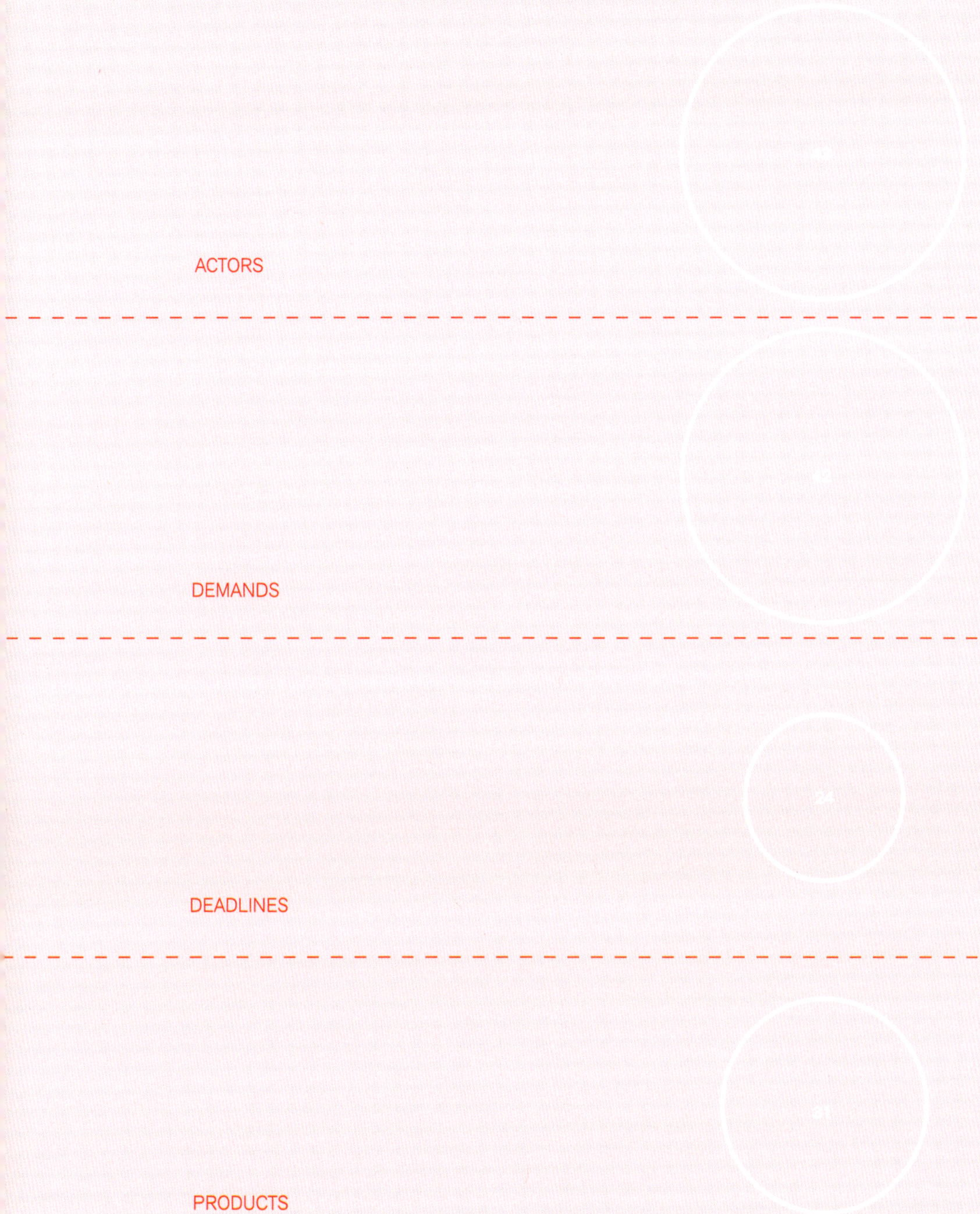

UTP Diagram organized and quantified by Actors, Demands, Deadlines and Products

SHOALING

The UTP is also a creative process, in which space and strategy are decisive factors. In order to achieve satisfactory results in this short period of time we adopt behavior that is similar to that of a shoal of fish: the UTP students move together, forming one organism with coordinated movements where their position defines their role and their personal goals.

The student swimming at the head, hungry and robust, directs the group's movements. Whoever chooses the risky sides opts for a personal and more creative position that is susceptible to many critiques, but which will no doubt be rewarded. In the center, the most timid positions shelter themselves but keep swimming all the same. The ones that follow behind use a smaller percentage of their energy, taking advantage of the slipstream as a survival tactic.

In this way, individual production has an impact on the overall development and vice versa. Each student tests his or her own limits within the powerful body represented by the UTP shoal.

COMMUNICATION

The students are faced with presenting their designs and exchanging opinions during the joint juries with the Design Critics, in what we interpret as training in coming to grips with their own ideas: presenting them, defending them and sorting through the feedback. The students also take specialized classes in Technical Practices. Just as with a professional project, they have advisors that benefit them and deepen their understanding of essential concepts related to important design decisions.

REWARD

The UTP is a commitment that closely resembles actual experiences in the profession itself and, without a doubt, it gives the students a taste of their first real work experience like professional architects in a firm. It is a complex and enriching situation, since it offers a dialogue that runs in different directions, which allows them to develop a rigorous design. The promotion and

The student swimming at the head, hungry and robust, directs the group's movements.

projection of this initial professional design is recorded through the edition and elaboration of the project material in a book and its display during a joint exhibition, *Finish Line*, which takes place at the end of the process. The best possible calling card is published in a format where, in addition to presenting the students' architectural designs, their specific skills and personal interests pinpointed at the beginning of a specialized presentation of each student's professional profile, with an eye to the job market.

The discovery of this other reality of the Thesis Project —one that is more versatile, dynamic and even pragmatic— becomes an exciting educational experiment, as students create a portfolio on a par with the strictest professional demands.

ACTORS, DEMANDS, DEADLINES AND PRODUCTS

BE WATER, MY FRIEND

The numbers that sum up the UTP IE 2013 are as follows: 28 students, 14 teachers, 20 weeks of production, 4 weeks of editing, 2 intensive introductory workshops of 15 sessions each, 45 design follow-up sessions, 30 technical practices sessions, 3 UTP directors, 4 guest professors as workshop directors, 2 technical practices professors, 5 design critics, 3 juries, 5 lessons in design skills, 1 exhibition, 1 formal lecture, 28 summary books, 28 final models, 28 projects handed in...

This numerical line-up lets us get a physical and temporal idea of what we have described above: the undergraduate Thesis Project as high-quality training, undertaken in a collective environment through the constant give-and-take between students and teachers with diverse backgrounds, allowing for osmotic learning as an update to previous teaching strategies and as pre-professional experience.

The density of actors, demands, deadlines and products requires a high degree of order and precision from teachers and an extraordinary exercise in rhythm, flexibility and adaptability from students. Over the twenty weeks,

122 — *Hypersensory Center* by Iñigo Arias Dávila

each student becomes a true Bruce Lee of the Undergraduate Thesis Project: "Don't get set into one form, adapt it and build your own, and let it grow, be like water. Empty your mind; be formless, shapeless —like water. Now you put water in a cup, it becomes the cup; you put water into a bottle it becomes the bottle; you put it in a teapot it becomes the teapot. Now water can flow, or creep, or drip, or it can crash. Be water, my friend."[2]

The total of 28 students includes the two groups—Spanish and English — from the first generation of architects trained at IE University. They have all worked their way through an ambitious undergraduate program that has prepared them to complete the UTP exercise successfully. They can begin their professional careers with the security of knowing they will be able to adapt to the professional demands they will face along the way.

DISTANCE RUNNING AND SPRINTING

The work began in January of 2013, with two initial workshops that lasted one week each. The first (January 14-18) was directed by Linna Choi and Tarik Oualoulou of KILO Architects and the second (January 21-25) by José María García del Monte and Laura Martínez de Guereñu.

On Friday, February 1, the weekly design follow-up sessions began, led by the three UTP directors. The Design Critics came onto the scene on February 15, during in the first combined group jury. The attendees were: Izaskun Chinchilla, Juan Elvira, Mónica García, Pedro Iglesias and Andrew Varela. From that moment on, the weekly rhythm became more intense, with Technical Practices sessions taught by professors Rafael Íñiguez and Manuel Pérez held every Tuesday until the end of May. In addition to the weekly sessions on Tuesdays and Fridays, the students received a series of lessons on design abilities—tools, concepts and methodologies—prepared by the five Design Critics for nine Wednesdays scattered throughout the course schedule.

On March 22 the second jury took place with the presence of the entire team of professors, marking the beginning of the final stage, which was more intense in terms of the workload and the number of sessions. Finally, as a climax to the production phase, for the final jury on May 31 the students prepared the best presentations of their designs in an effort to summarize all of their working formats—drawings, images, models, videos—taking advantage of their proposals' greatest strengths.

The hardest work had already been done. The month of June—with just one teaching session dedicated to identifying shortcomings and possible improvements—was used to complete the projects and edit all of the documents that had been generated. June 27 was the deadline for the final submission of the Undergraduate Thesis Project, accompanied by a book for each project that had been edited by the students themselves.

On the following day, June 28, Salvador Carmona, Dean of IE University, announced the opening of the Finish Line exhibition, including all of the work submitted by the students, held in the central cloister of Santa Cruz la Real in Segovia.

The icing on the cake was that, on that occasion, we had the pleasure of listening to a lecture given by Juan Herreros, head of the Design department at ETSAM and Chair Professor of Architecture at GSAPP-Columbia University, a speech filled with suggestions about architects, universities, architecture and the learning process.

1. This text is based on David Shapiro's interview with John Hejduk for the documentary film: John Hejduk. *Builder of Worlds*, © 1992, Michael Blackwood Productions Inc.

2. Lee, Bruce. *A Warrior's Journey*. Documentary by Warner Home Video, 2000.

IS INTEGRATION A NEW TEACHING 203 METHODOLOGY?

191 Manuel Pérez Romero

Technical Practices and Construction Systems Professor at IE University

> *"Whereas simplifying thought breaks up the complexity of reality, complex thought joins together symplifying modes of thought as much as possible."*[1]

It is worth explaining that one of the main reasons why the teaching of architecture is fragmented into different areas of knowledge is none other than a purely methodological reason. It is also important to remember that, although this training is developed on the basis of its parts, the final objective tends to be holistic. This seeming paradox is what has, to some extent, governed architectural instruction in Spain: we study the parts in order to comprehend the whole, although we know that the whole is more than just the sum of its parts. The current model for the UTP that is promoted here is based on a complex system directed at integrating the different areas of knowledge that an architect is expected to acquire. An architect's knowledge should not be compartmentalized, or divided, or reduced; it should be integrated.

Traditionally, architecture students have approached the UTP without the support of a clear teaching methodology. Suddenly and abruptly, students are asked to integrate all of the knowledge they have acquired throughout their university studies. But rather than basing it on an integrated system, the project is developed using an additive system—the result of the sum of the different areas that students are meant to demonstrate that they have understood and mastered.—Thus, the difficulty of dealing with a complex structure was reinforced with investing time and lots more time.

The challenge, then, is two-fold: on the one hand, to transform the UTP into an integrative system and, on the other, to reduce its length. Both factors are inherently related. With a more effective implementation of integration comes a greater reduction in the duration of the UTP.

In the specific case of the IE School of Architecture, the model for an integrated UTP is supported and promoted by the curriculum. Integration is present as a strategy throughout the entire degree program, in contrast to traditional course plans. In this sense, the UTP can be understood as the culmination of a process which begins during the first courses of the degree.

Fig. 1. Architecture: Traditional Plan of Studies

Fig. 2. Architecture: IE Plan of Studies

"IN-BOUND" INTEGRATION AND "OUT-BOUND" INTEGRATION

In general, integration systems can be classified in two groups: ones that are produced from within, and others that are brought in from the outside. In other words, "in-bound" systems and "out-bound" systems, respectively. Although a third model should be added, based on an overlapping of the two previous models. This last model is representative of the current UTP at the IE School of Architecture. Within the UTP, two professors with varying degrees of specialization organize the "in-bound" integration: one is dedicated more to design and the other to technical aspects, although the boundaries between the two are blurred. From the outside, a group of design critics manage the "out-bound" integration of the system. As such, the UTP is organized as a dual system that evolves both from within and from the outside. The UTP is the interstitial space between both integration models. A buffer space that is compressed and expanded in response to internal and external pressure. Thus, students should be prepared to encounter a non-linear teaching method that is based on the complex integration of knowledge. It would perhaps be useful to teach students to "surf" in between the "in-bound" and "out-bound" movements, seeing as this type of structure forces students to take on an open and flexible attitude. The traditional figure of the Thesis Project director is replaced by a complex system of relationships where each professor's role can be modified according to the demands of the project. Students may not refer back to a specific director, but they know who their coaches are.

INTEGRATION PROTOCOL

The short amount of time that students will dedicate to the UTP (compared to other architecture schools) makes strict adherence to an integration protocol a necessity. A large number of coaches for a UTP can create high noise levels, which students may be incapable of integrating. In order to muffle this more than probable noise and to achieve the spontaneous creation of an ordered structure, all of the professors must be coordinated through a schedule which takes all of the actors into account. What is more, the coordination should occur in a synchronized way. For example, if the "technical professors" come in too early, their work may be insubstantial, whereas if they come in too late, their contribution will consist only in verifying what has already been done.

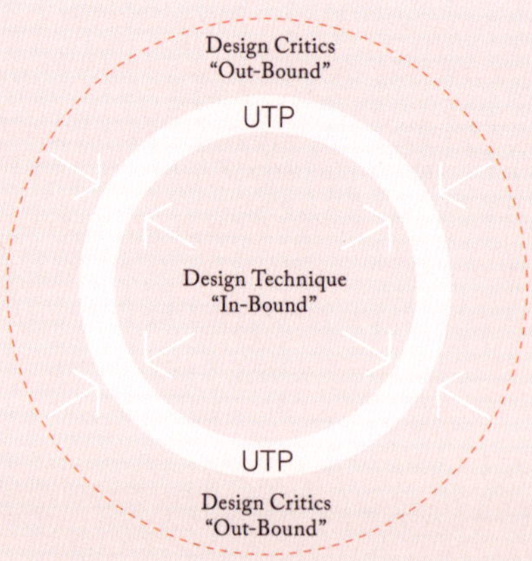

Fig. 3. Diagram showing the relationship between "in-bound" and "out-bound" integration models

...a complex system of relationships where each professor's role can be modified according to the demands of the project.

Cecil Balmond tells the story of how, when Rem Koolhaas called him to help define the structure for a house in Bordeaux, the two took a trip to the site to explore it together. Koolhaas wanted the house to float above the hill, looking out over the city of Bordeaux.[2] But considering the musculature required for floating, Cecil Balmond proposed a revision of the classical portico structure.

A soft and nuanced movement both vertically and horizontally. On the one hand, he shifted the axes of the porches outside the rectangle formed by the house's volume and, on the other, he emphasized the standing or hanging behavior of the structure. This example serves to illustrate the substantial capacity of any integrative system and how the decision about when technical components or other aspects should come into play is fundamental to the development of the design.

OMA's Maison à Bordeaux would never have been what it is without that early excursion between Balmond and Koolhaas. The rigorous planning undertaken for the UTP is focused on coordinating the integration of the different agents that intervene in the design process. On the other hand, however, the evolution of each student's project is highly variable, which requires precise organization that also needs to be flexible and adaptable. One of the metaphors that perhaps best illustrates the epistemology of complex thought is that of *navigating a sea of doubt amid islands of certainty.*

Those islands might represent the professors (though the intention is not to associate the professor with the truth, since students may always leave one island in search of another); while the number of islands, their location and distance will be defined by the integration method.

1. Morin, Edgar. *Introduction a la pensée complexe.* Thiron: ESF Éditeurs, 1990.

2. Balmond, Cecil. *Informal.* London: Prestel, 2007.

PRACTICING
TECHNOLOGY

204

191 Rafael Íñiguez de Onzoño
Technical Practices and Construction Systems Professor at IE University

> *"Young people go to university with the aim of becoming architects, of finding out if they have got what it takes. What is the first thing we should teach them? First of all, we must explain that the person standing in front of them is not someone who asks questions whose answers he already knows. Practicing architecture is asking oneseld questions, finding one's own answers with the help of the teacher, whittling down, finding solutions. Over and over again."*[1]

FORMAT

Technical Practices are part of an integration system defined as the Undergraduate Thesis Project, together with Design VII, the two introductory workshops for the UTP, and the individual sessions undertaken during the year, led by a group of Design Critics.

The TP sessions have been developed in workshop format, with the fundamental purpose of integrating the necessary technical material into the Undergraduate Thesis Project, based on the study and development of the technological aspects inherent in the proposed design. Deploying the knowledge that students have accumulated up to that point in order to establish their own voices, to tie their experiences together, allows for establishing the necessary connections between the different aspects of the Project from a professional dimension.

RESEARCH

The non-linear structure of the Workshop, closer to a true professional exercise than a strictly academic one, allows for engaging in a reflection that influences the evolution of the design concept through successive "circular approximations", with the idea of analyzing the different options at each point, in the search for the particular laws of the design. The student selects the tools for making decisions, in keeping with the conviction that the ultimate goal of a university education should be to teach students to teach themselves.

CONTENT

Based on a conceptual framework—tourism—and a common physical location for action—the Astur-Leonese basin—very different proposals were developed.

Accepting the limited usefulness of a strictly specific profile in terms of content, which is meant to be uniform across all designs, the initial conditions and the requirements for the final content of the projects were established from the outset through an essential set of themes:

TOPOS. Reading the place and the local determining factors as the true motor for the design proposal; the relationship with the terrain, understood as one of the areas in which architecture should develop the most sensitivity, allowed for multiple solutions: interventions that are firmly integrated into the land, as a part of it, shaping it, burrowing into it, floating above it, occasionally resting on it, submerged, suspended at the mercy of gravity... demonstrate the heterogeneity of convergence and divergence in the proposals.

ENERGY. ADAPTATION TO THE ENVIRONMENT. Explaining the proposal based on its behavior within its surroundings, the optimization of resources and the associated strategy, the use of passive systems for climate control and natural lighting... are decisive requirements when it comes to defining architecture in terms of energetic costs, achieved through the use of simple methods: reflecting sunlight, natural ventilation through convection, using the terrain as insulation...

STRUCTURAL SYSTEMS. It is necessary to emphasize the importance of the contribution of the structural component to the Projects in all of the exercises, including daring ideas that eschew the comfort of conventional solutions. Based on this tension, the Projects take advantage of structure's potential to enrich the architectural experience: the skeleton as a generator of spaces, beyond the primary function of transferring the load to the ground, as demonstrated once again by the wide variety of designs that include patterns based on grids, walls, lines, curves, membranes, etc.

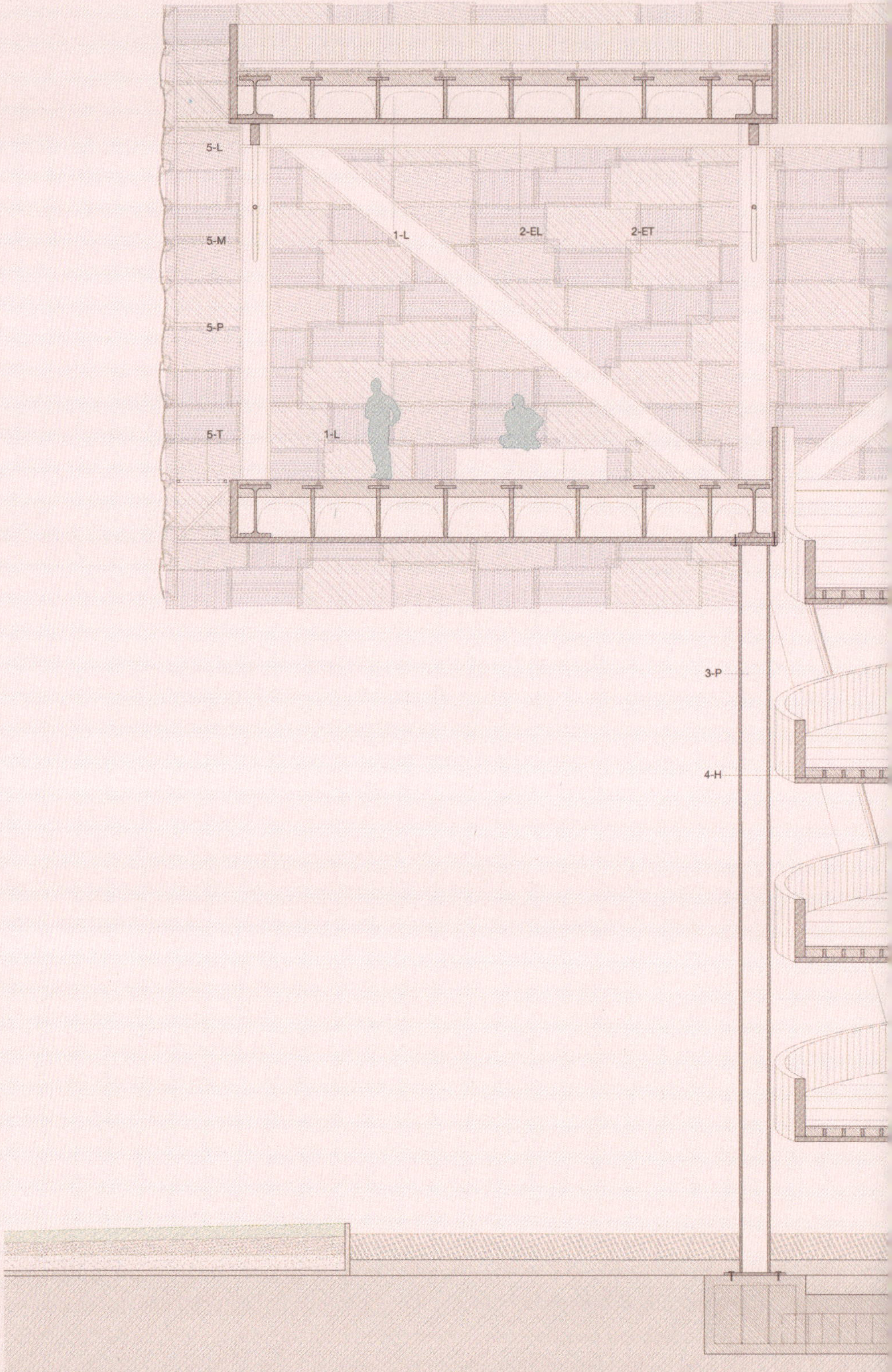

148 — *Car Museum* by Juan Moreno

MATERIALITY AND SYNTAX. The different strategies and scales of intervention on the site led to an equal number of different building approaches — from the forcefulness of using materials with a strong stereotomic component, establishing a dialogue with the terrain, containing it, to the option of selecting nearly weightless materials that float in the air— highligt the need to establish a material scenario and a specific design discourse for each project. The analysis of the unions between different materials and elements becomes an opportunity to test out the Project's validity.

OBSOLESCENCE AND EXPIRATION, PERMANENCE. Working on pre-existing architecture or sensitive physical frameworks determined the permanent character of certain proposals and the temporary or ephemeral nature of others, and it became an especially decisive factor in the explanation for certain designs, which were based on proposals that hinged on the scalability of the buildings or their total reversibility.

BUILDING PROCESS. Planning a suitable strategy for executing the exercise as a reflection that analyzes and detects the possible difficulties that might emerge during the development and conclusion of the Project, if it were to be built.

Finally, the intensity and commitment of the students should be recognized, no doubt shared by all of the professors who participated in the course, in facing up to the challenge they were given. Despite the initial uncertainty, since this was the first group of students to take on the new UTP project, the response was very positive, based on an attitude that was innovative from a number of angles (program, use, viability, suitability) and which we could interpret as part of the architect's "responsibility": an openness to new environments and disciplines.

1. Zumthor, Peter. "Teaching Architecture, Learning Architecture," in *Thinking Architecture*. Zurich: Lars Müller Publishers, 1998.

Deploying the knowledge that students have accumulated in order to establish their own voices allows for establishing the necessary connections between all proffesional aspects of the project.

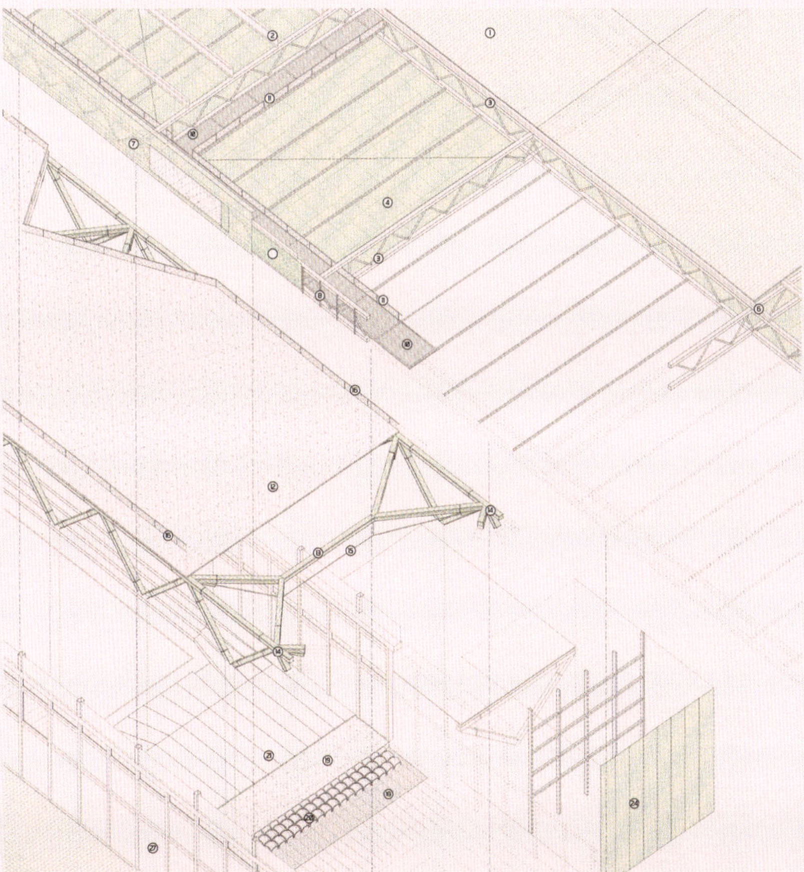

Sports Center by César Gusano —110

REALITY MAKES THINGS 206 FANTASTIC

192 Eleni Gigantes and Elia Zenghelis, in conversation
190 with David Goodman

I meet with Eleni Gigantes and Elia Zenghelis in the inevitably spectacular golden haze of a late Athens afternoon. My hosts are waiting for me in the terrace of a bar across the street from the Athens Hilton, and I arrive a bit out of breath after having walked too briskly from Plaka, across Syntagma Square—where the entire Greek National Police force seemed to be marshaled in anticipation (or provocation?) of anti-Troika protesters—past the presidential palace and the remnants of the 1896 Olympic games, down a busy boulevard choked with smog and French hatchbacks, and through a quiet neighborhood of sturdy and dignified neo-modernist 1960s housing blocks, where roughly half of the street-level storefronts stand empty and for rent.

I am greeted with a sincere warmth and familiarity that feels at once entirely natural and somehow surprising, as I have never before met Eleni, and have only met Elia once, a few months earlier, for a lecture and jury in Segovia.

At some point in our conversation, I take an absurdly large microphone out of my bag, turn it on, and we begin to discuss the first of the many questions I'd prepared. This is the only one of those questions we would address, as the conversation moves in fascinating turns I'd not anticipated, complete with brief engagements with psychic healing, Communists, snakes, and exploding mountains. Through it all: a focus on tourism, territory, infrastructure, and the possibility of intelligence in planning.

It is dark and we are hungry by the time I put the microphone away.

DAVID GOODMAN: I wanted to start by talking about the modern movement and tourism, because you could argue that they were born together. That is, I think you could make a case that a new model of tourism appeared more or less contemporaneously with the modern movement, and to some degree they come out of the same kind of hygienist ethos, and for a while, the same impulses that led to mass housing would lead to the phenomenon of mass leisure, the ability to have leisure time, and to even consider the possibility of going somewhere to enjoy it. All of this really does develop alongside the development of modern architecture. And to some degree, the same social motivations propelled the development of both. In fact many of the early moderns, like André Lurçat or even Le Corbusier are responsible for some very interesting projects dealing with tourism. But something happened along the way. I think it's safe to say that today, or in the century since the advent of modern architecture, we no longer necessarily see the link between tourism and an architecture of certain ambition. What happened? That is, if there was a divorce—and of course my question presumes that there was—how and why did the central current of Modern Architecture move away from dealing with tourism?

ELIA ZENGHELIS: So you mean the divorce between modernism and tourism? Well, the interesting thing is that—at least here in Greece—the opposite happened. Which is to say, modernism and modern architecture became part of the everyday. I mean you can see that the whole of Athens is based on this typical apartment block which is all around you. It is a byproduct of modernism. In fact one of the first archetypal apartment blocks in the center of Athens was admired by Le Corbusier.

But whereas modernism adopted these things that Athens is made of—this kind of pixel of Athens—with tourism, modernism, that is, quality modernism, was adopted. And most of the projects done for tourism in Greece, at least historically, were high-quality modernist. There is one particular architect, but there are more, who exemplifies that movement: Aris Konstantinidis. It's very interesting that there was no divorce, at least in Greece. On the contrary, there was a reinforcement of what is best about modern Greek architecture with tourism. It was a marriage.

GOODMAN: So what you're saying is that tourism is one of the places where a modernist ethic can still be observed?

ELENI GIGANTES: Not necessarily now, no. This was in the first period of tourism in Greece, which started in the 1950's. And that was a very specific program. What happened was that after the Second World War, Greece immediately plunged into a Civil War. And that finally ended in 1949, and it ended decisively. It was basically a fight about whether Greece would become Communist or not, but actually what had happened is that during the German Occupation, the true government of Greece had exiled itself to Cairo, and we had a Quisling government here that was collaborating with the Germans. And so most Greeks didn't agree with that and they took to the hills, and they formed resistance units, or brigands. Now, Greece has almost no plains. It's islands and mountains; highlands and islands. And some of it is quite impenetrable. And so the Greeks knew that territory. And the Germans, of course, didn't. Now, of the brigands, they divided themselves into those who were left behind who were not Communist, and then, the most effective ones organized themselves as Communist units. But more important than that, they went into the towns and they organized in the towns, and brought food to the people, because the Germans were taking the food away and sending it to Germany; 300,000 people died in Athens in one winter alone, in 1942. There was a terrible famine. And so while the proper government was in Cairo, the Communists basically made society function.

ZENGHELIS: The countryside was functioning very well because to the Germans it was inaccessible. And it was functioning in a very fair, and one could even say, very democratic way. It was communistic. Whether or not it would have stayed so, if the Communist Party had come to power, and then we had become part of the Eastern Bloc, is another matter.

GIGANTES: But basically what happened is that after the war, the Communists had made the state survive, made the Greeks survive, and the Greeks were very grateful to them. The government came back, and the miracle at Yalta had happened, that Greece would be in the western bloc.

ZENGHELIS: The deals were very....politically cruel.

GIGANTES: So what actually happened was that originally the British were to run Greece, not the Americans. But Britain was bankrupt, had no treasury. So in the first year of the Civil War they were here, but then they basically handed it over to the Americans to control. And so, what were they doing?

They were the ones who were supporting and giving aid to the non-Communist forces, because Greece was destined to be in the West. And the thing was that of the Communists, yes, some of them were practicing Stalinist Communists with all of the ideology. But others were just people who had joined because that was their village, or their group of villages, and that's how you survived. And it was the bread line, the food line, etc. Anyway, it was rather terrible, and in the end, the first jets ever developed were used in the Greek Civil War, we'll show you where, on Vasilisis Konstantinou, that side, was the non-Communist lines. And this side was the Communist lines.

ZENGHELIS: Vasilisis Konstantinou used to be a river, and there was a clear division. One side of the river was Communist, and the other side was British.

GIGANTES: And then American. So, the British had developed this jet.

ZENGHELIS: The Meteor.

GIGANTES: And they were tried out here in Greece. And they were tried out by bombing that green hill next to the Olympic Stadium, because that's where the Communists had buried their arsenal. And Elia, actually, lived on the other side.

ZENGHELIS: They would come down in front of our apartment. I would see the fire, the strafing, coming in front of the jets, and they would go like this. We had never seen anything like it: a jet!

GIGANTES: Nobody had. Greece saw jets for the first time.

ZENGHELIS: One day they hit the arsenal.

GIGANTES: The hill exploded.

ZENGHELIS: The hill blew up. We lived in a fairly solid modern apartment block. Everything broke. Everything inside broke. All our shelves, China, pictures. Everything.

GOODMAN: There's something you said that I want to tie back into the question of tourism. There was a moment where—and this is not related to tourism specifically in the case you mentioned—where inhabiting the landscape led to some sort of identity. The Greeks knew the landscape and the Germans didn't. The Greeks could disappear into the landscape, but the Germans couldn't follow them. It is that landscape that allowed the nation to survive, in a way. Certainly in terms of internal tourism, identity and landscape have been used to create nationhood, an idea of national identity, when it may never have really existed. So certainly in terms of an internal market, I think tourism has been used that way. Yet there's a more complicated relationship when it's incoming, or external, tourism. There's a very difficult relationship because it depends on a kind of hyper-defined caricature of an identity, right? The German or the British tourist wants to see a certain vision of Spain, for example, when they come to visit, and this vision may or may not actually correspond to the real Spain. Yet it needs to be provided nonetheless, to keep them pleased and to keep them coming back.

ZENGHELIS: Well, in the early years, Greek tourism was very much a cultural sort of thing. It was to visit important sites of antiquity and combine that with good weather and warm blue sea.

GOODMAN: That's quite different, of course, from what we see today. This morning, I was reading the in-flight magazine on Aegean Air, and what you see in every single advertisement in the entire magazine is an image of the horizon, the coastline, and an infinity pool. There's not a single picture of anything of antiquity.

GIGANTES: I know. It makes me vomit. First of all, no true lover of the Mediterranean wants a swimming pool. This is for the tourist from the North. I mean, you've got the sea there. Why this pool?

ZENGHELIS: However the recent issue of "Blue" is quite interesting. Because it doesn't have Athens or the Acropolis, OK, but what it does have is a lot about the islands.

GOODMAN: That's true. It seems to me, based on a very limited sample, of course, that the islands are quite present in the Greek consciousness. I've been here now for only eight hours. In the taxi, in the reception of the hotel, the woman cleaning my room in the hotel, they all said to me within 60 seconds of meeting me: "Athens is nice, but you have to see the islands." So it seems just initially to me that the islands are very present, even in the city.

GIGANTES: Yes. Actually, something else is very present but the summer tourists don't do it, and that's the mountains. And the real thing, the great tourist itinerary for Greece is to come to Athens, to go to Delphi, go to Meteora, and then you go to the Peloponnesus, and that's where everything is.

But I'd like to go back to what you said initially. And we have responded first by talking about Greece. I have spent my whole career working on this subject, and what I'd like to point out is that mass leisure arose with mass industry. The two went hand in hand, and this goes back actually to the 19th century. Even the Olympics arose out of this. For the first time you had world's fairs, that was something very spectacular. Look at the Chicago World's Fair. And the English had theirs, with the Crystal Palace of 1851, and so suddenly you were having these very large-scale mass events and people would cross the ocean in liners to visit the great exhibitions. This was huge. And at the same time, sport was becoming a mass activity. So this is very important for the Olympic movement. We were beginning to see these mass sporting events, like boxing, or like cycling, but they were all rigged. So Baron de Coubertin, who was this very protestant Frenchman, who was offended that the beauty and integrity of sport was being destroyed by money, basically. And that was one of the motivating forces for creating the Olympics, which was actually created by all the royal families of Europe. It was created from on high, and the idea was to re-institute the ancient Greek idea of the Olympics of peacetime, and then it's also about the healthy body and healthy mind that the English had developed, actually.

The thing is that tourism is something quite different from mass leisure. And tourism was always a very expensive thing. Mass leisure was living in Manhattan and being able to go to the beach at Far Rockaway, on the train, for the day, and come back. That's mass leisure. But there was no mass tourism, literally, until 1970. Why 1970? Because that was the year the jumbo jet appeared. And literally, there was no mass tourism before that. So, the idea of tourism before that time was cultural tourism.

ZENGHELIS: The '70s was also the apotheosis of the economic blossoming of capitalism, after the '50s in the west, and after that you start having series of economic crises that led to the present situation.

GIGANTES: I'm going to explain the Greek case to you. What happened was after the Civil War ended in 1949, America realized that Greece was the southeastern Mediterranean limit of its hegemony, Turkey and Greece. Greece had been literally destroyed by the Germans. As they left, they blew up everything. Everything. Every port, every road, every bridge. And it wasn't such an advanced country before. So, then the Civil War had been fought in the ruins. And so the Americans developed, before the Marshall Plan, the Truman Doctrine, which meant in part that America would send money to Greece and Turkey. And it was different from the Marshall Plan, which was more lend-lease oriented, you know, selling American products. This was literally rebuilding these countries, Greece especially, so that they could function. Turkey is another subject. But Greece, for example, had the great ports. And so the American naval bases were here. And so they gave a large sum of money to rebuild Greek infrastructure. And the very clever government at the time said, "OK, we're going to do that."

"But along with this, we're going to piggy-back onto it a plan for tourism." Now actually, that wasn't so extravagant. It wasn't like they were cheating the Americans. For example, to the main sites—Epidaurus, Meteora—they were building highways and roads, so actually they would build a paved road to that tourist site.

GOODMAN: Was the plan just to build the infrastructure, or to add tourist infrastructure to other infrastructure that was being built?

ZENGHELIS: You see, the Prime Minister at the time was a freak about infrastructure. He just built roads.

GIGANTES: He built roads, he built ports, he built facilities for electrification...

ZENGHELIS: That was aligned with this idea that Eleni has talked about, in tourism, which was linked, strangely, to an insurance company, Astir, which was created for this, and it was a branch of the Bank of Athens, back then. And Astir started building a series of beach resorts.

GIGANTES: So actually what happened was not only did they favor that electrical installations and water installations and road installations would to go those points that tourists that would come would want to see, but they realized that they had no infrastructure like hotels or anything like that, so they did a marvelous thing in that moment, in 1950, it was a watershed year, when the money from the Americans first arrived. What they did was to create the Ministry of Culture. And in the Ministry, there were two branches: there was the branch of archeology, and the other was the department of tourism. And so, of course, the two were completely aligned. And it was conceived of in this way: that the main archeological sites would have next to them a beautiful hotel, to the most modern standards, and modern roads going there for the tourists. None of this existed. If you were going there before, you'd be in tents, drinking from a brook, or a well, if you were lucky.

So they had to invent this infrastructure. And so they looked to Spain, because Spain in the '30s had started the idea with the Paradores, and had needed tourism. And Spain had looked around, and of course Spain has all this magnificent medieval architecture, which Greece doesn't. We have nothing. We're ancient, and modern. That's it. We have nothing in between. We have a few Byzantine churches, and the remains of some Byzantine buildings, but not much. So we didn't have what Spain has. So they looked at Spain and they did essentially the same thing, except that they didn't have the castles and forts and things that are the Paradores, so they said, "OK, we don't have that, but we'll do the infrastructure, and the electricity, just like Spain, and what we're going to do is we're going to have a program for architecture to have the most beautiful modern architecture from the best architects, and in each of these sites we go there and we choose the best site for the hotel."

ZENGHELIS: That was the difference with Spain. Because they selected specific points, rather than whole lines. And then, they legislated and extremely tough legislation where it became impossible to build anything along the cost. And that saved the Greek coastline.

GIGANTES: And it saved Greece.

ZENGHELIS: It saved the Greek coastline from becoming....

GOODMAN: From looking like Valencia?

ZENGHELIS: Exactly. And now they've passed legislation...

GIGANTES: Well, that's a scandal. That's troika. We'll get back to that. So actually in Greece, everyone has access to the coastline by law. I think it's European law. You can have no private coast, like in America. All building has to start a minimum of 50 meters from the coast, and if it's 50 meters back from the coast, it can only be 9m high. Progressively as you go back you can get higher.

ZENGHELIS: Even so...Even so...50 meters back it has to be in a zone where building is permitted. And if it's not a zone where building is permitted, nothing can be built.

GIGANTES: Not even a shack. You can have a temporary structure on the beach. Meaning you can have some electrical wires coming down to a refrigerator. But it has to go, at the end of summer.

Anyway, around this time, they created a whole government infrastructure, and one branch was for archeology. And with that, they created an archeological school, for guides. Meaning that they trained their guides. And it was a 2 year course. Very, very intensive. And also what they did is that all the various foreign universities that were working here, like the Americans who were working in the stoa, and so on, and they were working randomly—they were private archeologists from different countries—they forced them to work in schools. This was the American school, that's the Canadian school, that's the

Danish school of archeology – that's what they're called here. It doesn't really mean that it's a school. It really means, "institute". And they had to work with the Greek state. So every single archeological site is actually of course owned by Greece and it has its Greek archeologists, but it's handed over to the Americans or whomever, who dig, but it's overseen by the Greek archeologists. It actually works very well, there's never been a problem.

What they did on the tourism side apart from brining the infrastructure to the sites, and cleaning up the sites, and arranging all the workings and access to the sites on the archeological side. Was that they invented two hotel chains: Astir and Xenia. Astir is a five-star, and Xenia is a three-to four star.

ZENGHELIS: Xenia was also financed by Astir. And, as Eleni said, they thought, "OK, we'll appoint good architects."

GIGANTES: The best. So what happened is that this great architect, Konstantinidis, was put in charge of the architectural office, and he was the one who appointed what he thought were the best architects.

GOODMAN: And this was for inbound tourism, primarily?

ZENGHELIS: Well, Xenia, the name, comes from *philoxenia*, which is "hospitality".

GIGANTES: And *xenos* is "stranger" or "foreigner". And *philo*, is "friend". So it's the friendship of the foreigner, or of the stranger. And who were the people that came? At that time to live in England and think of going to Greece was like living in Brazil today and to think of going to Cambodia. It's a huge trip and you have to be well off. So actually only the very rich travelled. And the ones who came to Greece were the ones who were interested in the ancient culture. And so this was perfect for them.

GOODMAN: So it's the people who would have gone on the grand tour.

GIGANTES: Yes. It's like the modern grand tour. And they came on cruise ships, usually.

Anyway, what Konstantinidis did was he appointed great architects for these sites. Some of the sites are not so interesting, but they're always good.

And others are truly spectacular. They're so beautiful. And he himself, did many. So, perhaps you know Epidaurus was the great theater. You know, one thing I didn't know until my aunt told me—my aunt is a tour guide, and I always thought of Epidaurus just as a theater—and she said, "no, Eleni, actually from ancient times it's been a spa." It's been a medical center, because Asklepios had his wells there. You know the sign of the doctor, with the snakes? That's him. And Hippocrates, of the doctors' oath, was trained in the tradition of Asklepios. So actually what happened was before even the classical times, Greeks would come from all over to this site, Epidaurus to drink the waters and to be cured, so in fact it's a huge site and the ancient part of this site has this kind of amazing healing place, where people would go in for the night.

First, they would be cleansed, and they would go in for the night, and something very mysterious would happen with snakes, but it seemed to be a psychic healing. And they were healed. But there are hotels, or something like motels, all around the site. And then, they understood that the psychic healing could be pushed faster with theatre. And this coincided with the rise of the great tragedians. I don't know if you know any of the great Greek tragedies. Terrible. Horrifying. A mother eating her children, you know. And so they built the theatre. And so the idea was you would stay there for, let's say, two months; you would go to the theatre, you would go home, alone. You always slept alone, that was part of the healing process, and you had dreams that were cathartic to your psychology, and that healed you. These extreme dramatic situations precipitated your own drama and you could become psychically healed. So actually theatre was first tied to medicine as a kind of psychic catharsis, a healing.

GOODMAN: And there was this actual, physical, place where this would happen?

GIGANTES: Yes, in Epidaurus. You go there, and there's a huge site, and people only know the theatre, but you see the hotels and the healing spa, and then close to the sea, is the theatre. And the special rooms for Epidaurus were done by Konstantinidis himself. He was a great architect. And what's so fascinating about these rooms, is how he designed the rooms. Each room was for two people. But I was not a room in which you would leave the theatre, go and get drunk and have sex. No. It was like you would have this profound experience in the theatre. And then he replicated the cathartic rooms of healing in these beautiful series of rooms built into the landscape. And so each room is something like two and-a-half meters wide and five meters long. Two beds, very narrow, one after the other. A very narrow place just to hang your clothes, and it was specifically designed for this. It was unpopular for tourists, and now they just use it for the acting troupes and the people working on the archeological site. He was always just using natural materials, and he was just this calm structures guy, you always see the exposed concrete. Beautiful. It's just so Greek.

And what's so interesting about the Kalambaka one, when you go to Metora, it's this freaky landscape. It's got these strange pop-up hills and then on top there are monasteries. And so in the town of Meteora, you're below, and the monasteries are up like that. And what he does is that he just tilts the roof of the hotel's main lobby, so that you have before you the whole of Meteora like a picture. The weird landscape and the strange monasteries on top.

So what we had, from all of this, basically from the American Truman Doctrine, we had a golden age of architecture in Greece. Actually, they produced this amazing modern architecture in Greece that later went into the cities. But basically it all came to an end with the Junta.

ZENGHELIS: Now, look, this is the Hilton. (Points across the plaza). It's very beautiful. It's been spoiled, but it has a very beautiful lobby.

GOODMAN: It's Saarinen, no?

GIGANTES: Saarinen sketched it, and it was done by well-meaning Greek architects but what it has is that wonderful '60s generosity of lost space. You know, just space where you can breathe.

GOODMAN: Sure. Do you know the original Fontainebleau Hotel in Miami Beach, by Morris Lapidus? It has this mezzanine that only exists so that you can be seen coming down the stairs from it. It has an elevator in the lobby that goes up to a little platform with a grand stair which you can be seen descending. That's it. That's the only reason the stair and the mezzanine exist: so you can be seen.

GIGANTES: Well, I like to think that this is a little better than that! The beauty and generosity of the '60s. It was a whole ethos. And with it was this kind of splendid ease about space, and indoor/outdoor space. And so Saarinen came and he designed the old airport, and he was invited to give his ideas for the new Hilton. He managed to do it on the back of an envelope or something, god knows, and he came up with this first idea of a boomerang beholding the whole landscape. And behind all the mountains of Athens, and it's spectacular.

GOODMAN: Now...that shape, that boomerang. In your work, it seems like it may have been in your head. Maybe you weren't aware of it, or maybe you were. But now that I see this hotel, I see it in your work, all over the place. The Hilton is there, somehow.

GIGANTES: Yeah, of course. That's true, but strangely enough that wasn't the one. I originally studied biochemistry, actually. I loved nature and gardens and I loved architecture but my falling in love with architecture was Saarinen. And that was when he had just built that wonderful airport in Washington, Dulles. And I think about a month after it opened, my parents were coming back from the Caribbean and I was about six years old and I remember: we were driving down this straight road, and there it was in the distance and all you could see was this flat roof, and you could see through it! And I thought, "This is beautiful." And the planes were coming down behind it, and you could see the planes! That day, somehow the light was shining and you could see. It was an ur-moment for me. It was, "Wow!" So this was my idea of architecture from the beginning.

And so I didn't know when I left bio-chemistry if I should go into landscape or into architecture, and I decided architecture would give me more tools, and I could always do landscape. And the people I really loved during the time I was at school were very unfashionable, Saarinen, of course. Roberto Burle Marx, and that was before he became so fashionable. Geddes. Affonso Reidy. I was obsessed with him. More than Niemeyer actually, because Niemeyer has sometimes a too-easy looseness. But he's great, too. And Reidy only did a few projects.

GOODMAN: Actually, you know, I was going to bring that up —I think you see a lot of that Niemeyer casino, the Pampulha Casino, in your work as well.

GIGANTES: Well the funny thing is that I did that work before really knowing that casino. Actually, Reidy was the person who taught me about geometry. And Elia is the other person. He is amazing with geometry. I would draw something, and I would say, "I want it like this." And he would literally sit there with a compass. And long compasses and short compasses. They were very accurate drawings I was giving him, but he would make them perfectly accurate. With all the center points and joining points so that we could draw the second line, the thickness, so there would be a template, because of course this was ink drawing. So, he's a genius.

GOODMAN: And these are the things that look free and loose, and that are imitated by people imitate without necessarily having that discipline.

GIGANTES: Well, the thing is that architecture only works in geometry. And I don't know if you've seen this Ashikita that I did. It's a Japanese resort. Well, every Japanese prefecture has a House of Youth, in the most privileged spot, far from the cities. And they build dormitories and another building where they can do lectures and art projects, building projects, and activities. So our house of youth was in Ashikita, in the south of Japan, and it's semi tropical. On Kysushu.

When I started the project, I thought of it. I wanted them to feel that they're camping under the sky. It's like a tent. So I originally started it like this Frei Otto thing, but more accurate in the curves, with a three-dimensional tenting system. And of course when I went to present it in Japan, it turns out that there are only local builders. So I said, "Forget it." I understood that I had to make a two dimensional thing. And, of course, it was fantastic. Reality always makes things fantastic.

But what was fascinating was they didn't know how to start building it. They could figure out the setting out points for the ground. That was standard. But how do we calculate the roof? So actually we had this amazing drawing looking at the roof straight on, and how far it comes down and every single beam is calculated from the ground: "this beam is 6.73 meters from the ground, this one is 8.51 meters from the ground." That's literally how they build it. So actually now that I see this computer programing for three dimensional things, it's quite interesting because truly geometry makes things beautiful. I mean, I don't know if you consider that beautiful, but it's strange. It has an impact.

GOODMAN: So today on the airplane over here, I was reading in the *New York Times* about how, as the United States pulls combat troops out of Iraq and Afghanistan, all of this excess military hardware is showing up in local police departments. So suddenly, a town in Wisconsin has, for example, a tank. Or an armored personnel carrier that they never asked for. And of course, they have to use it, because they have it. Or instead of riot gear, they have body armor that was designed for combat. So all of this hardware designed for foreign occupation is basically coming home. And it was never meant for that, but ultimately it ends up getting deployed on the local population.

This is the negative version, maybe of what's possible with tourism. That is, tourist infrastructure is, perhaps, only incidentally meant for the local population. But is there a possibility of a bleeding off of benefits? You create these little microcosms of an ideal world.

A hotel is an extremely idealized vision of housing, to some degree. Just as that machinery of war can have a negative sort of bleed-over into daily life, can tourism lead to that idealized vision being eventually applied to everyday life?

GIGANTES: Ok, there's two things, to answer you. The other thing I didn't mention was something that my father was specifically in charge of, as Culture Minister, which was the islands. So, we had this very high-end modern architecture, which actually is extremely modest and the idea is in the generosity of space, like in the Hilton. The internal spaces are usually rather small, but the indoor/outdoor spaces, are very beautiful architecture. And that bled off into basically cafés in good places, private homes, and that kind of thing. But it didn't affect the main architectural thinking. What did affect it was that the islands were, from the beginning very heavily policed, architecturally. Every single year, they had to repaint everything white, by law. And nobody could build modern things, and any new buildings on the islands had to be like fake old buildings. So in the Ionian, which has pitched roofs and the red tiles, everything new had to have that also. In in the Aegean, where you see white cubes, everything new needs to be a white cube, and you can't go over a certain height. So actually, what's interesting is that over time, the islands have acquired tons and tons of living spaces which are empty in winter. Some islands go up to 10,000 people in the summer and they go back down to 500 people in the winter. And not only that but there had to be a whole infrastructure for the islands, and they also made tourist police, police that spoke English, and that took care of the tourist.

ZENGHELIS: And now they're learning Russian, and they're giving Russian lessons to restaurant owners and shopkeepers.

GIGANTES: But there's another problem, because you have these little islands that had somehow their own self-sustaining economy, but very basic, right? And then suddenly you have these very sophisticated tourists coming in. And so what happened was that you had to build electrical power lines under the sea to each island, but major ones. Because of course every hotel had to have air conditioning. The Greeks don't need air conditioning in the summer on the islands, but the English or the Germans come into their rooms and they turn on the air conditioning, and worst of all, they go for the day, and they leave the air conditioning on. So horrendous, you know?

And another thing is water. A lot of these islands don't really have enough water, so it was always a limit to their population. So in fact, some islands, like

Hydra, have very little water. It's a dry island. But to all of these islands, all of them, these tankers come dragging water, twice a week. So there's an infrastructure where electricity is supplied, where water is brought by boat, where food is brought by boat, where frozen fish from Spain and from the Atlantic is of course flown in.

And what happens if there are accidents? So there's a whole infrastructure of emergency helicopters because all of the islands are basically a half-hour helicopter ride from the main trauma hospital in Athens. And so from the beginning, every island or group of islands had an emergency helicopter that could fly accident victims within half an hour to the roof of the main accident hospital. So there's this whole invisible infrastructure that goes behind these supposed beautiful minimal islands, untouched by humans. Incredible.

And also you go to the islands and you see shops everywhere. But there are a lot of Greeks who made their living by being on the islands from the beginning of May to the end of October, with shops. And whatever the earned in those six months had to last them through the winter. They would come back to Athens, with their stuff. The shops were shut for the winter. They paid the bills during the winter, and they would come back and they'd work like crazy, from morning to night, selling things.

So there's this whole strange life that's behind the reality of the islands, at tourist season, they come and it's delightful: there's air conditioning, there's water, you can have showers, there's all these lovely shops that are open until midnight, you can wander the streets after eating. But all of this shuts down and it goes. So actually the winter version of the islands is completely different, and on some of the tiny islands, and also in the mountains, in remote villages and islands their children spend the week in another place. On the islands, they go by ferry to the bigger island, and in the mountains, they go by bus to the bigger town, and they live in dormitories during the week and they go to school. And on the weekends they're bused or ferried back.

Greece has the most airports in Europe. There's no way you can get to Athens to Ioannana except for driving fourteen hours over mountains. Or you can have a 20-minute flight to Ioannina. And you have main islands that have airports and some of them have extended runways so they can take flights directly from London, or from Berlin. So we have something like 35 airports. And how many ports? Every island has a port. All along the coast, there are ports to be maintained by coast guard, by port pilots. Actually, we have an exceptional need for civil servants.

So, in the end, Greece has this incredible infrastructure that's different from the rest of Europe. Incredible infrastructure. Of course! We have to.

3

PROJECTS

THE FIVE LANDSCAPES OF TOURISM

214

190 Fernando Rodríguez, Pablo Oriol and Lina Toro
190 Directors of Undergraduate Thesis Projects IE University
190

The Undergraduate Thesis Project proposes a reading of architectural design as a tool capable of generating an urgent and necessary progress, in opposition to the stigma it has taken on during the last decade as an element intended to demonstrate economic success. Architecture becomes an indispensable means of ordering reality, similar to the role of infrastructures in developing a territory. The *infrastructural* nature of architectural design imbues the architect's creative capacity with the *healthy ambition* of transforming a territory into a landscape of new opportunities.

In order for this teaching approach to be possible, the UTP has to be articulated as a complete territorial hypothesis that has to be defended, developed and corroborated. In order for this hypothesis to have a chance at success, it must be included in an existing *contemporary debate*, it must refer to a *broad context* and it must be formalized in a *specific setting* that allows for working with real variables.

ARCHITECTURE, TOURISM AND ACTION

In the debate over updating the models for the development of tourism, which have brought so much delight to the national economy, the *Architecture & Tourism* research project was created with the aim of increasing the value of design strategies in the process of reformulating the Spanish tourism offer, established within the theoretical and research framework for the development of the UTP. The authors of the projects presented here are invited to work within the scope of the complex relationships between architecture, territory and tourism, a question that is current, geographically close, politically pertinent and capable of generating sustainable and necessary economic progress.

In the background of this debate about the role of the architectural professional in the development of the tourism supply and demand resides the conviction that a new interpretation of the territory is desirable, and that the success of this renewed thought has to be transferred to the existing tourism offer through the appropriate communication formats, complimenting the well-known and successful formula of sun and surf with unexpected strategies and programs. These new architectures are described using new vocabularies—extreme landscapes, reversible architecture, industrial beauty—as well as others that are already incorporated into our discipline—exchange, event, time offering, heritage, and human and natural landscapes—.

As such, design becomes a tool for economic, political and administrative management, encouraging all proposed actions-interventions to be beneficial to new users as well as local users, and guaranteeing the creation of environments with their own particular identity, which can be the seeds for architecture that is capable of coexisting with the pre-existing landscape, whether it is natural, architectural or urban.

TOTAL IBERIA

This new perspective on the pair *Architecture & Tourism* uncovers a recent change in scale that operates on two levels. On the one hand, the time required for movement changes, reducing the space-time relationship of the whole as a result. On the other hand, the territorial dimension within anyone's reach is also modified: access to the remote areas is universalized and the radius of the area that can potentially be visited is increased.

Given this new dimensional horizon we propose a framework for intervention that we call Total Iberia: the Iberian Peninsula understood as a single tourist destination with the potential for global impact, which can be visited from its airport hubs and train stations, and is accessible through its networks of roads, and can bring together a clear Iberian identity—which is cemented as an international topic—with the specific identities of the different destinations. This is an attempt at reorganizing, imagining and strengthening a unique and

Architecture becomes an indispensable means of ordering reality, similar to the role of infrastructures in developing a territory.

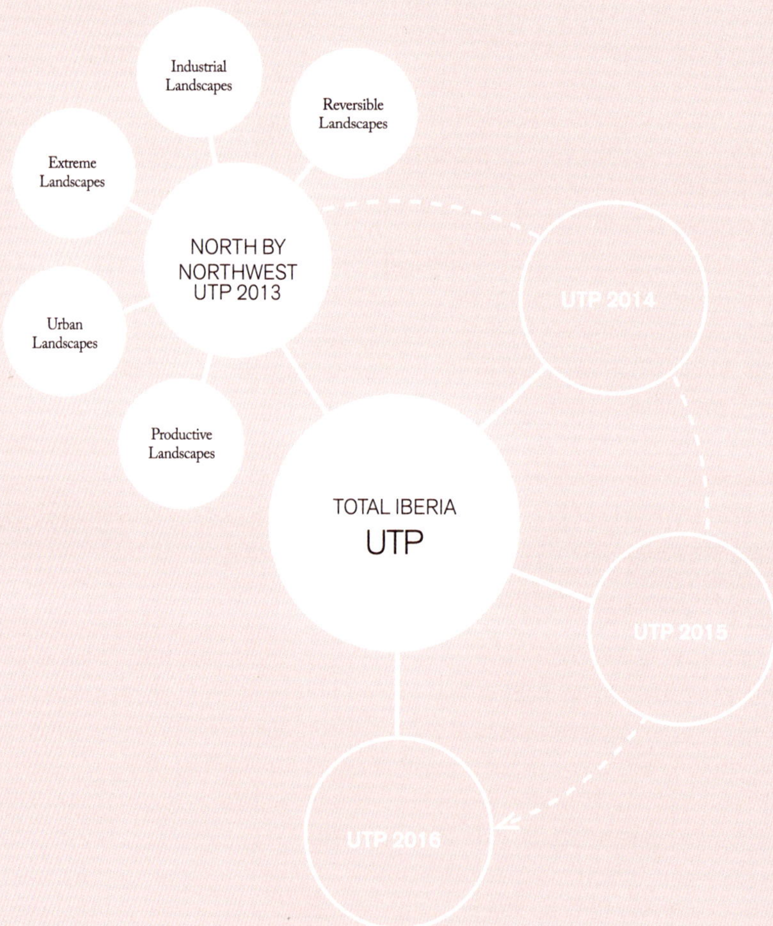

Diagram showing the UTP structure. *North by Northwest* is organized into five kinds of landscapes special tourist network that is articulated strategically on a territorial scale and that transcends the scale of a *singular destination*.

The projects completed within the framework of this UTP therefore respond to this double condition: they belong to networks that reach far beyond them and they play a role as catalysts for placing value on specificity.

NORTH BY NORTHWEST

The proposed setting for developing this first UTP is the corridor that runs along highway AP-66 and links the city of León with the Cantabrian Sea.

Historically part of the Vía de la Plata, the Roman road that connected Astorga to Mérida, the stretch in question is one of the first highways to be constructed in Spain and was definitive in the industrial development in the north and the northwest of the peninsula. Important population centers, both administrative and productive, have lined up along it for centuries. The dismantling of industry in the 1980s marked the beginning of an economic decline that still persists; socioeconomic conflicts derived from the closing of mines have been cover stories in international media and they highlight the need to provide a possible future for this corridor.

As though it were an enormous *Infrastructural Landscape,*[1] this setting presents a series of overlapping characteristics that portray a territory where a design analysis encounters different areas of opportunity. Urban, rural, infrastructural, heritage and natural aspects express themselves with force in this fragment of Total Iberia: the Metropolitan Area of Asturias brings together more than a million people in a system of towns with a relatively low, nearly rural, index of concentration. The extraordinarily dense transportation network combines conventional railways and stretches of narrow gauge, roadways and highways, secondary roads and local mining routes that ensure high accessibility ratios. There is a high concentration of assets with historic-artistic interest and a vast industrial heritage, as well as a natural heritage made up of coastline, valleys and mountains, and a National Park: the *Picos de Europa*.

THE FIVE LANDSCAPES OF TOURISM

Based on this shared understanding of the territory as a total design setting, the UTP students were asked to select a place, a user and an architectural image in order to put together a proposal for an intervention within the framework of this relationship between Architecture and Tourism.

Their reflection on this relationship and analysis of the territorial context revealed areas of opportunity that naturally came together into groups focused on similar issues. The working process, involving the combined efforts of the 28 students and the UTP directors, resulted in a basic taxonomy for ways of generating new and unexpected tourist scenarios, which came to be called Productive Landscapes, Urban Landscapes, Extreme Landscapes, Industrial Landscapes and Reversible Landscapes.

Productive Landscapes attempt to activate entire communities through didactic-experiential communication centered on the production processes that serve as the foundation for the local economy: the rise in ecological and gastronomic tourism and the attractiveness of a return to responsible direct consumption, cutting out intermediaries, are the main assets behind these proposals, which present a high degree of viability.

Urban Landscapes are the setting for the reactivation of dense city centers, based on leisure programs with a metropolitan character that can be incorporated into circuits focused on culture, sports or artistic creation with an international scope. These interventions are generally tied in with heritage protection, and they provide strong support for urban tourism.

Extreme Landscapes take advantage of the enormous landscape potential of the natural environment in the Astur-Leonese region and the proposals include different types of infrastructures intended to make the most of it. The exclusive nature of the experiences and the proposed scenarios justify extreme proposals, as is anticipated by the name.

Industrial Landscapes mirror a wealth of experiences that, like in the case of the Ruhr valley in Germany, attempt to make use of the existing mining heritage to promote a change in the economic model. The enormous richness of the examples that can be found in the area allows for the appearance of diverse proposals, all of which are high in intensity.

Reversible Landscapes display a special sensibility when faced with the possibility of intervening in sensitive natural contexts that demand temporary architectural proposals that allow for an intense use of their landscape value.

Thus, without losing sight of a specific socioeconomic reality, the Landscapes of Tourism developed during this year's UTP seek to string together a network of potential tourist settings that articulate a new vision of the territory. They propose strategies that provide a glimpse of unprecedented projects for entire communities. Ultimately, they seek out hypotheses for complex realities.

1. Bélanger, Pierre. "Redefining Infrastructure." In *Ecological Urbanism*, edited by M. Mostafavi and G. Doherty: Harvard University GSD. Lars Müller Publishers, 2010.

WORKSHOP 1. TOURISM: IDENTITY, DESTRUCTION AND DESIRE

216

191

Linna Choi and Tarik Oualalou
KILO Architectes

Within the framework of the *Total Iberia* architectural studio, this one-week workshop explored the margins of established perceptions of tourism and investigated why questions of tourism have stayed outside the contemporary discourse in architecture. The workshop attempted to redefine tourism not in terms of policy, but through architectural and urbanistic means. Through the exploration of several themes and four case studies, the students worked on collective research projects which aimed to push the limits of architecture's role in the transformation of tourism in the 21st century.

THEME 1: TOURISM AND IDENTITY

This workshop examined how the architecture of tourism attempts to create unique environments specific to their locales while creating generic environments for perceived needs of convenience and comfort. The workshop explored how a sense of identity and destination can be created through architectural means that do not fall prey to the theme park model.

THEME 2: TOURISM AND DESTRUCTION

This workshop investigated tourism centered on destruction and catastrophe and architecture's role in defining these new territories of tourism. Some examples we studied were the following:

Chernobyl: Described by *Forbes* magazine as among the "world's unique places to visit", last year Chernobyl hosted thousands of tourists interested in catastrophe tourism.

Berlin Wall: Almost all of the 160 km of wall that encircled West Berlin was torn down or chiseled away after it was breached in 1989. However, after tourists started asking, 'Where's the wall?', the city began to reconstruct segments of the wall. Part of the rebuilt section is composed of authentic slabs, some of which were purchased for €1000 each from a private collector.

DMZ: On the 38th parallel, this zone is 250 km long and 4 km wide and is the most heavily militarized border in the world. It is also a popular tourist attraction, with propagandist 'peace villages' built on either side, presenting two very different histories of the same conflict.

THEME 3: TOURISM AND DESIRE

This workshop examined tourism's need for the iconic and architecture's role in making the intangible (desire) tangible. We investigated examples of architecture's role in creating a sense of desire in blank territories (Dubai, Perla de Las Dunas, etc.) and depressed regions (Bilbao, Lens).

The students worked on four case studies:

Case Study 1: The De-Militarized Zone between North and South Korea (DMZ)
Two groups of students posited opposing scenarios: the first scenario was based upon the continuing presence of the DMZ and the second scenario was based upon the assumption of reunification of the two Koreas. The first group explored the nature of border conditions around the world and their spatial

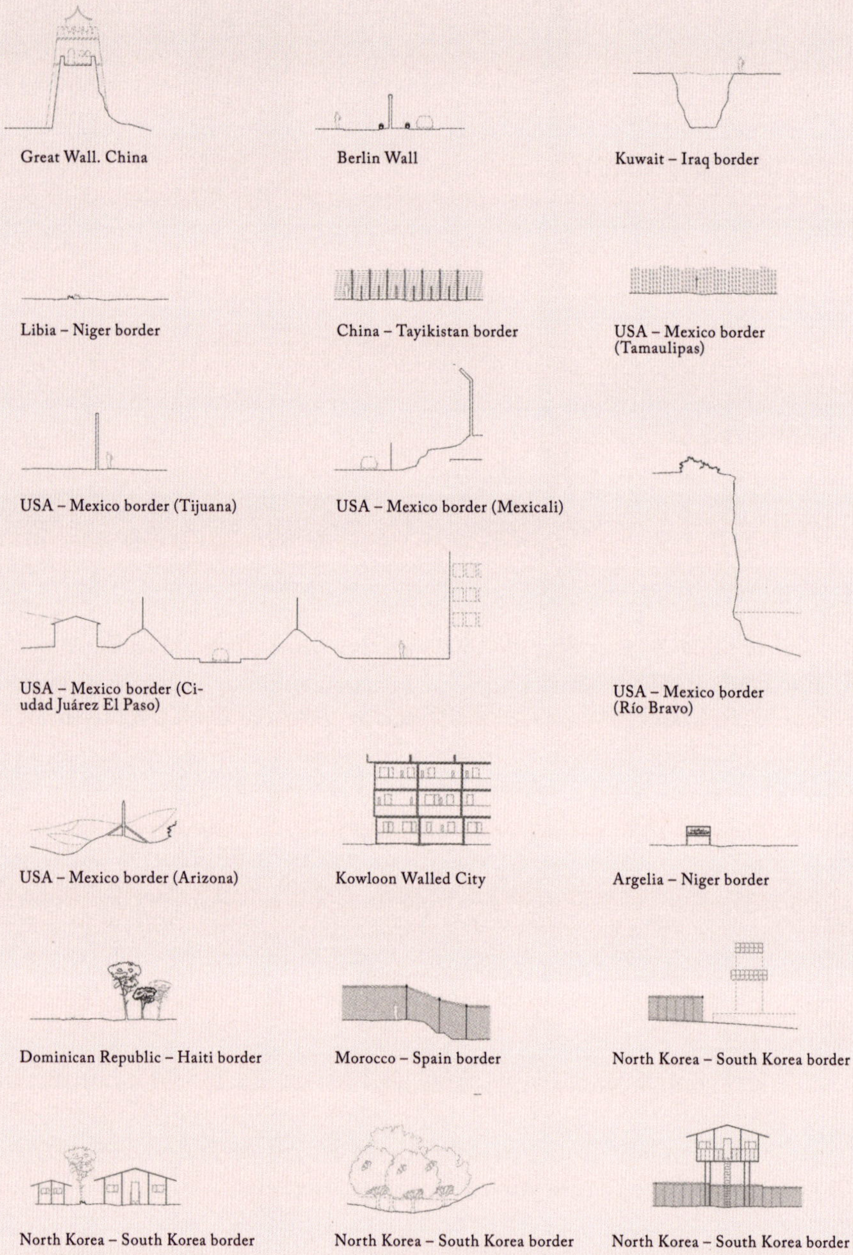

Case Study 1: DMZ. Border catalogue. Research by Iñigo Arias, Juan Gilsanz and Juan Moreno

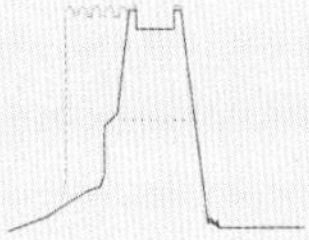

Avila wall

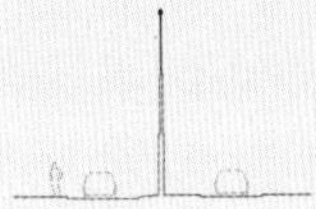

Belfast border

Firebreak

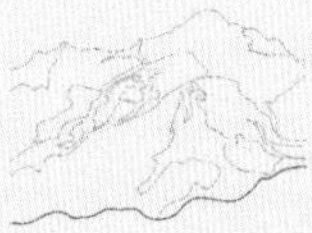

Spain – France border

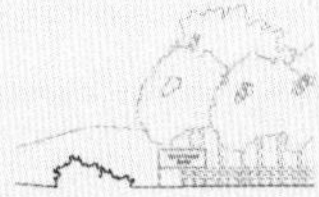

Spain – Portugal border

USA – Canada border (Niagara falls)

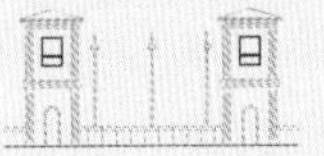

Uruguay – Brasil border

China – North Korea border

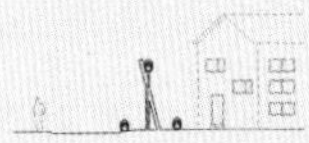

Jewish Guetto Wall

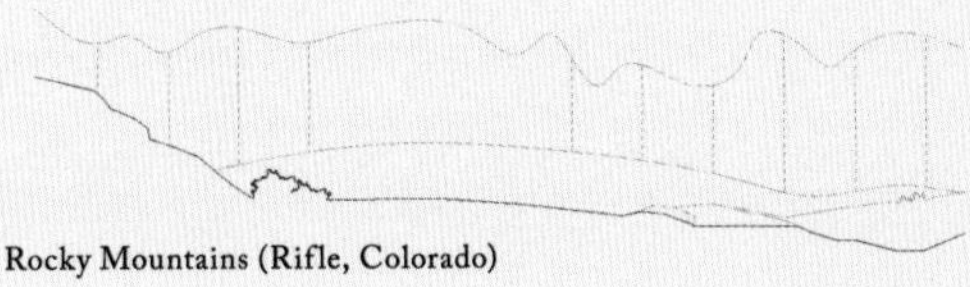

Rocky Mountains (Rifle, Colorado)

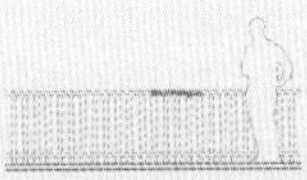

Paraguay – Brasil border

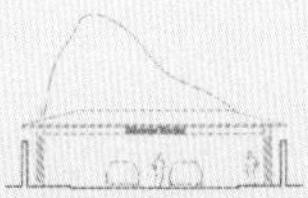

Gibraltar border

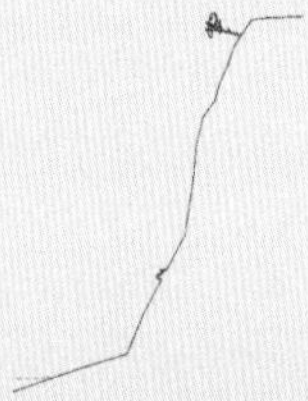

Spain – Portugal border

USA – Canada border

Germany – Netherlands – Belgium border

Nepal – China border

USA – Rusia border

Sudan – South Sudan border

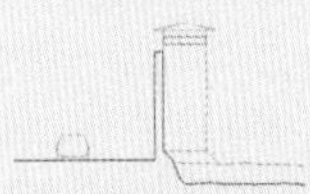

Israel – Palestina border

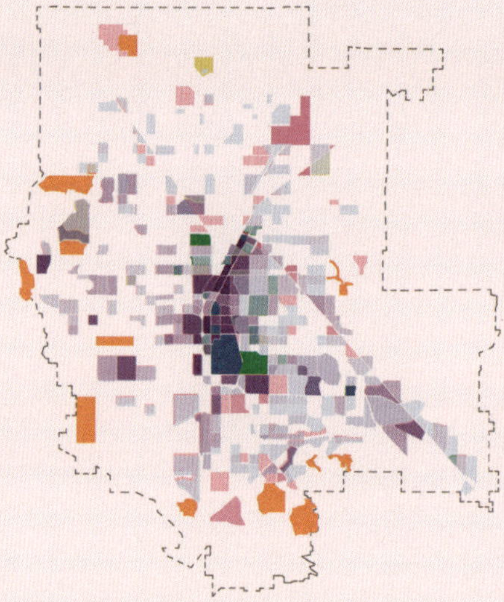

Case Study 2: Las Vegas. Diagram of city tourist nodes: museums, golf courses, chapels and airports. Project by Clara Bueno, Tamara García and César Gusano.

implications. The investigations of the second group led to such proposals as the transformation of the DMZ into a nature reserve or the center of a new urban conglomeration.

Case Study 2: Las Vegas

One group of students tried to reconcile the presence of Las Vegas's touristic heart with the exploding suburban fabric mushrooming around it. No longer merely an island of tourism in the middle of the desert, Las Vegas suffers from uncontrolled growth and the undesirable leftover spaces that rapid growth invariably creates.

This group investigated possible scenarios for injecting desirable programs into these leftover "pocket" spaces which would benefit both tourists and local residents. The second group of students examined the complex sectional relationships on Las Vegas Boulevard ("The Strip") and proposed transformations to knit the two sides of the Strip into a more accessible urban fabric.

Case Study 3: Seaside, Florida – A Tourism of Nostalgia

Seaside is an example of tourism's success in creating desire for a place based on nostalgia, a longing for an ideal place and time. Based upon the notion of an old-fashioned beach town, Seaside's success stems from its sense of small-town community, which is created by its carefully designed urban codes and highly informed vernacular architecture.

A victim of its own success, Seaside is undergoing expansion beyond its originally designed limits. The two groups of students explored the ramifica-

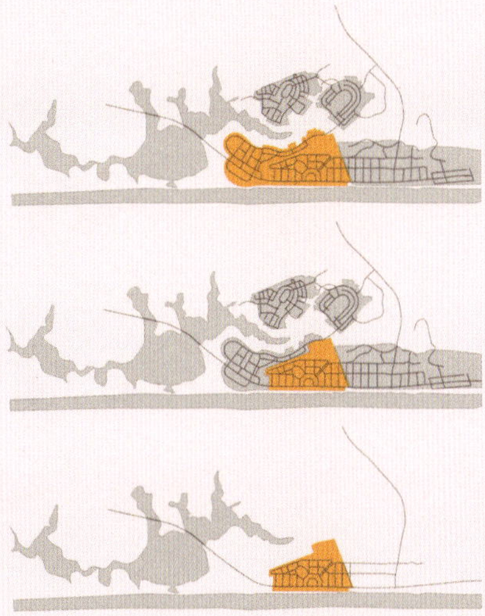

Case Study 3: Seaside, Florida. Diagram of city showing growth vs. identity landmarks. Seaside's proposal is an imaginary belt as a boundary.

tions of such an expansion: Are there fixed limits to the fantasy? Does the dreamscape die after a certain scale?

Case Study 4: Marfa, Texas – A Tourism of Pilgrimage

This group explored tourisms of pilgrimage, from the historic religious pilgrimages to Santiago de Compostela to modern-day pilgrimages to meccas of art and architecture, such as Marfa, Texas, the home and studio of Donald Judd and a center for Minimalist Art. One group investigated the journey to Marfa as "stages" of a pilgrimage experience, in time and space.

The second group examined the development of this small town's urban grid in response to the pressures of tourism and its consequences for the social and architectural coherence of the town.

Case Study 4: Marfa, Texas. "This is what Marfa attracts.... but this is what Marfa is." Research by Leticia Merino, Valentina Occhini, Claudia Maneti and Cecilia Marina.

REAL MARFA

WORKSHOP 2. RESEARCH AS DESIGN: 217 FRAMING IDENTITY

193 Laura Martínez de Guereñu
Project Design professor at IE University

The "Research as Design: Framing Identity" workshop was the students' first contact with the territorial framework of the Asturias-León region (ACTAL). Over five consecutive days of work, students tried to envision this region's identity—pinpointing what makes it different from other places—in order to identify possible intervention strategies with the potential to attract tourism. The definition of tourism that was used as a foundation came from the British sociologist John Urry, known primarily for his book *The Tourist Gaze* (1990) in which he argues that tourism is a leisure activity that presupposes its opposite, i.e., regulated and organized work. As a result, tourism is a "manifestation of how work and leisure are organized as separate and regulated spheres of social practice."[1] This difference implies that tourists only notice the aspects of the landscape and the built environment that "contrast with their everyday experience". This is true to such an extent that the central aim in guaranteeing consumption through tourism has to do with "capturing the tourist's gaze". This gaze is founded on contrast, which enhances other elements of our perceptual experience and which architecture, as a discipline that acts as a framework for our lives, can clearly highlight. The workshop focused therefore on architectural design as a tool for emphasizing these differences, which are necessary to ensuring tourism consumption. From the very beginning, the research was given a collective character. The main objective was to arrive at an idea of the territory that could be understood as the sum of places with the potential for transformation. Places where different intervention strategies could be implemented, which would allow for "capturing the tourist gaze" and which could later be transformed into individual design proposals. Therefore, the analyses undertaken by individual students during the workshop would accumulate and be shared until all participants could ultimately develop their own idea of the place's identity. Many questions were raised: What are the basic aspects that construct the idiosyncrasy of a place? How many distinguishing elements need to be found? Which of them make a territory an attractive place for tourism? In answer to these questions, four categories of analysis were developed which were generic enough yet had the potential for capturing the specificities that led to the selection of ACTAL as a territorial framework.

The categories were: "Events", "Landscape/Infrastructure", "Built Environment: taxonomies of deindustrialization" and "Timeline: historic signposts". Each of the four days of collective work focused on one of these categories, leaving the final day of synthesis for the presentation of individual results. As a lead-up to drafting the final graphic document, students analyzed the latent information within each of the categories and mapped them, together with the potential for intervention that they identified in the area. Each working day was divided into a theoretical session and a practical work session and, beginning with the second day, a session was added for correcting work from the previous category. The first day focused on the "Timeline" and featured a presentation on how the ACTAL territory had developed from an economic, political, social and cultural standpoint. The historical impact of tourism in the area was also analyzed. The aim of the analysis to be performed and mapped was to identify "the historic signposts", the years of change that had been vital to the history of the ACTAL territorial framework. This change could be understood broadly, with the aim of identifying the signs that displayed the idiosyncrasies of the place. The second day focused on the "Built Environment" and featured a presentation of possible approaches to the existing industrial

Category: *Events*. Video Story Board by Marina Carretero

00:06
00:08
00:10
00:14
00:15
00:16
00:22
00:23
00:24
00:28
00:29
00:30

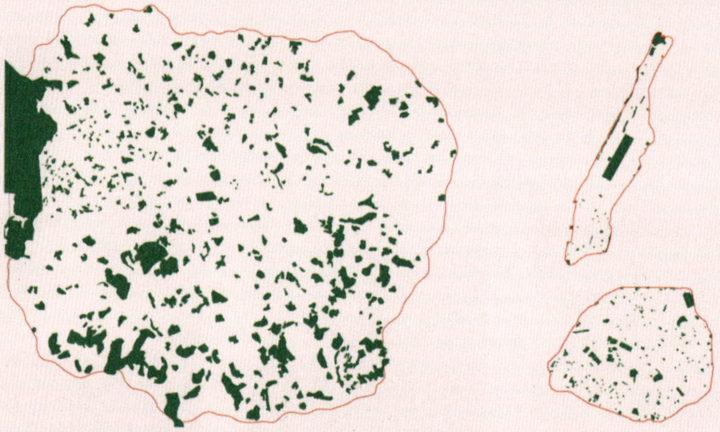

Category: *Landscape / Infrastructure.* Diagram of city voids as alternative spaces for tourism by Clara Bueno, Tamara García and César Gusano.

heritage in the area. The abandonment of coal mines and the mining conflict that had taken place in the area were not isolated incidents. While it was a very depressed area, it also offered very good opportunities for developing alternative urban models. The interiors of some of the industrial buildings and the exterior landscapes of others offered a unique potential for creating new settlement models. The objective of the analysis was to map the "taxonomies of industrialization" and determine the conditions and opportunities of the existing industrial landscape as the first step toward an overall understanding of the existing built heritage. The third day, called "Landscape/Infrastructure", included a presentation that differentiated the categories of the vernacular, the picturesque and the sublime into different case studies. The aim was to analyze the natural environment as the meeting point between the natural landscape, the industrial landscape and infrastructures. The goal was to understand landscape as a material product of human actions and also as an object of aesthetic appropriation. Whereas the area's patrimonial heritage had been clear in the previous map, in this case the aim was to analyze the potential of the cultural landscape. The infrastructures and the different types of routes had to be expressed graphically. The fourth day, called "Events" featured the presentation of opportunities for positioning regions in the tourism market, as is the case with the competition between cities to be named European Capital of Culture. Two case studies were presented —one on the coast and one in the interior— to understand the various difficulties that cities come up against in their attempts to become more legible and consumable. The analysis of the cases focused on the buildings and infrastructures that need to be created to ensure a continuous and uninterrupted flow of visitors. Certain city mottos used in European

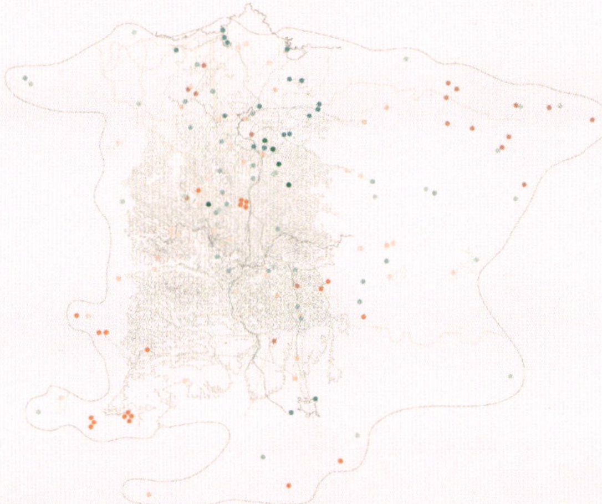

Category: *Built Environment: taxonomies of deindustrialization*. AP-66 route analysis by Cristina Moreno Cabello.

capitals were also studied to understand the importance of a slogan: how to make the transition from a myth to a brand and build up an identity that can attract tourists. The collection of information and the mapping of pre-existing conditions and the potential for each of the categories resulted in four complementary approaches that came together in the overall design approach. For the final hand-in, on the fifth consecutive day of work, each student produced an individual synthetic map showing his or her particular vision of the identity of the ACTAL territorial framework. These maps reflected a preference for promoting a specific potential and, to a certain extent, indicated possible programs for intervention with the potential for attracting tourism. A SWOT analysis, in which students identified the territory's strengths, weaknesses, opportunities and threats, complemented the graphic syntheses. Different design types began to emerge. Some of them aimed to intervene in the mining heritage, others would try to activate the natural landscapes, still others would focus on creating new cultural opportunities in urban areas. Students waited until after the workshop to visit the location. Thus, their first encounter with the territory occurred more gradually, when they already had a clear idea of the elements they wanted to promote. The transfer of the workshop from the territory to the UTP was achieved through a shift in the means of representation. A video/storyboard, created with stills from the student's individual maps and their on-site visits, served as a point of departure for the UTP.

1. John Urry, "The 'Consumption' of Tourism," in *Sociology*, vol. 24, no. 1, February 1990, pp. 23-35. Online version at http://soc.sagepub.com/content/24/1/23.

Category: *Timeline. Historic signposts.* Maps of the built environment and timelines at the area of study. Project by Beatriz Fernández Gómez.

PRODUCTIVE LANDSCAPES

General axonometric view of Llumeres Yum! by Teresa Rodríguez-Gimeno Wiggin. The project is a man-crafted ecosystem based on a design philosophy that combines architectural strategies with horticulture, ecology, finalncial management and community design.

THE STAGING OF THE AGRICULTURAL PRODUCTIVE
218 LANDSCAPE AS A TOURIST EXPERIENCE

193 Andrew Varela
Desgin Critic, FTP-DSVII, TOTAL IBERIA 1.0, IE University

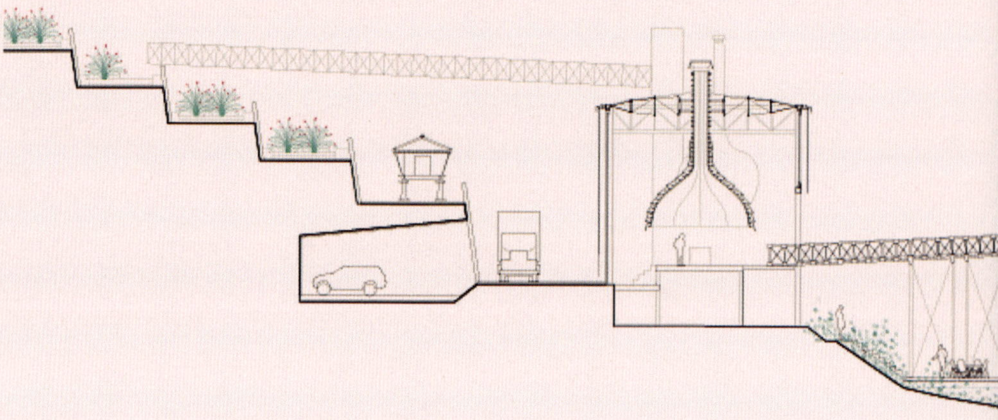

Productive landscapes reveal how as a society we make use of the land, whether it is for basic survival necessities, such as the production of food, or for the economic and cultural systems that structure our society, like the production of energy. The relevance of productive landscapes has increased over recent years as the interest in issues of sustainability have permeated every aspect of our daily lives, resulting in many instances in the promotion of geographic proximity as something good, particularly when it comes to the production of food. Agricultural production is as specialized and as efficient as most other production systems of contemporary capitalist society. Food is produced in massive quantities ready to be exported to global markets for the biggest economic gain. Local food production as something more than a small niche market is not a viable option, given the restrictions one would face in terms of limited food options, cost, and use of land and water supply.

In the ACTAL, a territory that has suffered economic, social and material devastation due to the closing of the mining industry, small scale agricultural production is pursued as a strategy for the creation of tourist destinations capable of becoming nodes of reactivation and regeneration for the region. Small-scale agricultural production is employed here not as an alternative to the current global agricultural production organization but as part of the staged experience that defines tourist activity.

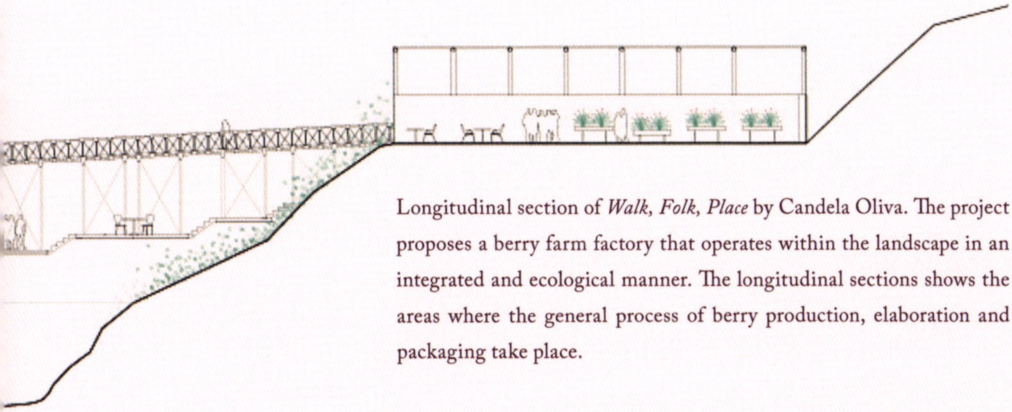

Longitudinal section of *Walk, Folk, Place* by Candela Oliva. The project proposes a berry farm factory that operates within the landscape in an integrated and ecological manner. The longitudinal sections shows the areas where the general process of berry production, elaboration and packaging take place. 90

In a region whose identity is so linked to the inner depths of the earth and the extraction of fossil fuels, these projects seek its regeneration through the reactivation of its outer layer, its soil, and the latent potential it holds. The success of these proposals as points of tourist activity is based on their ability to create a new physical environment that is distinctive and can "signify an experience which contrasts with everyday experience."[1] In the pursuit of that distinct environment, the projects reconfigure the productive capability of the landscape and its associated building fabric into a new agricultural environment. The built configurations that responded to systems of production related to mining are transformed into new productive organizations related to agriculture and, in doing so, create a new distinct landscape that imbues the region with a new identity potent enough to become a catalyst for regeneration. The projects result from the implementation of a broader touristic regional strategy and are therefore conceived as nodes belonging to a larger network of proposals that, together as a whole, have the potential for the transformation of a particular region within the ACTAL. This network approach not only provides a more economically sustainable strategy but offers the potential of linking to other tourist routes at the national and international level. In their programming, these projects surround agricultural production with complimentary experiences of consumption, not only to make the proposals financially viable but,

88 — Main section of *Economy behind Tourism through Cosmetics* (E.T.C), by Carmen Mencos. Existing infrastructures are reused mixing the old mining uses with the processes of cosmetic fabrication, involving locals and tourists to achieve the goal.

more importantly, to create the desired touristic experience where "everything is a sign of itself."[2] Restaurants, artisan food processing, tasting facilities, hotel and exhibitions amongst others, are all devised to promote and enhance the experience of a different lifestyle.

The experience being sold here could fall under what is known as "slow life", "slow food" or a "farm to table" type of experience. At a time when most of the food we consume is processed and packaged for delivery, when we are debating whether to have labels on our food that identify GMOs (genetically modified organisms), when food is sold and distributed by fewer and fewer worldwide conglomerates, these proposals stage the experience of locally grown produce, processed in non industrial ways and consumed with extreme pleasure on site. The touristic value of these types of experiences is based on the lack of connection we currently have to the food we eat and to the processes that make it. It is the activation of the senses that one experiences in these environments that qualifies them as out of the ordinary, making them a desirable tourist experience.

In a region whose identity is linked to the depths of the earth and the extraction of fossil fuels, these projects seek its regeneration through the reactivation of its outer layer, its soil.

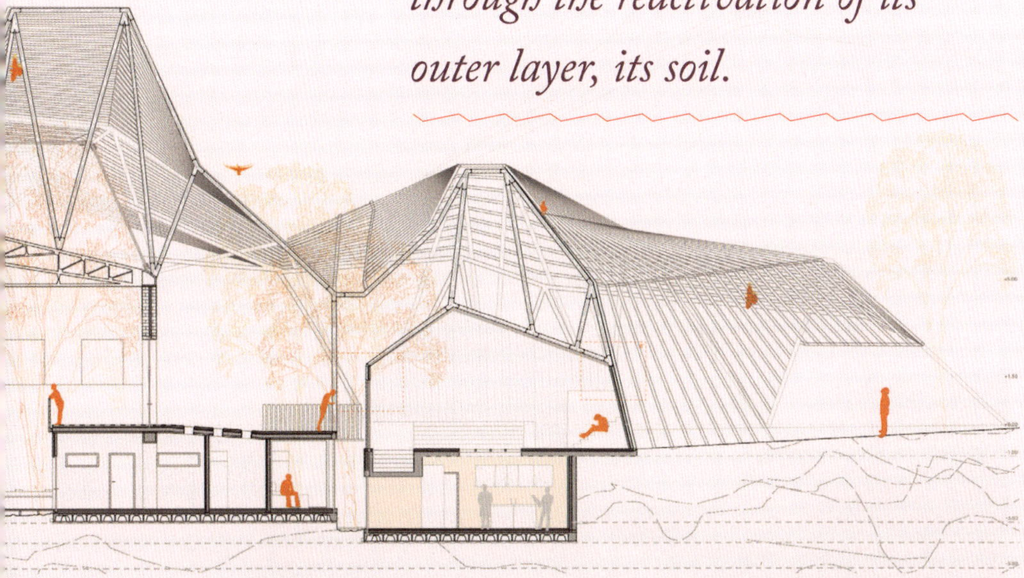

Here, the tomato tastes better! One can grow, pick, prepare, smell and taste food in ways that we typically do not.

In a world where no authentic tourist experience is available, and when local food production as a universal solution is an impossibility, these projects represent a "staged authenticity"[3] that presupposes that the berry coop, the farm, the cosmetics center, or the fungi museum cannot exist without the income provided by the tourist who eats at the restaurant, makes the jam, tastes the mushrooms, stays in the hotel and gets pampered at the spa.

1. J. Urry, "The Consumption of Tourism." *Sociology*, vol. 24, No. 1, February 1990, p. 26.
2. J. Culler, "Semiotics of Tourism" *American Journal of Semiotics* 1:127-40, 1981. Cited by J. Urry, "The Consumption of Tourism." *Sociology*, vol. 24, No. 1, February 1990, p. 27.
3. D. MacCannell, *The Tourist. A New Theory of Leisure Class.* London: Macmillan, 1976. Cited by J. Urry, "The Consumption of Tourism." *Sociology*, vol. 24, No. 1, February 1990, p. 34.

220 RETHINKING THE MONASTERY

Fernando Jiménez Salmerón

This project is a reaction to the current sociopolitical situation caused by the rural exodus that comes from the closing of the mining companies around Langreo. It aims for a viable solution that revitalizes these areas to save the villages from disappearing. The project is focused on La Cruz with a cooperative berry farm and housing for 30 people, providing cyclical tourism and economic support. It is meant to create a ripple effect on the surrounding villages. To achieve this, the core idea of a working retirement is proposed. Like in old monasteries, where the way of life was working retirement, now the concept is exploded into a contemporary materialization. The proposal is based on four actions:

1. First the location in a peaceful natural environment with a strong identity.
2. An outer protection in the form of a wooden fence.
3. The program distribution in the shape of permeable rings.
4. The self-sustainability ideal materialized through the fog catcher and year-round vegetable cultivation.

The horizontal language is the main figure as organization of space

General plan

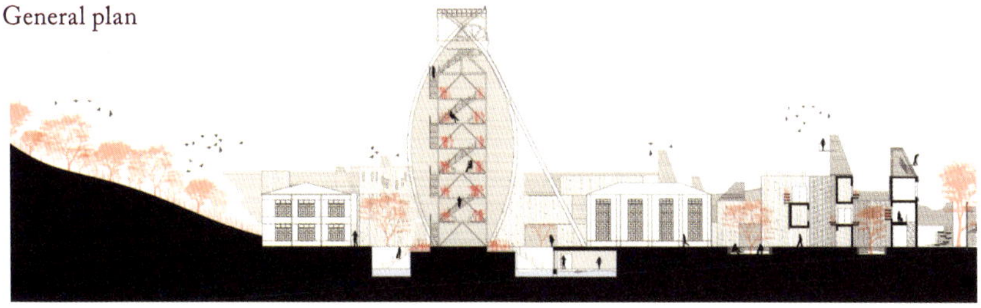

General section

220 — E.T.C

Carmen Mencos

Economy behind Tourism through Cosmetics (E.T.C) consists in the rehabilitation and reactivation of an abandoned mine through a specific market: cosmetics. The project aims not only to create a new tourist attraction in the area, but also to create jobs with existing raw mining materials, this time targeted at a very specific new market. The combination of tourism and employment creates three different kinds of tourists: international, national and local. They all depend on how much time tourists want to spend, from weekly to daily experiences. A close relationship between worker-visitor and also between local-foreign is promoted. There are many differences between the mining process and the process of cosmetic elaboration. One is composed of a series of steps including extraction, classification, production, storage, transportation and sale; meanwhile the other is based on conservation, production, investigation and experimentation. The project mixes both processes, trying to use the existing building as support for the new cosmetic fabrication. The sequence of conservation-production-investigation-experimentation is also designed for tourists to enjoy and engage with.

General view

Solar protection and secondary wood structure

Wood primary truss structure

Existing brick and plaster building ruin

0/-1 Plan

Floor plan

Basement floor

220 — WALK, FOLK, PLACE

Candela Oliva

The project is a reaction to the current social situation in rural Asturias, desolated since the mining industry began its decline. A cooperative berry farm is placed next to the river, at the bottom of the Nalon valley. How can we work with landscape so that we can achieve efficiency in a productive process? Are economy and ecology necessarily two opposed terms? This is a proposal for a humanized, hands-on kind of industry, one that does not lose contact with nature throughout the process. From the moment of the harvest on the hillsides, to the cooking down at the processing core, to actually tasting the fruits and jellies beside the river... The interior space is organized into a sequence of different chimneys.

These are light structures that house diverse activities underneath, and which never touch the ground. There are therefore two worlds in this jelly factory: ground and air. The earth is "shaped" in the form of concrete platforms that raise the activity to a level above ground.

General view

Types of chimneys: Smoke, Light, Sound and Smell

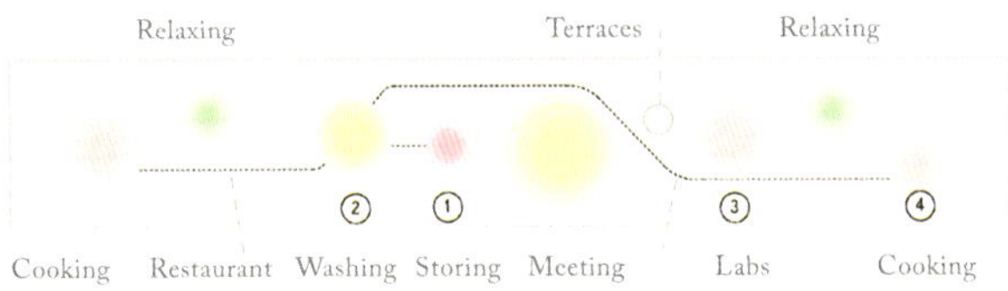

Process diagram

Plans and longitudinal section

In the berry farm the fruit moves down the valley through the whole process: from harvesting on the hillsides, to cooking at the processing core on the river banks, to actually tasting the fruits and jellies above the river.

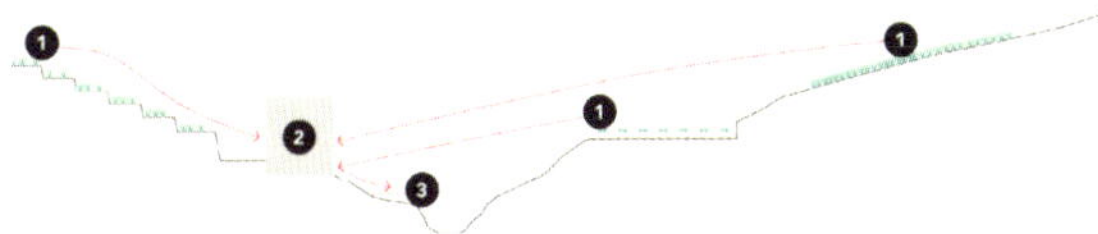

Diagram that depicts the movement of the fruit down the valley.

Every chimney has a specific function. For instance, the sound chimney has a shape that is meant to amplify the tapping sound of the rain for the person that stands underneath. Its function is also the collection of water for the garden below the building.

220 — LLUMERES YUM!

Teresa Rodríguez-Gimeno Wiggin

This project is not (only) about architecture. It aims to create a sustainable system that provides for its own needs. It is a man-crafted ecosystem based on an integrated design philosophy that encompasses gardening, horticulture, ecology, money management, community design and, last but not least (and not more), architecture.

It aims to revitalize the site by transforming the use of its soil, which has been degraded by years of iron mining activity, its subsequent abandonment, and the existing eucalyptus cash crop. With the ruin as a base, the different elements (orchards, grassland, stables, chestnut walk...) evolve into the landscape, adapting and making the most of the environmental conditionings of the site.

Local knowledge is essential to the project, from subsistence farming to vernacular architecture, as is sharing these elements that create a sense of "place" with the rest of the world through the tourism-oriented part of the program.

The aim of the project from the beginning was never to approach the site from a naive or condescending point of view, but to extract as much knowledge as possible.

So, don't you think it's time you got your hands dirty?

Seed bombs

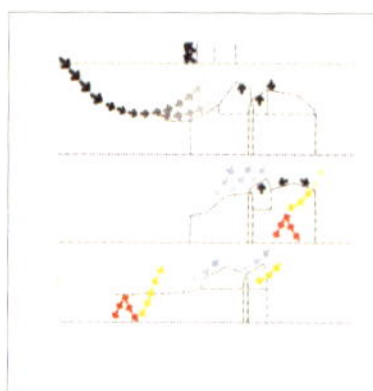

Rooms

Seed Tree

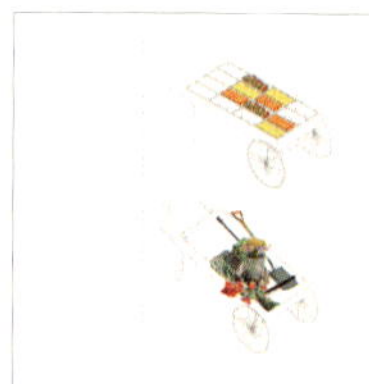

Carts

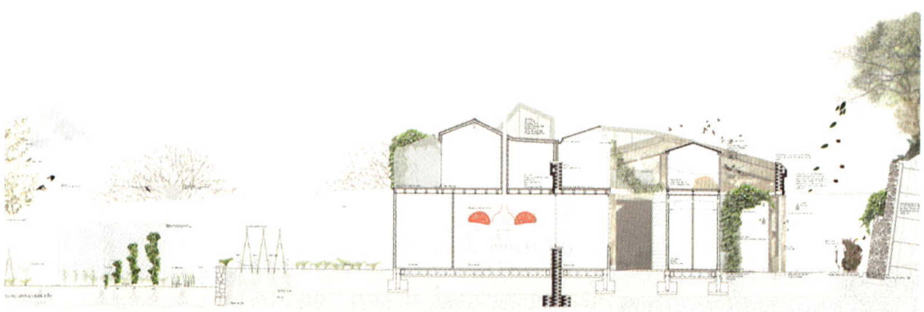

Longitudinal section through the community building

no heavy machinery
cowpat
citrus limon
prunus armeniaca
partenocissus quinquef
sylvia atricapilla
farmer
organic vegs
castanea sativa
fagus sylvatica
tilia platyphyllos
turdus merula
nendo dando
experimental tourist
vaccinum bluecrop
betula celtiberica
taxus baccata
carduelis carduelis
seeds
passiflora edulis
rubus ulmifolius
arbutus unedo
sorbus aucuparia
carduelis chloris
birds
malus communis
rubus idaeus
acer pseudoplatanus
crataegus monogyna
erithacus rubecula
wildlife
juglans regia
ribes rubrum
visteria sinensis
quercus robur
hirundo rustica
indigenous plants
fortunella margaritus
ribes nigrum
yellow rose
jasminus officinalis
motacilla alba
the sun
ficus carica
pyrus communics
trachelosperum jasm
salix fragilis
muscicapa estriata
the moon
corylus avellana
punica granatum
campsis radicans
castanea sativa
passer domesticus
amazing soil
citrus sinensis
prunus persica
honeysuckle
corylus avellana
pyrrhula pyrrhula
compost
citrus nobilis
prunus domestica
pandorea jasminoides
populus nigra
saxicola torquata
free range chickens
citrus medica
prunus avium
passiflora edulis
laurus nobilis
serinus serinus

220 — MYCOLOGY SCHOOL

Paula Álvarez

The aim of this project is to attract mushroom hunting tourism to Tabanedo (León), an ideal place for picking wild mushrooms. It proposes a rapid and efficient construction method, which responds to the irregularity of the terrain and its orientation. To ensure that the existing buildings maintain the importance they deserve, it relies on local construction methods and the use of traditional materials.

Triangular shells made from ETFE membranes are placed on top, which provides a certain amount of freedom in meeting the program needs and provides sufficient transparency for distinguishing what is happening inside.

The envelope of the existing buildings is resolved using glulam beams and ETFE membranes. Translucent membranes in soft colors are used for the southern-facing areas, as an environmental strategy for reducing direct sunlight in summer.

This approach contrasts with the rigidity of the traditional buildings, through a combination of effects and volumes that maintain the dynamic composition of the interior.

The design attempts to take advantage of the freedom provided by the natural environment, capturing as much light as possible and allowing for enjoying views of the landscape.

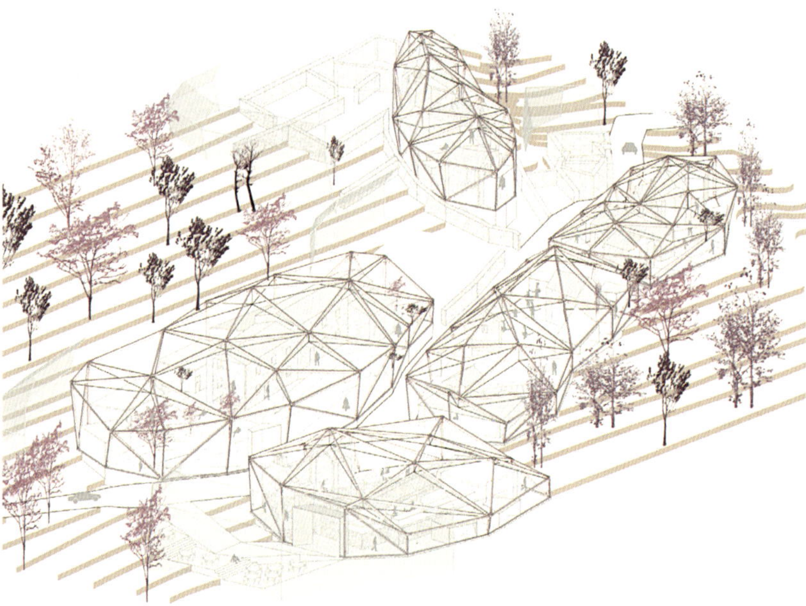

Axonometric view

Cross section and longitudinal section

General plan showing the existing ruins and the new intervention

URBAN LANDSCAPES

City of Fashion by Cristina Moreno

220 CHANNELING THE SPEED OF CHANGE

193 Pedro Iglesias
Design Critic, FTP-DSVII, TOTAL IBERIA 1.0, IE University

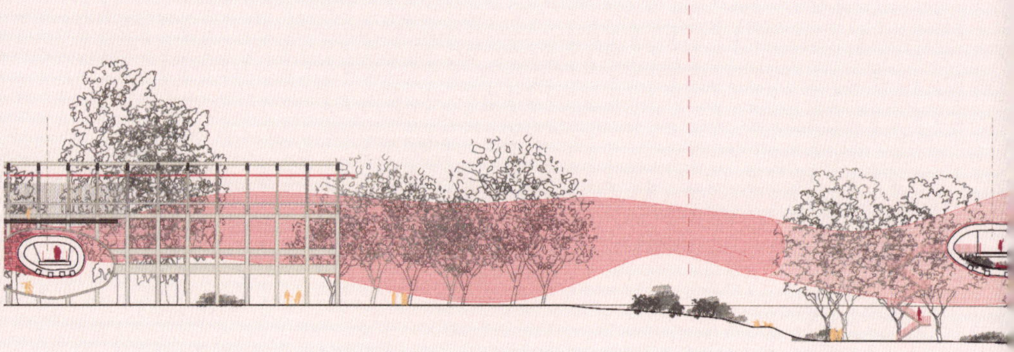

In his delightful book *Apuntes de viaje al interior del tiempo* (Notes from a Voyage inside Time), Luis Moreno Mansilla talked about architecture as "life pretending to be nature."[1] He wrote about travel, anecdotes, architects and landscape: landscapes where "architecture prowls", where life has deposited layer upon layer of information, leaving behind traces of countless generations' desires and aspirations in their attempt to emulate nature through architecture.

Luis used his trip through Italy as a pretext for reflections on architectural design and the title made it clear that everything would tie in with that great human invention, time. Time was always present in Luís's conversations about architecture. Time—necessary for life to be able to produce architecture—is difficult to understand, or even to describe, but little by little it leaves its mark on urban landscapes.

Renaissance and Baroque artists used architecture as a metaphor for time. In the 15th century, painters like Vittore Carpaccio painted landscapes that included buildings of an unknown perfection in their conception, details and finished to represent the utopia of future days, while in the 18th century painters like Canaletto framed their landscapes with buildings in ruins to evoke the nostalgia of past splendor.

Today, landscapes and architecture are mainly associated with movement.

School of Heat by Maria Elena Cardiel 104

Since the democratization of travel, which has become almost a right in industrialized countries, a growing number of landscapes have become part of the collective imagination of generations of both amateur and seasoned travelers. Different outlooks have woven together a network of places in constant transformation, which are interconnected yet not necessarily by their physical proximity, and they have shaped multiple visions of a reality that is changing at an ever-increasing rhythm.

Focusing architectural design on the landscape has made it easier for students to address the slippery nature of time, and it has helped them see that the first step in imagining new architecture is positioning oneself in a different time; new architecture cannot be produced with the tools of the past or the present. It has to be attuned to the dizzying changes in our society to avoid falling into irrelevance.

The first group of projects chose the former Nitrastur factory, popularly referred to as "el Nitrógeno", in the La Felguera neighborhood of the Asturian town of Langreo. Time suddenly changed speed there at the end of the last century when the production of synthetic products began to flag. When the compound was abandoned in 1997 the large-scale industrial warehouses built by Fernández Casado began to deteriorate progressively, and what had once

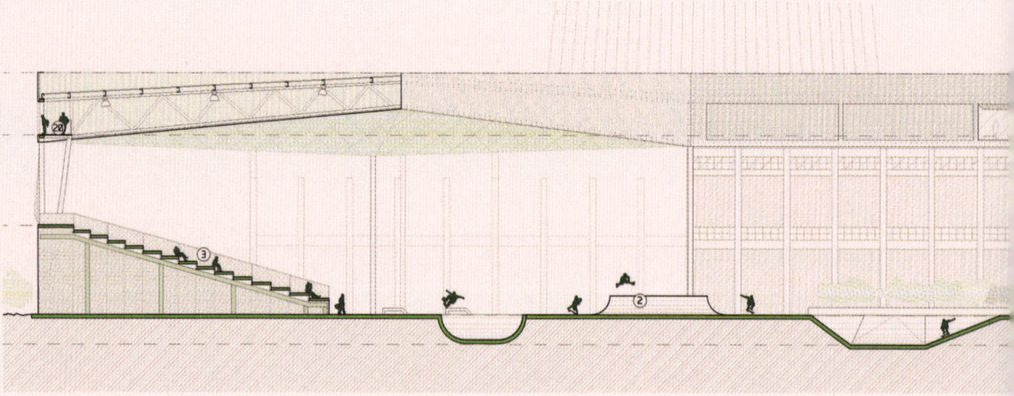

been a city within the city became a huge void, a barrier that divides Langreo in two, with an industrial scale that stands in violent contrast to the surrounding small-scale residential fabric.

The proposals begin by imagining new activities for this dead city, as a first step toward designing architecture with the potential to have a real effect on the social and economic reality of the region. Based on very different approaches, the projects all use a similar strategy. They maintain the ruins as they are, as remnants of the past, while taking advantage of the potential for contrasting new architecture—a new time—with the old industrial structures, so that the traces of history are not erased, playing with the possibilities for dialogue between past and future. Thus, the designs transcend what could have been a merely disciplinary exercise in order to offer solutions for urgent social problems, with clear references to similar experiences in Europe.

Another group of designs is located in a very different landscape: the center of Oviedo. Whereas Langreo was inextricably linked to its industrial activity, Oviedo's identity has been shaped by the slow trickle of innumerable biographies, many of which remain anonymous and only show through in the traces they have left behind in the urban fabric. These designs attempt to make those echoes heard, to add new layers to the complex structure of the landscape, intensifying the play of resonances with the aim of channeling the speed and intensity of the changes. Each change opens up a new area for economic and

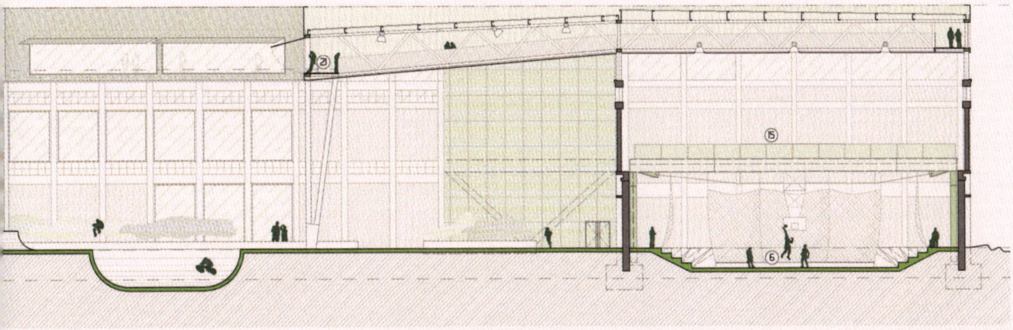

Sports Center by César Gusano 110

social development linked to artistic activities with high added value. Whereas in Langreo the goal was to provide a solution to urgent problems, in Oviedo the strategy aimed at exploring a rich world of suggestions and possibilities. Understanding architectural design as a necessary mechanism for shaping the urban landscape allowed for discovering a series of hidden or underused spaces where the intensification activities could be undertaken, through the introduction of the new program.

Each of the projects presented here enters into a dialog with the different times corresponding to the urban landscapes in the mining region, and all of them move beyond the traditional limits of architectural design to seek out new developmental avenues for the profession. They all make a conscious use of the architect's ability to spread out across time, bringing together past, present and future by designing activities and installations intended for an imaginary, potential time, which give shape to the aspirations and concerns of the inhabitants. All together, these proposals constitute a series of perspectives which help us adopt a different approach to their respective pasts.

1. Moreno Mansilla, Luis. *Apuntes de viaje al interior del tiempo*, Ed. Fundación Caja de Arquitectos, Barcelona, 2002.

222 SCHOOL OF HEAT

Mª Elena Cardiel

The project is located in an urban area in central Asturias, home to a key element in contemporary Asturian-Leonese industrial heritage. The proposal attempts to reactivate and reorganize the abandoned Nitrastur industrial complex using a provocative and cosmopolitan program: a Sexuality Center linked to an aromatic garden. The entire project is part of a tourism strategy founded on belonging to a consolidated European territorial network. In the first place, the design is related to the modern style warehouses by Fernández Casado, which are in ruins and have taken on a monumental character. In the second place, the proposal includes two aromatic gardens and two large built volumes. The introduction of a public urban aromatic garden incorporates a new use into the municipality and reactivates the empty space of the Nitrastur complex, occupying the entire plot and connecting the two adjacent neighborhoods. The new volumes take on a geometry that is completely different from the existing buildings, providing each of the buildings with a personal character by contrasting them strongly and clearly. These new volumes connect the warehouses and allow for creating a semi-interior private promenade and garden.

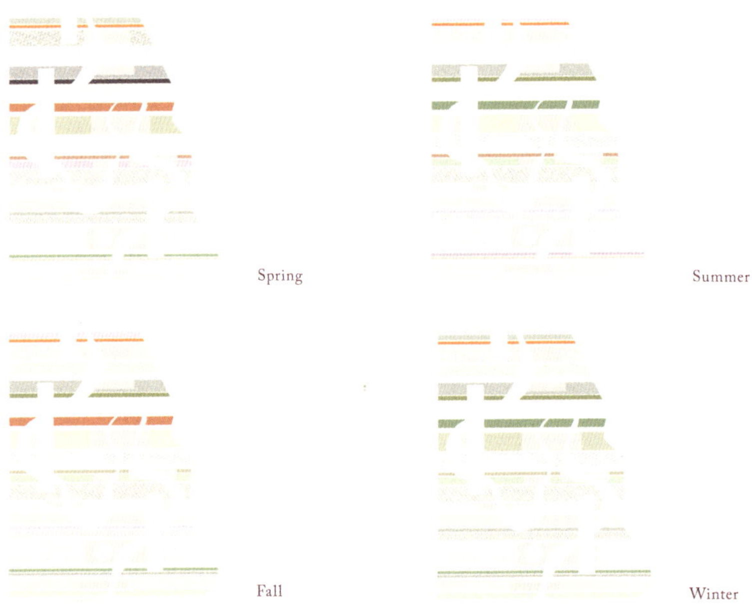

Seasonal landscape change

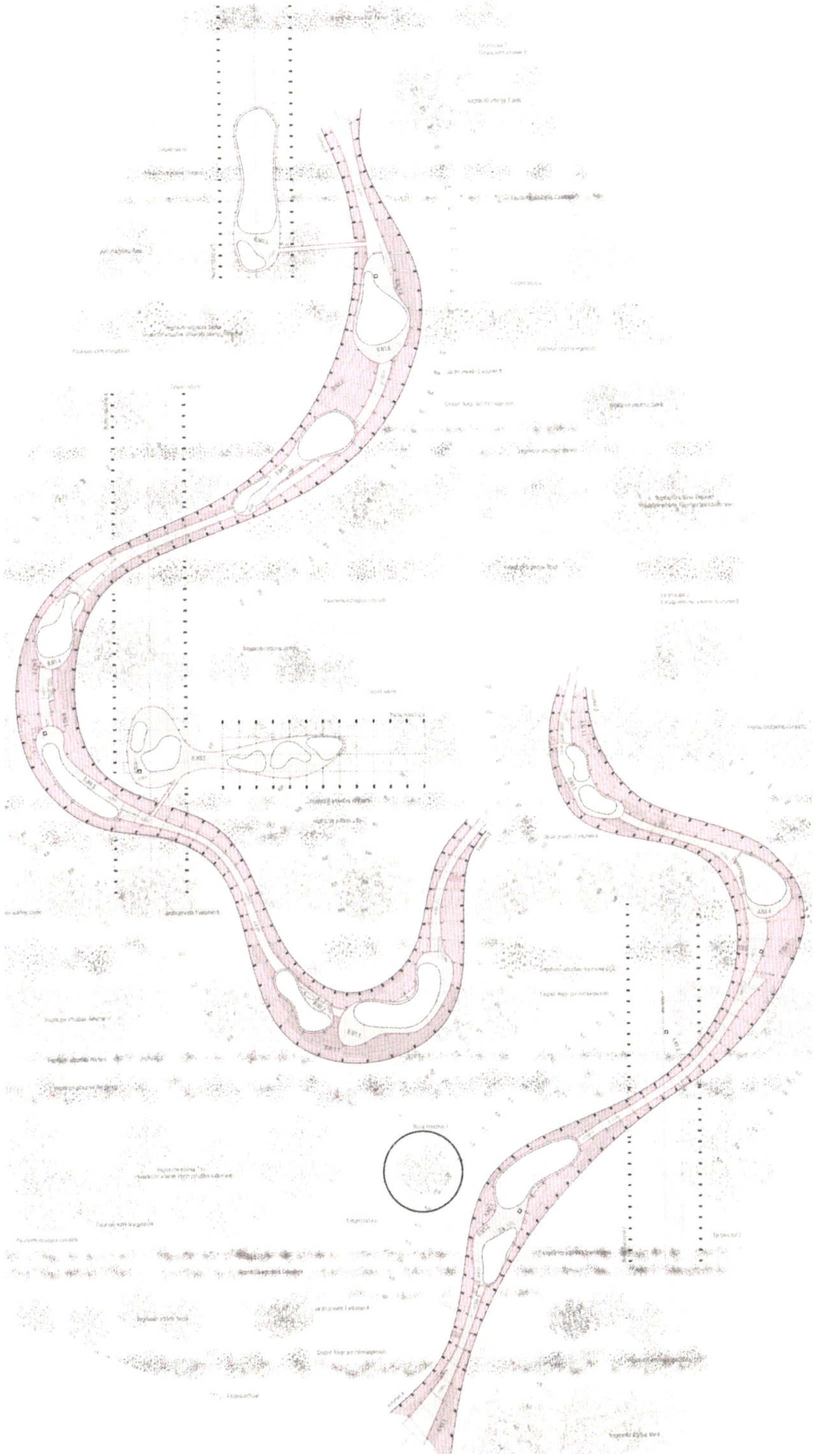

Ground Floor Plan

222

FORBIDDEN SCENARIOS

Ana González Granja

Where is the limit between prohibition and desire? To attract tourism a space should offer identity and be desirable; it should be limited in time and conditioned in context. Forbidden Scenarios pursues a unique encounter and a particular identity for Oviedo. It wants to make the invisible visible We are going to taste through emotion, through a gastronomic experience associated with dance. Where is the limit, if there is one, between the physical and non-physical components of a city?

Pre-exisiting conditions understood as potential spaces, allow us to create architecture inside architecture. An engagement is produced between the visitor, the interior-exterior, the context and the experience. Six inaccessible spaces whose limits leave voids full of memory are invaded in the city of Oviedo.

Inside Forbidden Scenarios pleasure is served. A new gastronomic experience linked to dance, where three scenarios are associated with three places for tasting.

The space, understood as a continuous architectural choreography, is anchored to a context full of character and memory. An urban performance reveals the secrects of what was hidden.

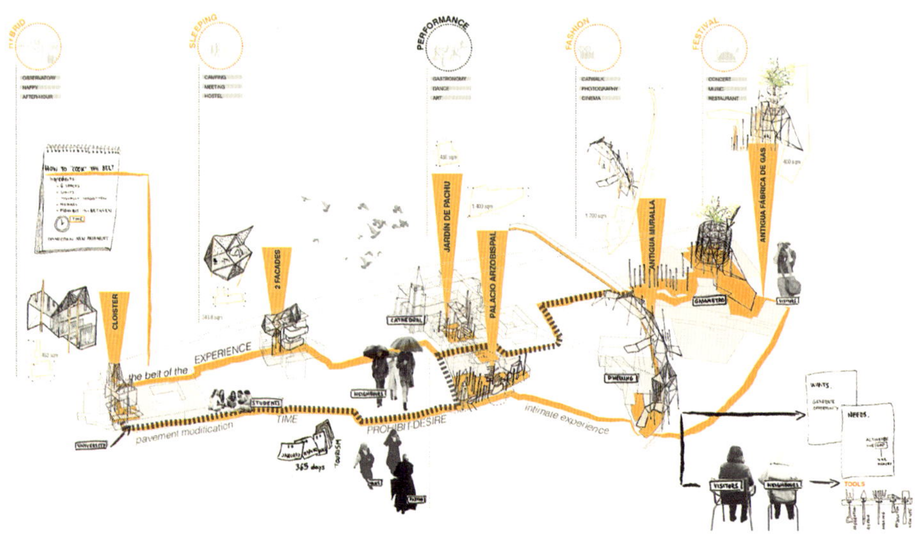

Project diagram

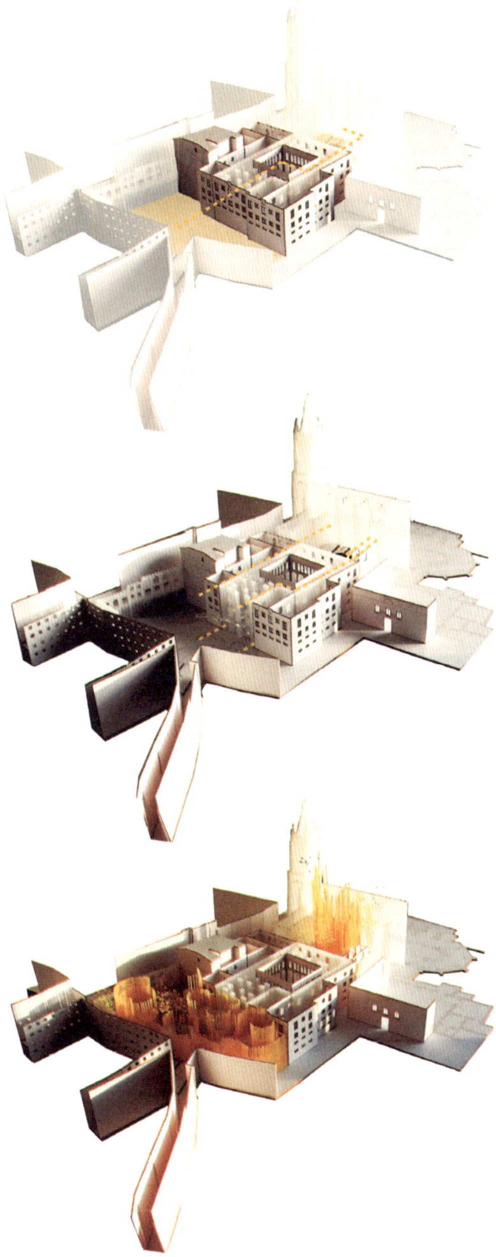

Model

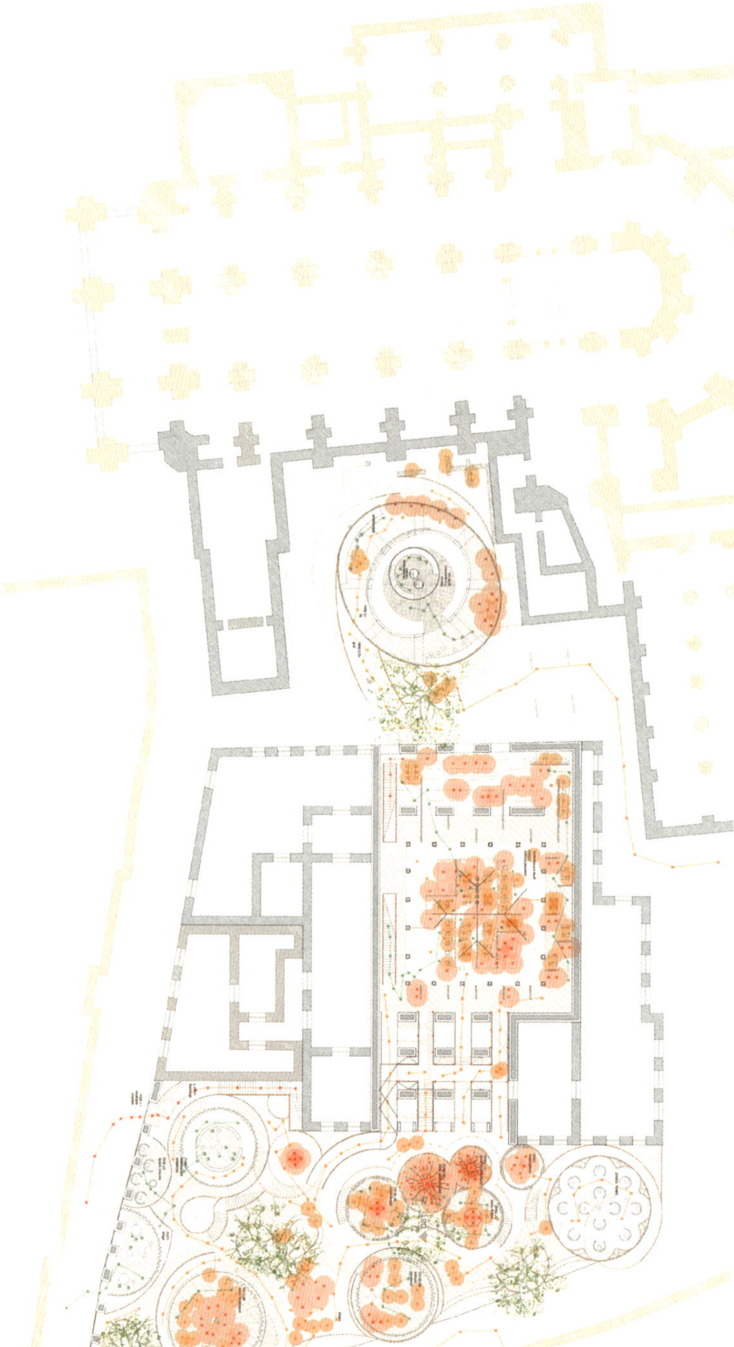

General plan showing the existing structures

Views

222 — SPORTS CENTER

César Gusano

The growing interest in sports tourism and the shortage of facilities for certain newly established disciplines are the main reasons behind this project. Sports such as skateboarding, rollerblading, BMX, parkour, etc. are commonly practiced in urban environments that have not been adapted, and this design is intended to respond to this need.

Imagining a place for practicing these sports is synonymous with imagining new topographies. In addition, these sports require a dry, covered area.

Thus, the most important operation in the design is the introduction of a large roof over the existing buildings, in conjunction with the space that is generated between them. This creates a large outdoor public plaza that is ideal for the proposed sports activities and it constitutes a new protection for the interior spaces. As a complement to this large roof, a series of topographical variations are introduced into the terrain to generate hollows or protrusions, which serve as the surfaces where most of the program is developed.

Model

View under the roof structure

222 OVIEDO IN THE MOVIES

Beatriz Fernández Gómez

This project is developed at a time when urban tourism in Oviedo is *in crescendo*. It not only relates with people, but also with legacy, topography and boundaries (both natural and artificial), which hold back a lot of possibilities that can make a city grow and work not only for the locals, but also for the tourists.

The project pursues the transformation of the empty spaces of the city into places for people to meet through the concept of cinema.The cinema world is created with scenography. In order to shape the spaces, several scenographic resources have been extracted from the cinema world.

The different techniques to amplify spaces in cinema are summarized in the mirror reflections, using a movable LED façade, stroboscopic spaces and mirror effects at the main entrance, facing the cathedral square.

This threshold amplifies the space and shows the diverse activities that take place, from information points, to the stairs that climb up to the auditorium/cinema passing through the cafeteria, which are open to a more touristic use.

Movies shot in the area of intervention

General view of the project with the cathedral tower in the foreground

222 CITY OF FASHION

Cristina Moreno

The project is based on the idea of rehabilitating some of the buildings in the Nitrastur compound in an "unconventional" way, using a walkway that connects two warehouses. Qualities such as ephemeral, lasting, temporary, timeless, static, mobile or adaptable have been characteristic of 21st century architectural language. Similarly, these concepts also appear in historic fashion dictionaries. Throughout the centuries, fashion and architecture have shared an aesthetic stage and have developed in parallel, growing ever closer. This design develops a device to provide a new purpose for the existing warehouses. Without it, their use would not be possible. An idea as simple as installing a catwalk connects us to the world of fashion. This space, which can be transformed over time using both fixed and variable program, will attract people to the key locations in the area, creating prominent viewpoints. A light and articulated structure penetrates into the buildings, allowing for an ample capacity for transformation. A catwalk draws us directly into the world of fashion.

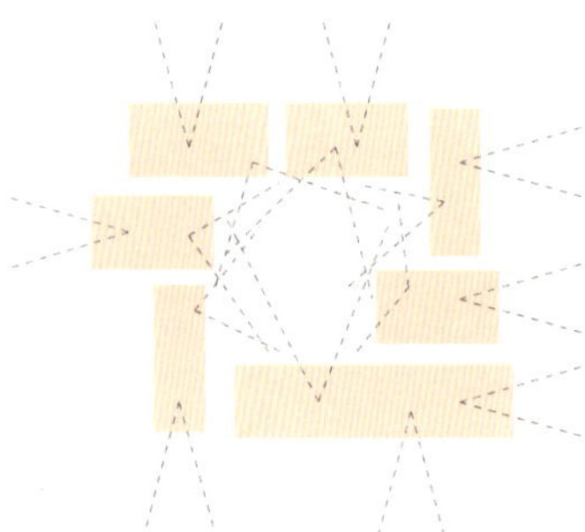

Potential connections

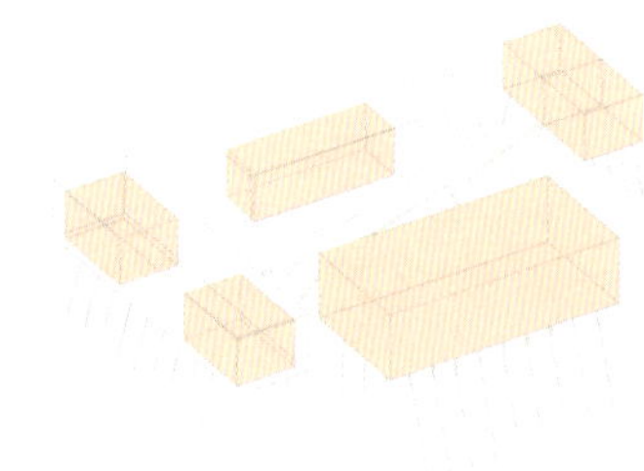

Infiltration

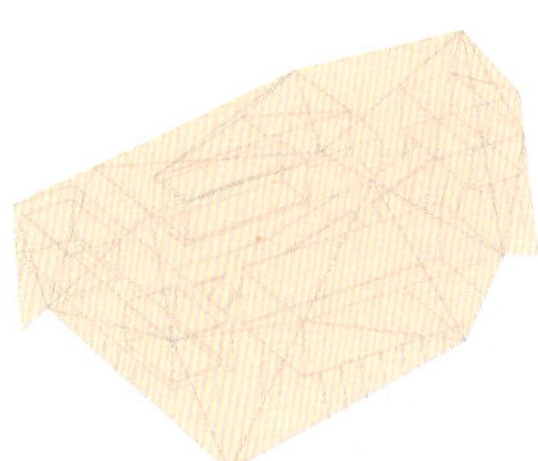

Envelope

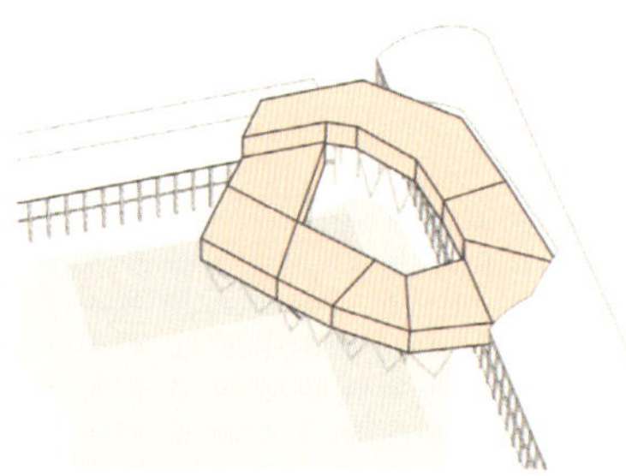

Proposal

Organization diagrams

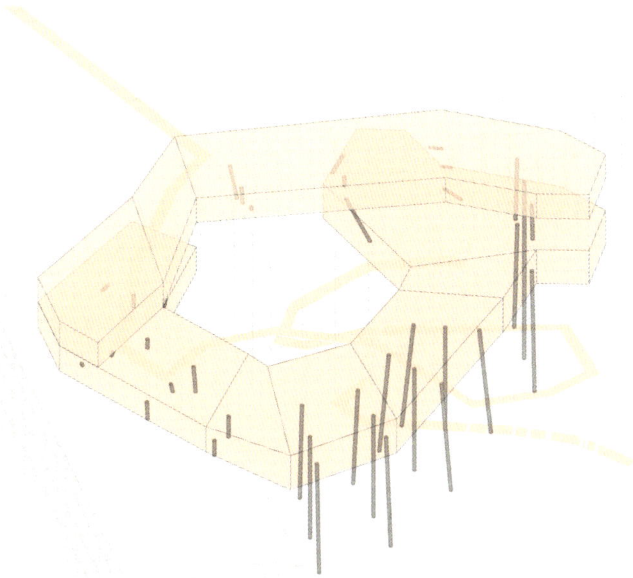

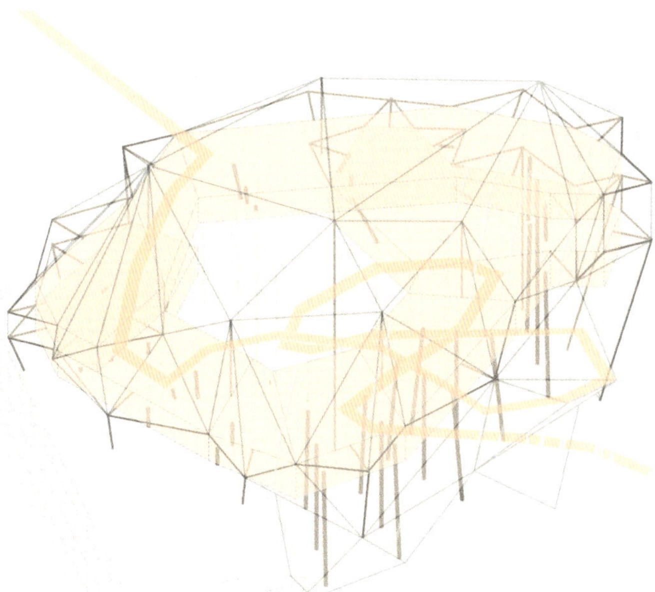

Axonometric studies

EXTREME LANDSCAPES

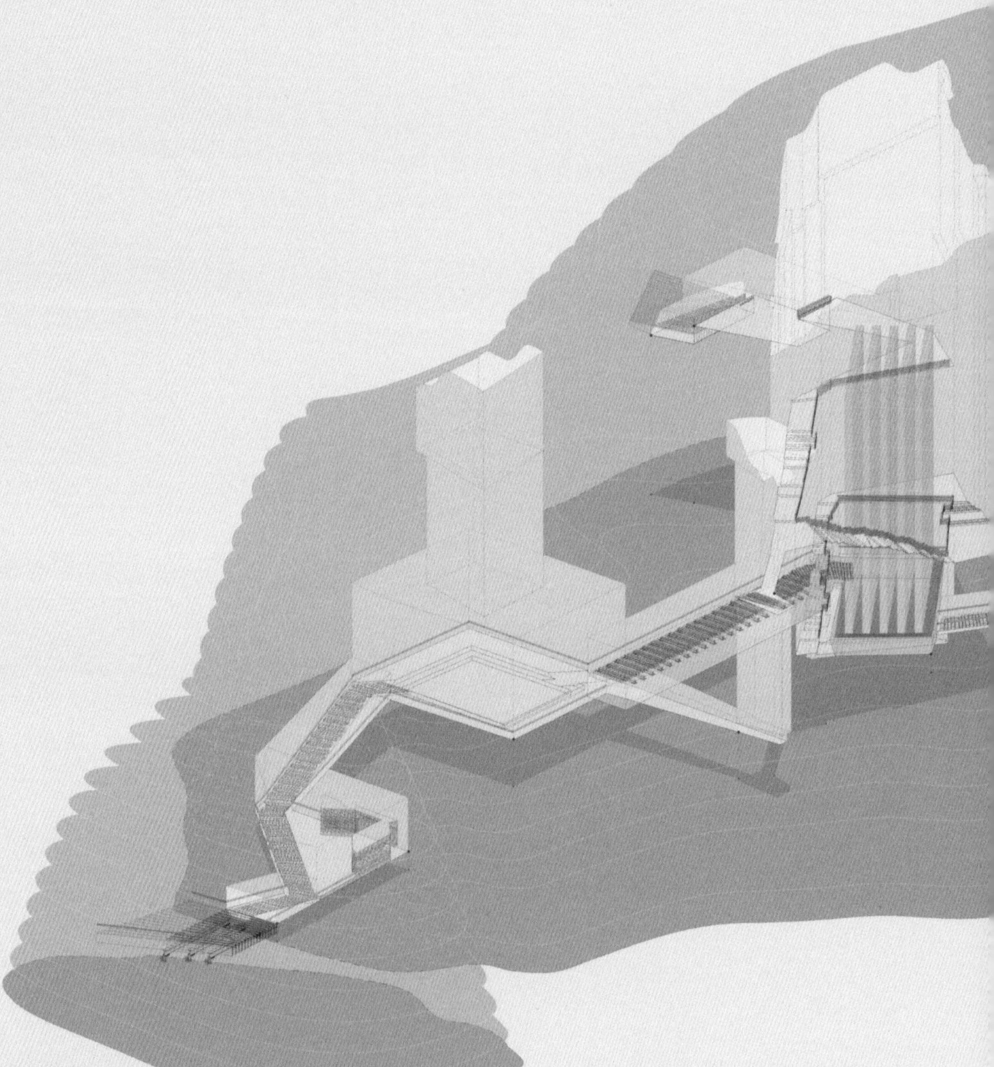

Paths of Perception by Cecilia Marina. Speculation on an underground landscape at Erbosa Island aimed to capture the phenomenological essences of the landscapes in Asturias and Leon.

223 — MEDIUM AND PLASTICITY

192 — Juan Elvira
Professor of Urban Workshop and Design Critic, FTP-DSVII, TOTAL IBERIA 1.0, IE University

In order to address the architecture of extreme landscapes, we first have to determine the meaning of this natural category. Extreme landscapes are not just riverbeds or high mountain lakes. They can be any place where architecture seems unconceivable: like a mountain cliff, inside a body of water, or the rocky heart of a geological formation. In an extreme landscape nature is perceived as an unlimited extension, where architecture is not only absent, but forgotten.

The central quality of designs that operate in them is their landscape dimension. For two reasons: first, because they intervene in a natural surrounding and their presence is significant on a territorial scale. Second, because they reproduce the characteristics of those natural spaces in their interiors. Extreme landscapes contribute to the idea of landscapes within architecture.

Independently of their scale, these designs combine architecture and infrastructure. They take on certain qualities of territorial infrastructure, but they also incorporate a capacity for functional reprogramming, which is characteristic of architecture. They are flexible; they are open to change. That is where one of their greatest potentials lies, since they propose appropriations and interventions that are open to different uses—a condition that infrastruc-

Hidden Underwater by Vanesa Payo. An unprecedented take on the 136
reservoir infrastructure, very common in the Spanish territory. The construction of new reservoirs during the sixties led to the flooding of vast inhabitated areas. The immersed building acts as a filtering device and a diving facility.

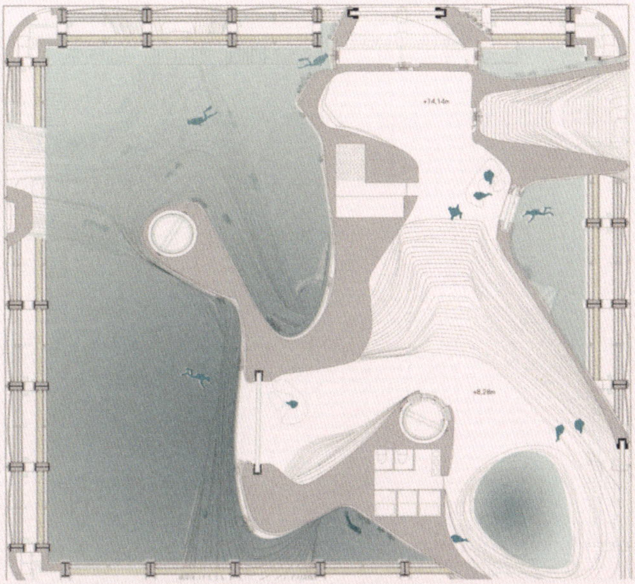

tures normally do not fulfill, strictly speaking—allowing them to avoid an otherwise inevitable obsolescence.

Another of their qualities is ambiguity. The architecture of extreme landscapes stands at an equal distance from invasiveness and mimicry. It bluntly deploys all of the artificial means at its disposal, while coexisting harmoniously with its surroundings, generating habitats that exist in a fascinating intermediate state. Looking on, we ask ourselves if we are standing before a ruin designed to be immediately invaded by vegetation, water and land, or whether it was conceived as an architectural invasion of nature.

In this sense it is significant that these interventions, far from falling into nostalgia, display an ability to manipulate nature, the plasticity of the medium. Although these designs don't imitate nature, nor do they employ the rhetoric of preservation or the absence of any impact, they do avoid negating nature. They do not dramatize sustainability or ecology, but a certain naturalization of architectural organization is evident in them. Architecture that we might call "extreme" owes this ambiguity to the desire to articulate the conflicts present in the medium in which it operates, working with the potential of its surraings.

124 *Ecological Bridges* by Clara Bueno. This new infrastructure extends the series of paths and animal tracks that cover the entire area of Valle del Lago near Pola de Somiedo. A set of platforms hang from the main structure, housing different program related to tourism.

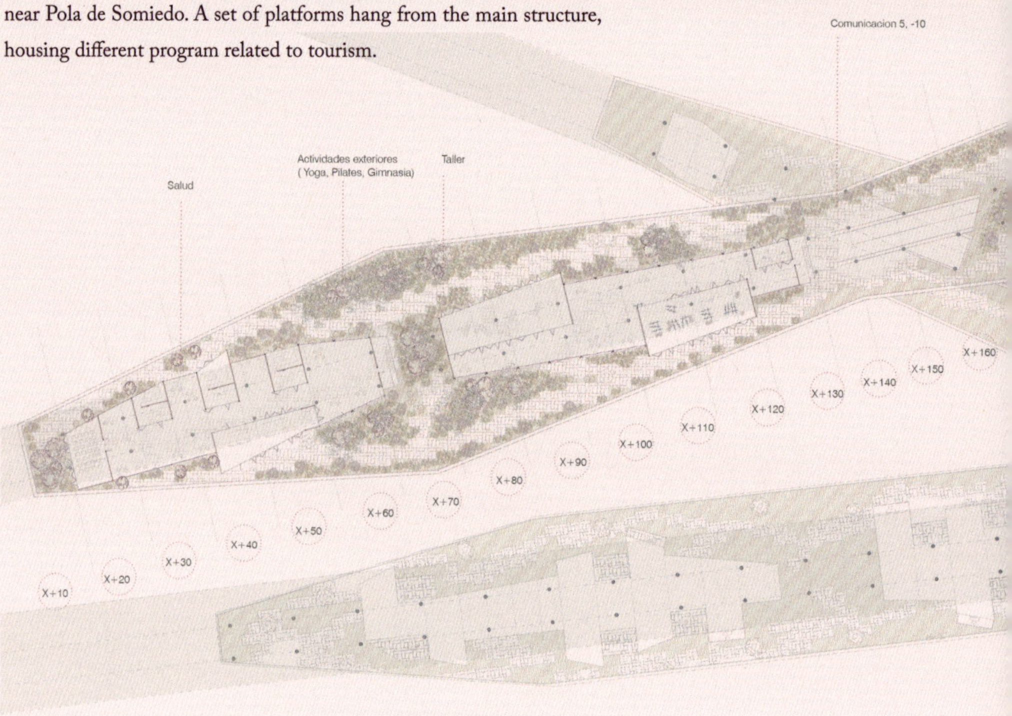

The preparation of an analytical understanding of the context and a natural sensitivity play a fundamental role. Each agent, force and process is present. Beyond design, we can assert that they cultivate actions in the landscape, following a logic that intertwines with that of the medium where they are developed. Therein lies its proximity to environmental sustainability.

Far from being autonomous and self-referential, this architecture is strictly cultural (in the sense of something that is cultivated) because it accepts its artificiality in relation to the medium and deliberately exhibits this quality. They are "second natures" in a double sense. The first refers to what takes shape with what seems like inherent ease, though that is only an appearance because it is rooted in a profound knowledge of the medium. The second alludes to the construction of an alternate nature, where architectural action dissolves into the medium in which it operates, amplifying it. The architecture of extreme landscapes uses occupational logics that are characteristic of nature. It frequently resorts to patterns to define laws for occupying the territory. Its limits are imprecise or they are the result of outlining a regular perimeter onto the abstract texture of the organization, which could otherwise extend indefinitely.

The architecture of extreme landscapes short-circuits preexisting topologi-

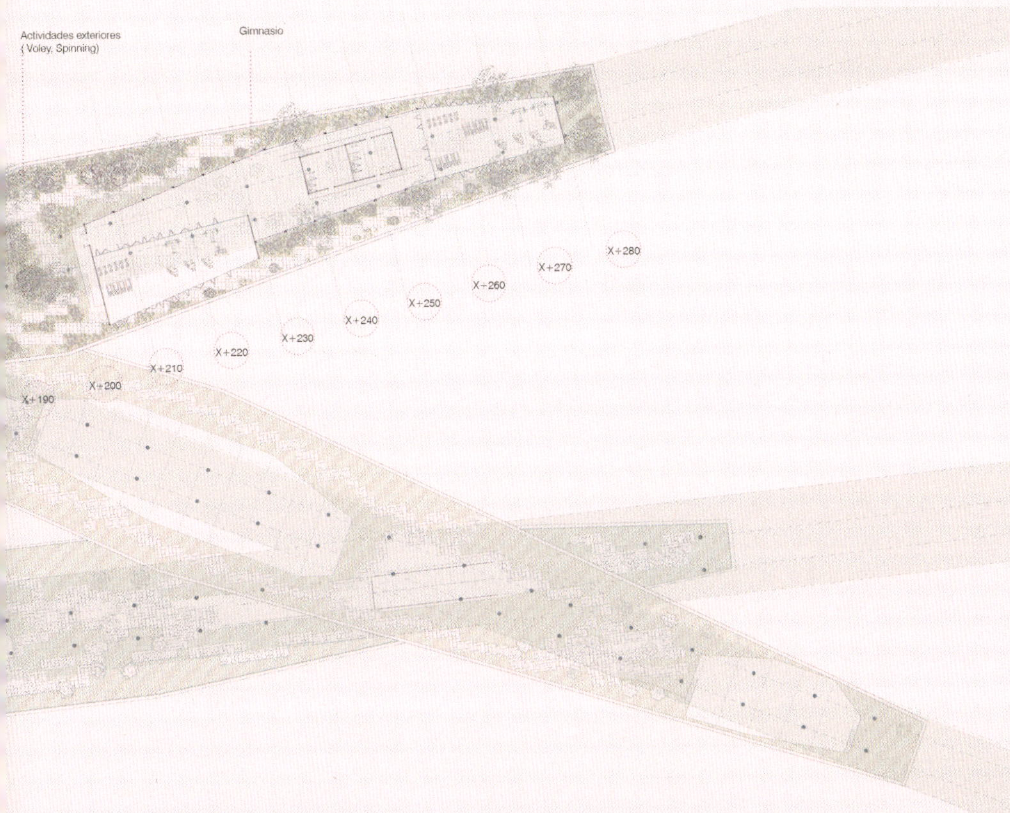

cal relationships; it modifies them. It constructs altered natural conditions. It reproduces "extreme" experiences in nature —like mountaineering, speleology or diving— which condition how they should be experienced. It projects unprecedented environments that are meant to be discovered, explored and colonized. Exploring them implies foraying into places where the rules don't follow the usual codes of architectural design. This architecture is meant to be climbed, to dive into, to get lost in. It is an untamed space, an unpredictable landscape that has to be explored.

We find ourselves before architecture that, in the end, we could classify as wild. No doubt unexplored nature is an increasingly rare commodity and any that does still exist is subject to protection and preservation. The wild —far from instilling fear and serving as the setting for monstrosity— now needs to be protected, with the support of those who used to fear it above all else. Perhaps that is why, more than ever, we need feral untamable architecture that is identified with extreme landscapes, that integrates the qualities of experiences in nature.

Architecture that aims to be mountain, cave, river, lake.

224

HYPERSENSORY CENTER

Íñigo Arias Dávila

Moving through this building brings us closer to the hidden history of the towns that lie beneath the dark waters of the Barrios de Luna reservoir. The project is rooted in the tensions emanating from the surroundings. The hill where it is built has a steep slope, which allows for views of the surroundings and the fields of León on the horizon. These tensions are summed up in the thick concrete walls. The organization in plan presents a complex space that has to be discovered as you move through it. The project is planned as a twinning of different spaces, where the need to reach the next location creates a new and different view, which then links into another space and the cycle begins again.

The Plant Spine is the key element that runs through the building, consisting of a series of spaces that are combined disjointedly. Along this spine, the courtyards are strung together as condensed points of activity. This provides a smooth flow of circulation, where the simplicity of the geometries helps us decipher the space around us.

Context tensions and general view

Site model showing the overall plan organization

224 — ECOLOGICAL BRIDGES

Clara Bueno

We are in the Valle del Lago, near Pola de Somiedo. A series of paths and animal tracks dominate the area and serve as the starting point for the proposal.

The project is an Eco-Bridge that acts as an extension of these paths through the valley, to make it easier to cross from one side to the other, and to provide new expansion routes for the local flora and fauna.

A number of platforms hang from the main structure, each with a different program. The first is the knowledge platform, where all the activities intended to improve tourist efficiency and to expand their knowledge of the area and the sport they are going to participate in. The second is the food platform, which houses the restaurant and bar.

Finally, the third platform is for relaxing, where there are rooms intended for tourist lodging. All together, it creates a focal point for tourism in Somiedo Natural Park.

Bridges' crossing paths

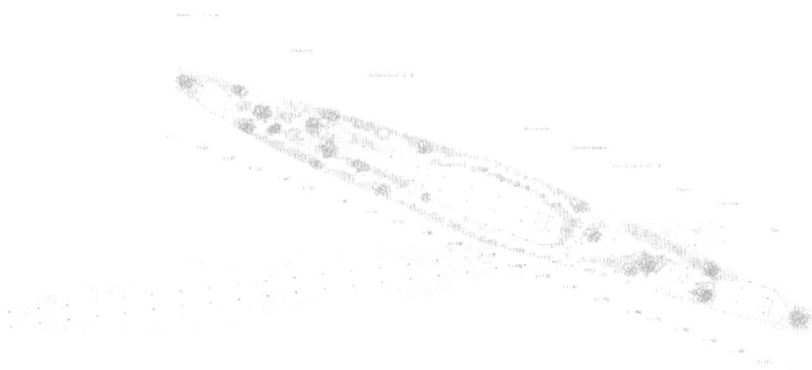

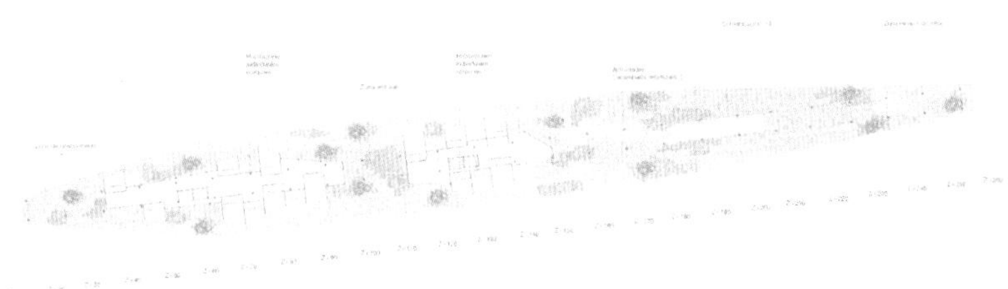

Plans

224 —

EXCAVATION BETWEEN TWO LANDSCAPES

Ettore Disconzi

The main concept for this project is the orchestation of a sequence of actions in the natural landscape.

It is planned in time through three main stages. The first stage is rock excavation. The second, the positioning of the post-tensioned concrete. Finally, the third stage involves reusing of the excavated rock.

Globally, it aims to design an artificial landscape where the natural materials are rearranged with new architectural qualities.

The general organization combines two types of limits. One is precise and accurate, the other is soft and organic and faces the sea. Between both of them, several collective functions are organized.

Dwelling units are designed to achieve the maximum light throughout the day.

Project stages showing the topographical formation of the project

Model showing the traces of the interior volumes

224

HANGING BY A THREAD

Juan González

Sometimes we look out over a cliff but we don't dare jump.

Architecture is that big cliff, where the formula for getting a good result rarely involves cautiously peeking into the abyss. We have to take the risk although it may sometimes leave us hanging by a thread. This design is based on the idea of inhabiting different vertical walls through a temporary system of colonization, with the aim of promoting varied natural settings, using extreme sports as a tool for taking advantage of all of its possibilities. The building is a high performance center for the practice of extreme sports and training. The strategy temporarily colonizes different vertical walls of the boundary between the provinces of León and Asturias.

The project program cannot be enclosed within a building. It is not a static program; timing and seasonality are fundamental, and it varies depending on the time of year.

Among other references, the proposal refers to the systems used by climbers to temporarily inhabit the high mountains.

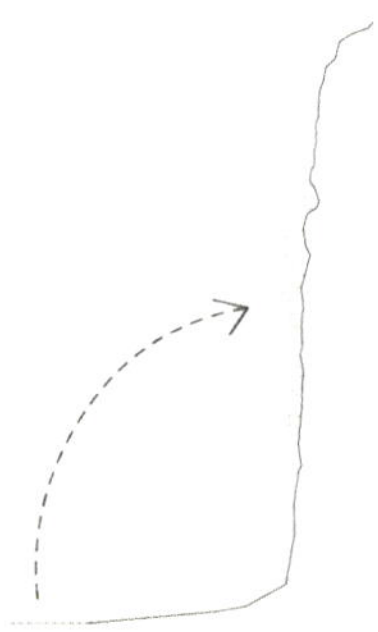

Action

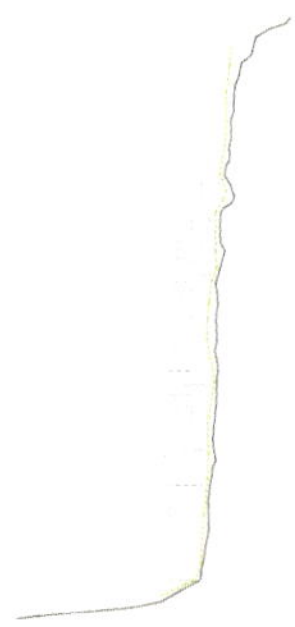

Colonization

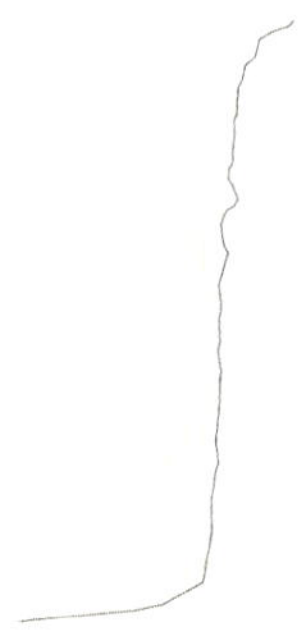

Structure

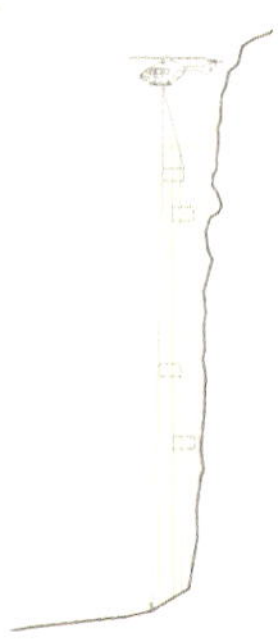

Implementation

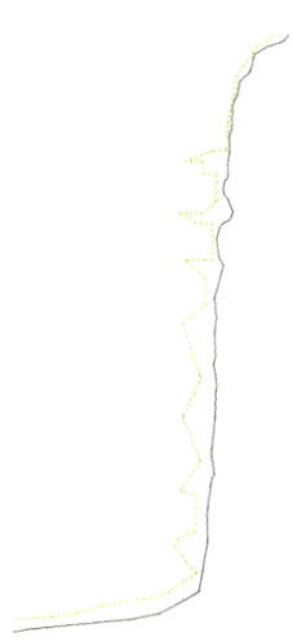

Routes

Proposal

Technologies

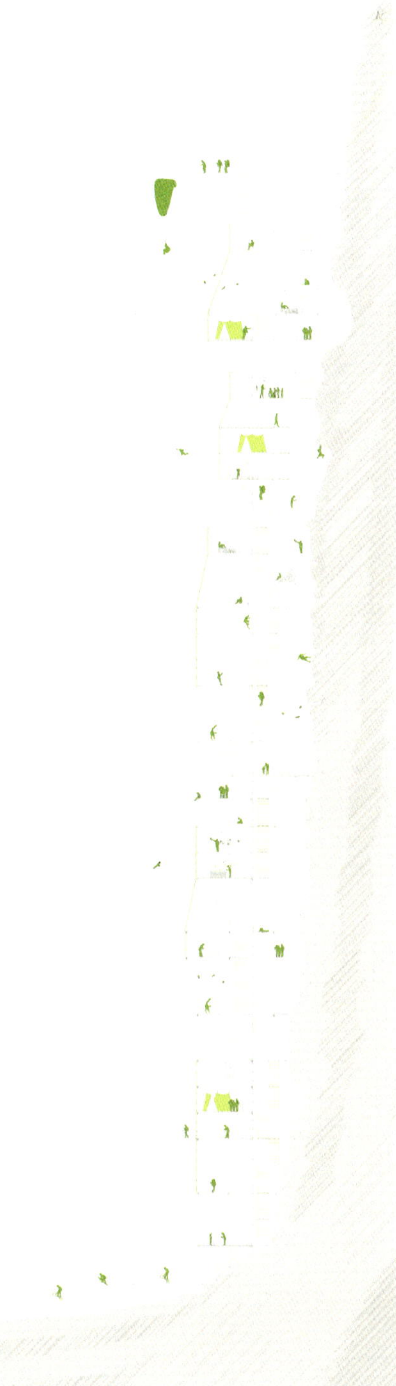

Cross section with upper and lower accesses

Appropriation of textile structures

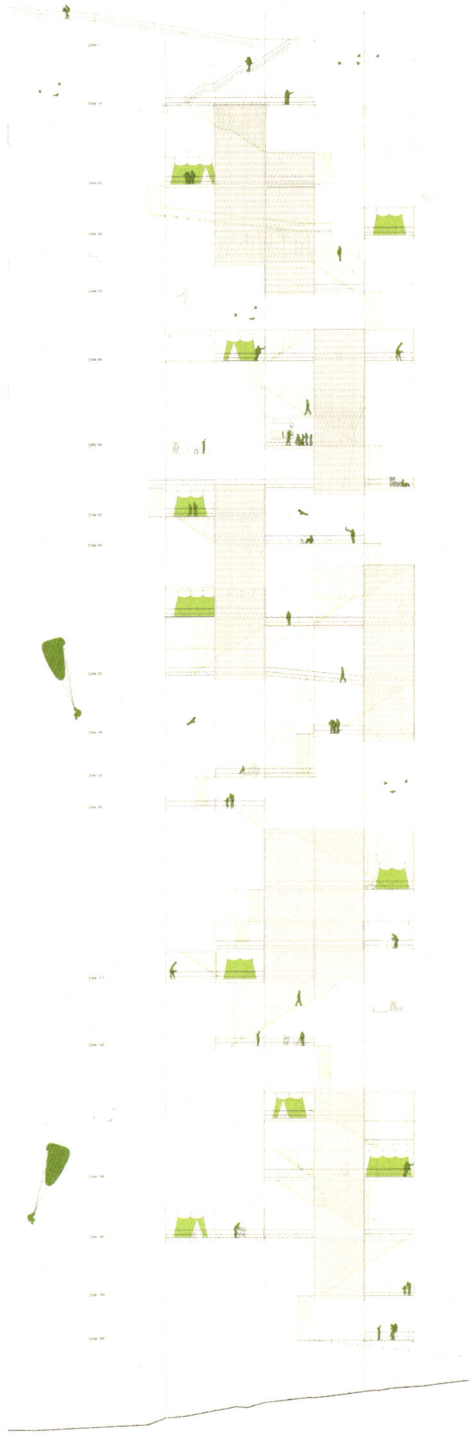

General elevation

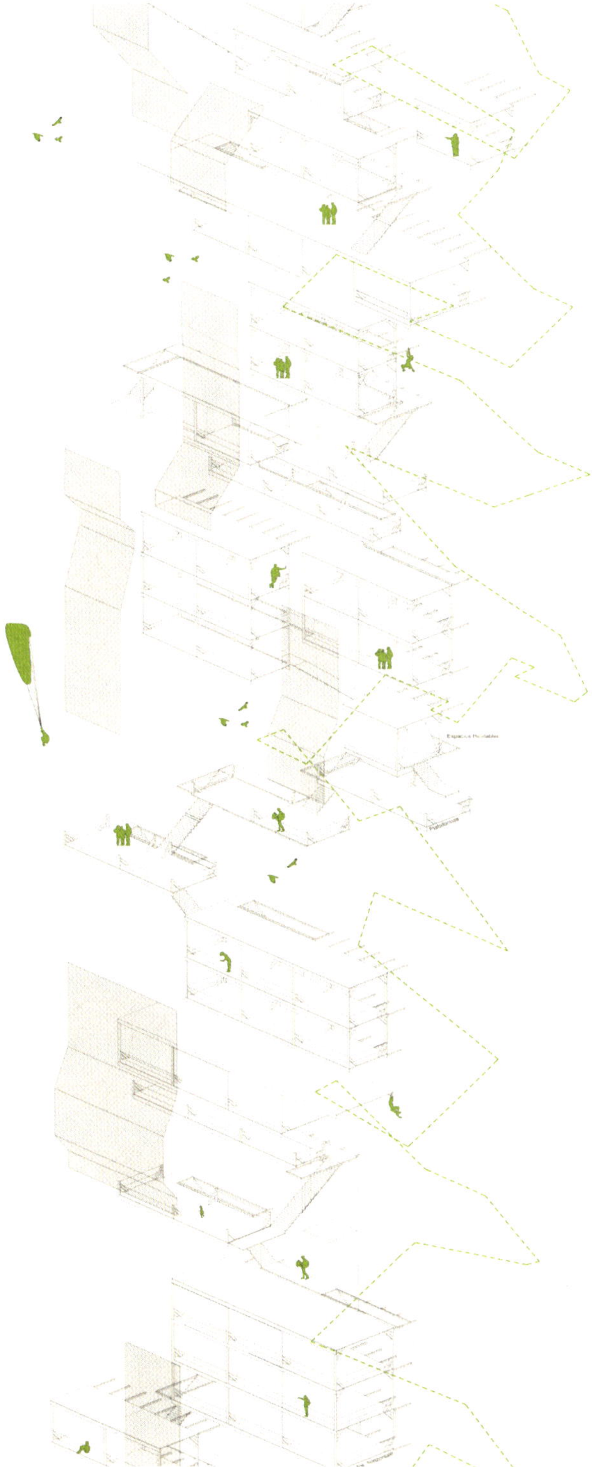

Analysis of structural and spatial components

224 PATHS OF PERCEPTION

Cecilia Marina

Gardens in the Asturian-Leonese landscape on Erbosa island are a natural environment where visitors connect with the essence of these distinctive places. They attempt to concentrate the perceptual essences of the landscape in Asturias and Leon in one specific place.

Faced with the immobility and the forcefulness of the site, these spaces for sensory connection use the climate and the environment to establish a new internal dynamism.

While the weather is of great importance in the project, water also plays a key role.

The project is a natural machine where the local climate is brought into the garden, modifies it and transforms it into a dynamic space.

The space is neutral, sturdy and empty, capable of housing different sensations in its interior without detracting from any aspect of the program.

The interior of the granite becomes a neutral space that is charged with meaning, where interventions by different artists associated with the world of sculpture temporarily provide meaning to the empty spaces.

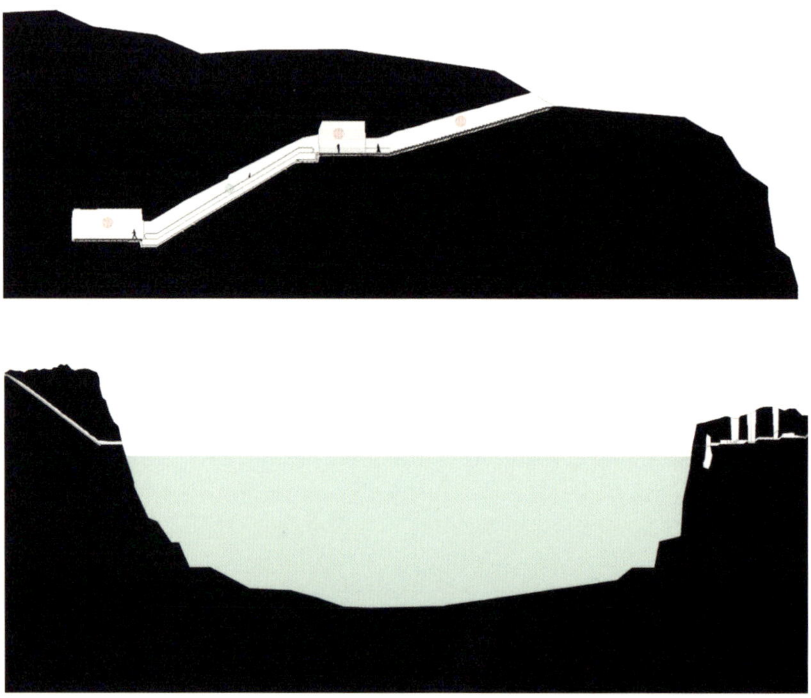

General sections showing the project carved on the rock

Cross sections

224 — HIDDEN UNDERWATER

HIDDEN UNDERWATER

Vanesa Payo

Water decides when to reveal the treasures it contains.

Building reservoirs in Spain was a very important operation, often repeated throughout the peninsula. This is a fundamental fact regarding the context of this project.

The construction of these infrastructures caused some controversy since when they were built priority was given to irrigation at the expense of numerous small towns that were flooded, forcing residents to find new homes.

Specifically, the waters of the Barrios de Luna reservoir hide the ruins of the twelve villages that were flooded. The building proposed here is also immersed in the reservoir. This situation generates a location that is identifiable and attractive for tourism.

Enclosing a portion of water within a porous cube creates a space around the ruins of the church of the flooded village, Miñera. The façade is designed as a mechanism to filter the water, so that it is suitable for diving and allows for visibility of the ruins.

The project maintains part of the memory of the Barrios de Luna reservoir and its former village, making it visible.

Overall section showing the project immersed in the lake Barrios de Luna

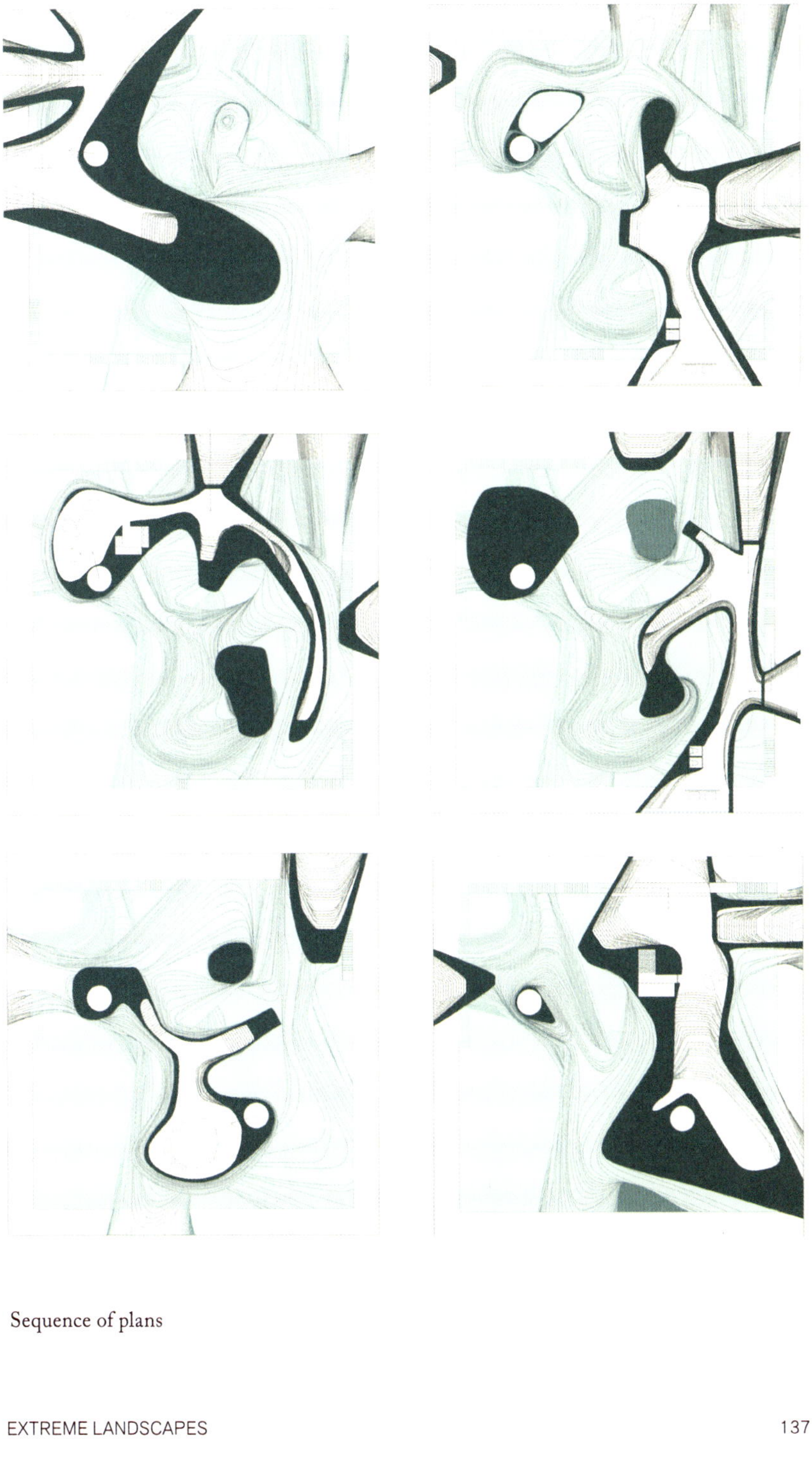

Sequence of plans

225 — EARTHEN

Marina Carretero

The project sits upon a slate vein, a geological dike near a river. It aims to study different ways of approaching the site and let people enjoy it in a gentle way. The program becomes a spiritual retreat unveiling the most hidden nature, such as the inside of the vein, allowing users to approach this uninhabited area. Therefore, the way the project touches the ground, and the way the project is designed, result in unique spaces for users to find themselves in nature, through architecture. From the shaping of the vein to the stacking of rocks in the walls, the architectural design becomes a full experience of what nature can give us, allowing users to experience a unique kind of solitude, viewing nature and architecture as if they were one.

The project strategy splits the full program in different volumes, proposing a coherent route all through it, merging visitors who have just entered with other visitors. This proposed—but not mandatory—route allows for housing different programs in the campus, creating spaces for different kind of tourism (hiking, working, etc.) giving the site a renewed but respectful use.

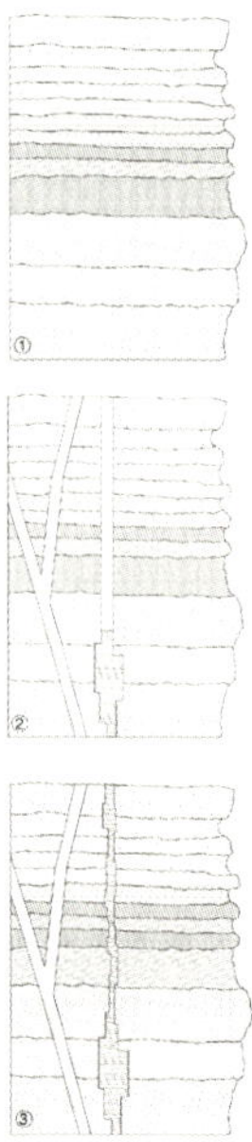

Occupation patterns Sitemap

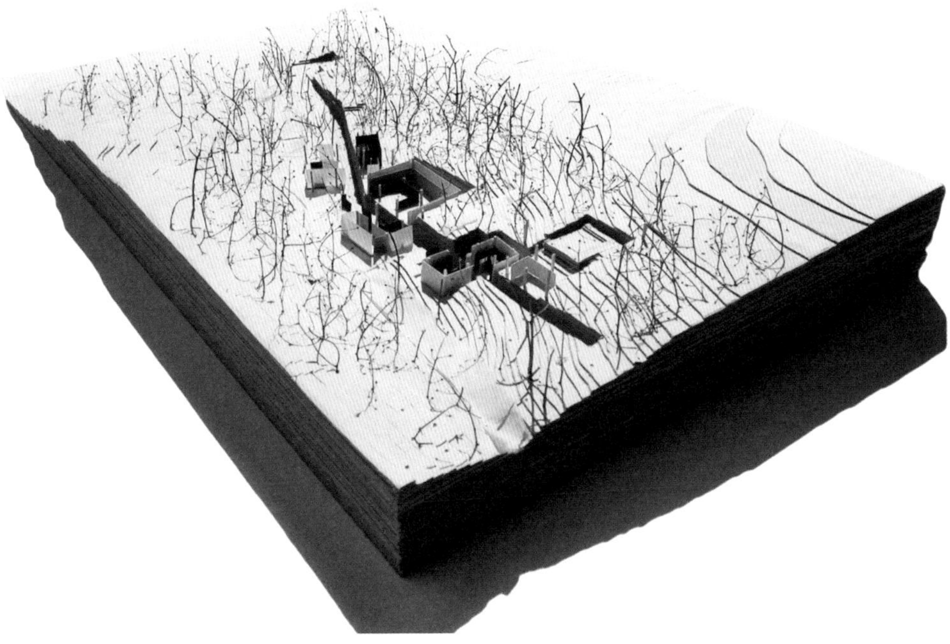

Voids running along the slate vein

INDUSTRIAL LANDSCAPES

Asturias' Loudspeaker by Leticia Merino. Six spaces contained in six bubbles related to sound production inside an abandoned industrial chimney.

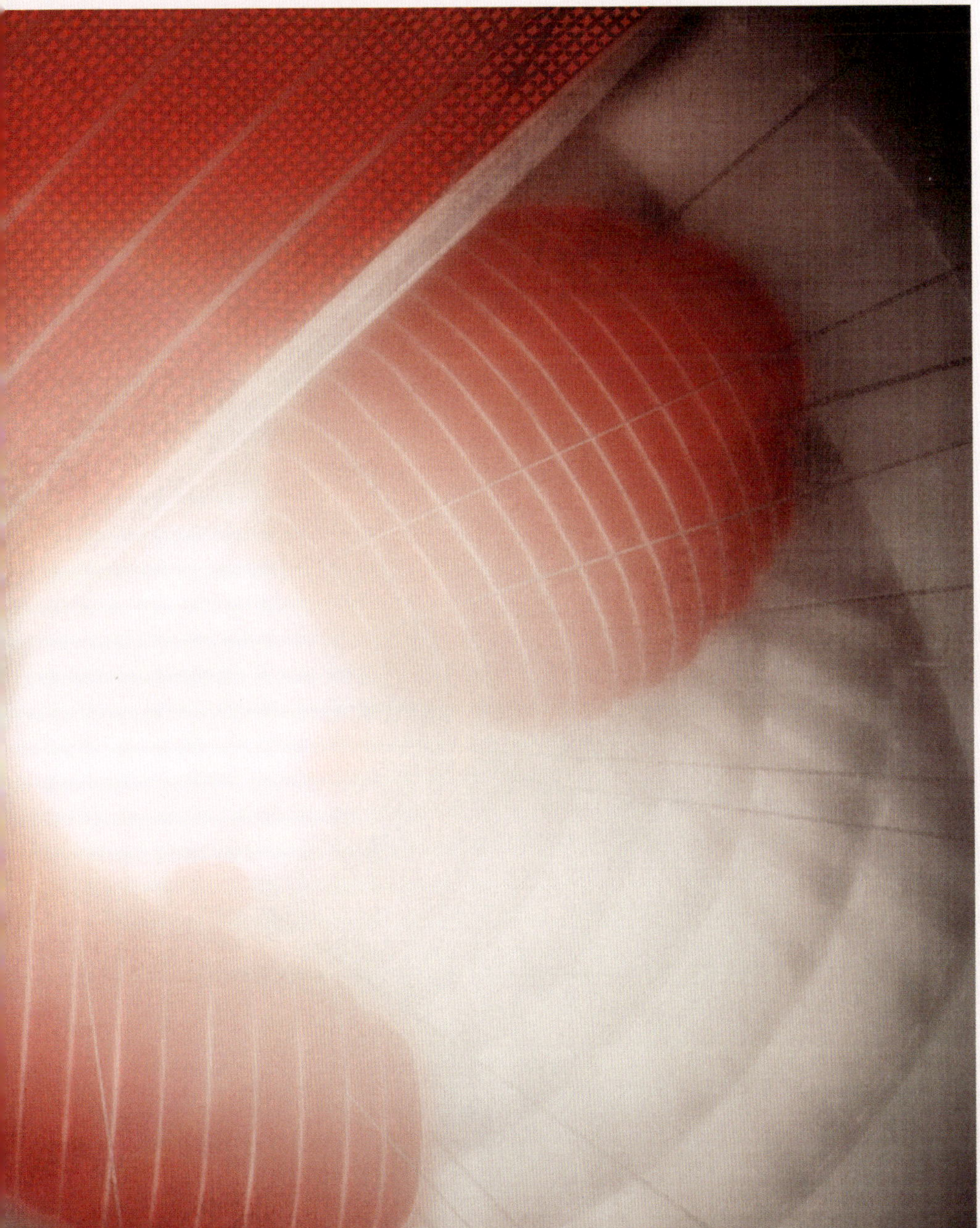

225 — # MEMORY AS A MATERIAL OF ARCHITECTURE

192 — Mónica García
Design Critic, UTP-DSVII, TOTAL IBERIA 1.0, IE University

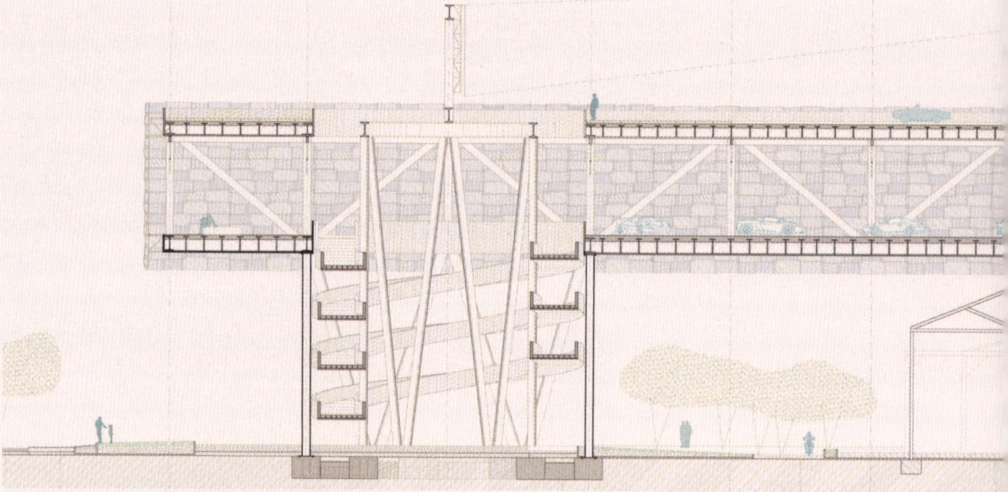

The concept of an industrial landscape is included within the wider theoretical framework of a cultural landscape, a historical series of natural values along with values resulting from human action. The possibility of linking the terms "industrial" and "landscape", which are in principle mutually exclusive, is relatively recent. The shift in the concept of landscape —from a fixed image of nature to any product of human activity, be it rural, urban or even industrial— has made this alliance possible. In Discovering the Vernacular Lanscape (1984) John Brinckerhoff Jackson offers the following formula for landscape: *a composition of man-made spaces on the land*.[1] The landscape, the cultural landscape, is therefore a synthetic space, an artificial system of overlapping spaces that function and evolve, not only according to natural laws, but to serve a community.

The industrial landscape in the Astur-Leonesa (ACTAL) tourist area extends beyond the series of factory buildings, mining constructions, storage tanks... heritage objects, inert morphologies. It has the ability to represent the nature of the territory, the raw materials and their transformation, how the industrial events are linked to the systems of social organization, and ultimately life itself. Those landscapes are imbued with the memory of work and the recent history of the industrial communities that cherish them. Working on industrial landscapes is aligned with a statement of urgency proposed by the fledgling discipline of industrial archeology: recovering and placing new value on our industrial heritage, which is highly fragile. While industrial heritage is the most elaborate and complex form of territorial occupation, it is also one of

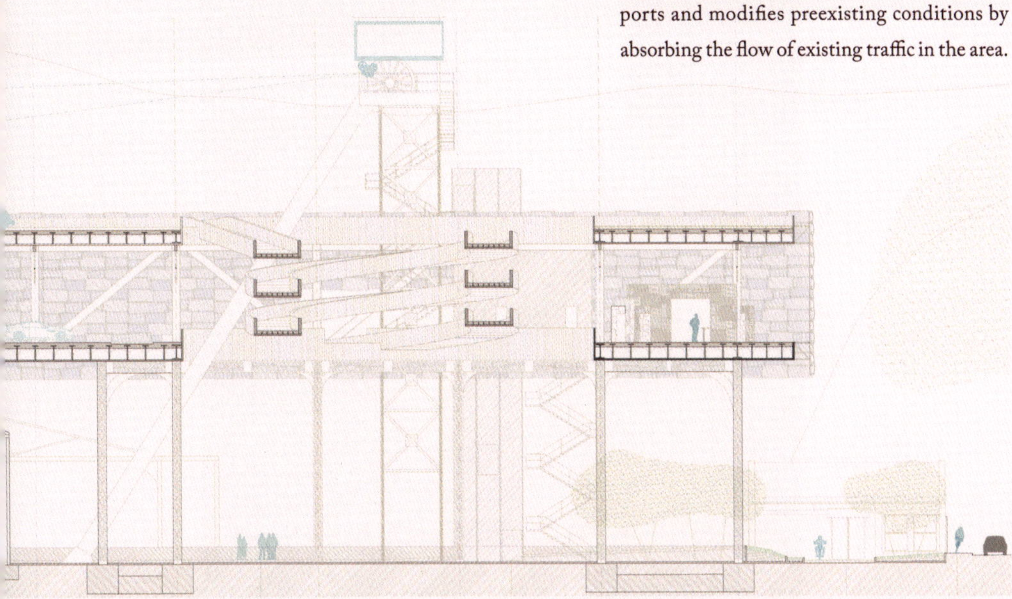

046

Car Museum by Juan Moreno. The project supports and modifies preexisting conditions by absorbing the flow of existing traffic in the area.

the most temporary structures. Compared with rural colonization, the landscapes that emerged from the development of industrial activities are much more recent, more localized and ultimately more vulnerable because they are more superficially rooted. Their traces can disappear very rapidly, making them an endangered species.

The need to recover our industrial heritage connects with contemporary society more profoundly than other legacies, given the abundance of shared sentiments in territories with industrial traditions that are on the verge of extinction. The coincidence in time and the direct knowledge of territorial structures inherited from industrialization, which have left their mark on the living landscape, add value which lends vigor and dynamism to its enhancement. These proposals bring together two interests: on the one hand, recovering the collective memory of work in the territory and bolstering self-confidence, by reaffirming the local identity of citizens in the area; and on the other, promoting new activities linked to tourism with the aim of reactivating the local economy. The industrial heritage in ACTAL offers significant resources for the development of tourism, not only due to the quality of its singular buildings and the system of relationships that they establish with the territory, but because of its potential for re-establishing meaning and implanting new programs that tap into the real significance of the area. The tourism industry looks at this landscape covetously. Traveling in time and space are fundamental premises underlying tourist demand. Now more than ever, clients demand

de-contextualization (or re-contextualization). Managing cultural or historical specificity becomes a necessary tool in rebuilding a setting that has the power to elicit emotion, which houses a "genius loci".

In the ACTAL area, there is no need to create a stage set, to generate fictions like in the theme parks we are used to encountering; the landscape merely needs to be interpreted, its identity needs to be rebuilt. Far from employing mere formal "regionalisms", the proposed interventions are supported by the existing industrial heritage in order to lend "meaning" to the entire body of tourist activities. Their operations are based on a careful reading of the place which allows for connecting its history with the present —building a living tradition, a narrative in progress—. Design becomes a tool for delving into the territory, paying attention to the overlapping layers of time and positioning memory as an active element. Just as Sébastien Marot suggested in Sub-Urbanism and the Art of Memory (1999), a process is established in which place, the exploration of the "space-time layers" of the territory, is a matrix for architectural design: "architecture as an instrument of memory and memory as a material of architecture."[2]

The capacity for stimulation among the new cultural or educational programs that are introduced depends largely on their coexistence with the industrial activity and their degree of connection with the territory in general. The

The need to recover our industrial heritage connects with contemporary society more profoundly than other legacies, given the abundance of shared sentiments in territories with industrial traditions that are on the verge of extinction.

(Opposite page). *Mining Logistical Center*, by Álvaro Bravo. An obsolete mining infrastructure is reused both mantaining its industrial and its symbolic uses. Hydrology and geospatial localization are key elements in the project. The image shows one of the inhabitated "deepenings" that contain different built structures. 150

interventions act on meaningful architecture, nodes in the industrial landscape, without forgetting that it emerged together with the corresponding infrastructures that tie it into a territorial network. The new models for tourism develop the concept of roving, which is based on the regeneration of paths or different categories of roads. This varied mobility network connects the different tourist offerings in a global system. The proposals for activating the inherited industrial landscape should respond to a globalizing concept; they should be able to create synergies and to promote sustainable development on a regional scale, particularly when the industry is the direct result of society's use of the natural environment as a whole. As opposed to assuming nostalgic positions, we should take a lesson from industry's strategic occupation of the territory. Acting in this way, we provide continuity to the region's own history, as well as its heritage, which is connected due to its historical functional development and encompasses supralocal, regional and international spheres.

1. Jackson, John Brinckerhoff. *Discovering the Vernaculas Landscape*, Ed. Yale University Press, New Haven and London, 1984.
2. Marot, Sébastien. "L'art de la mémoire, le territoire et l'architecture." In *Le visiteur*, nº4, June 1999. (*Sub-urbanism and the Art of Memory, London*: Architectural Association Publications, 2003).

226

ASTURIAS' LOUDSPEAKER

Leticia Merino

The design program is directed at experimenting sound, enhanced through architecture.

There are six spaces, contained in six bubbles, dedicated to research and a large open space for playing high-decibel music. The quality of the sound wave, how it spreads, or the path it will follow have been studied in depth for the project to work properly and to enhance the desired situation. To that end, each bubble has been treated differently, both in terms of geometries and materials.

Their situation responds to the desired type of sound, but it also has to do with the use and the size. The bubbles are suspended in the air using 20mm diameter steel cables. The arrangement of the cables is determined by a preexisting grating on the bottom, duplicated on top and reinforced by a light substructure made from steel tubes.

This creates a network of points used to hang the cables. The top structure supports all the weight, and the bottom serves to provide stability.

Existing structure

Pods

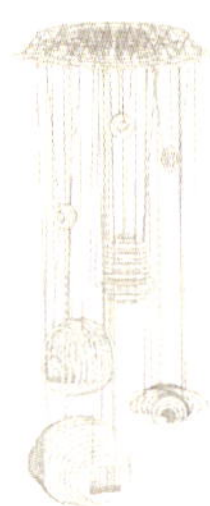

New structure

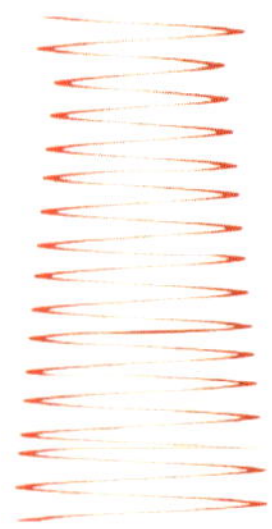

Movement

Orchestra

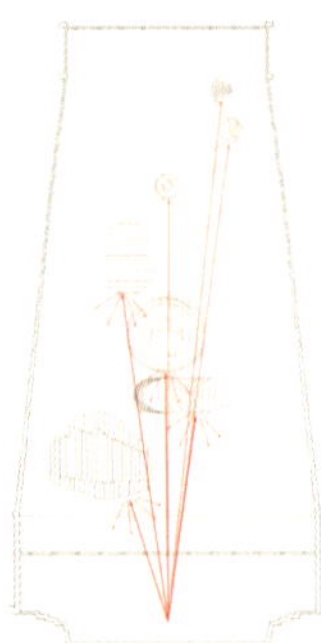

Hall

General scheme

Collage

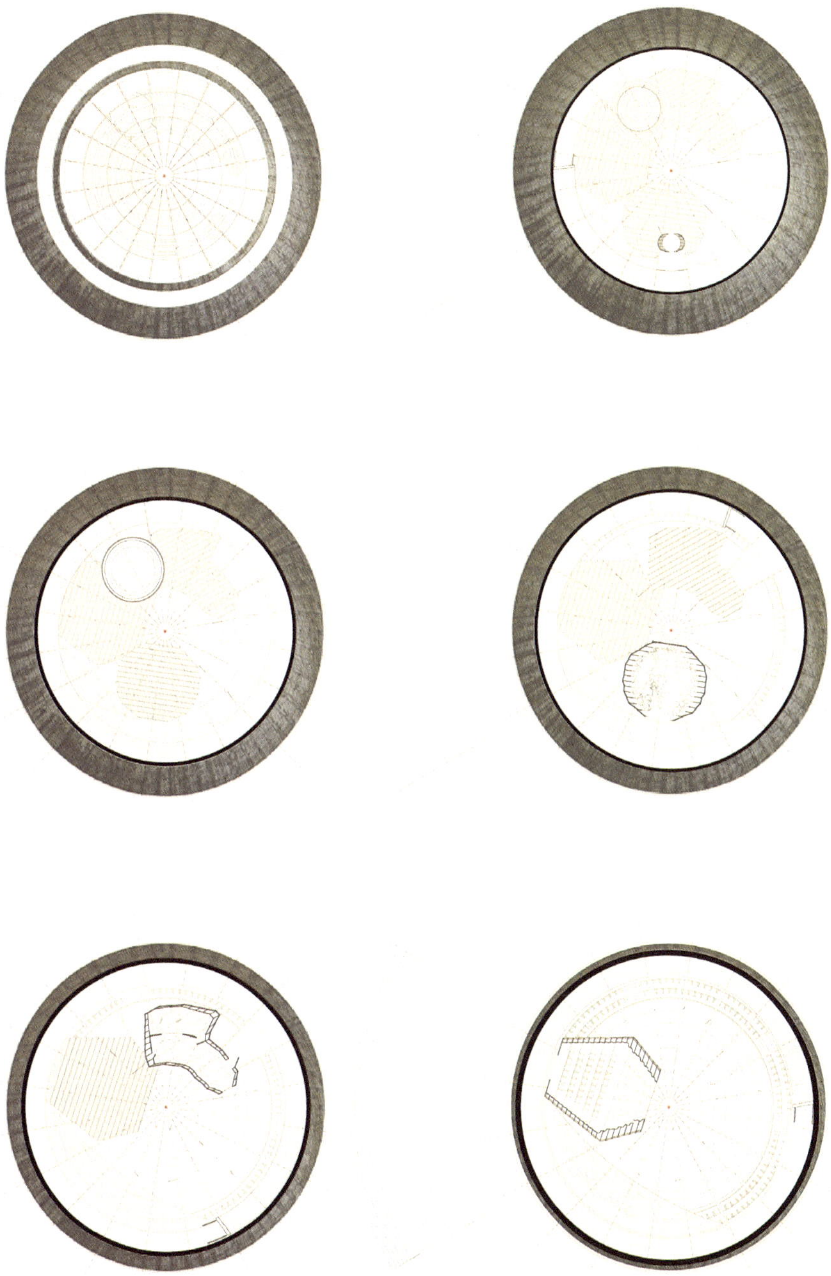

Plans of the new pods inside the existing industrial chimney

226

CAR MUSEUM

Juan Moreno

The purpose of this museum is to house and promote motor tourism in the area. The Motor Museum in El Sotón supports and modifies unique preexisting conditions shifting and absorbing the flow of vehicle traffic, providing for the possibility of visiting and experiencing all the activities from inside a vehicle. Because the idea is for tourists, drivers, to experience this design from behind the wheel of their cars, the program is distributed on the ground level.

The final distribution responds to different criteria. One of them outlines circulation patterns based on the existing ones, within the plot itself yet redefining, structuring and organizing them. Another separates the visitor circulation from campers' movements, making the camping area more private. And the last one creates a "patch" of interrelated activities. The private camping area overlooks the river, separated from the public area by the access road for campers. The most public programs are arranged within the closed circuit intended for visitors. The uses are identified by changes in the surface height and the material used for each type of use: soft surfaces for pedestrians and hard ones for wheeled traffic (roads, parking areas and exhibitions).

Museum Access

Drive-in Cinema

Museum

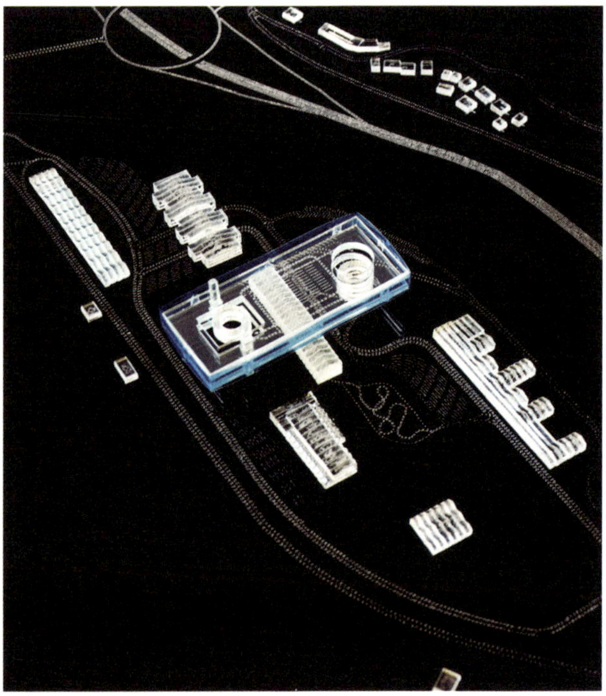

Museum and surrounding structures

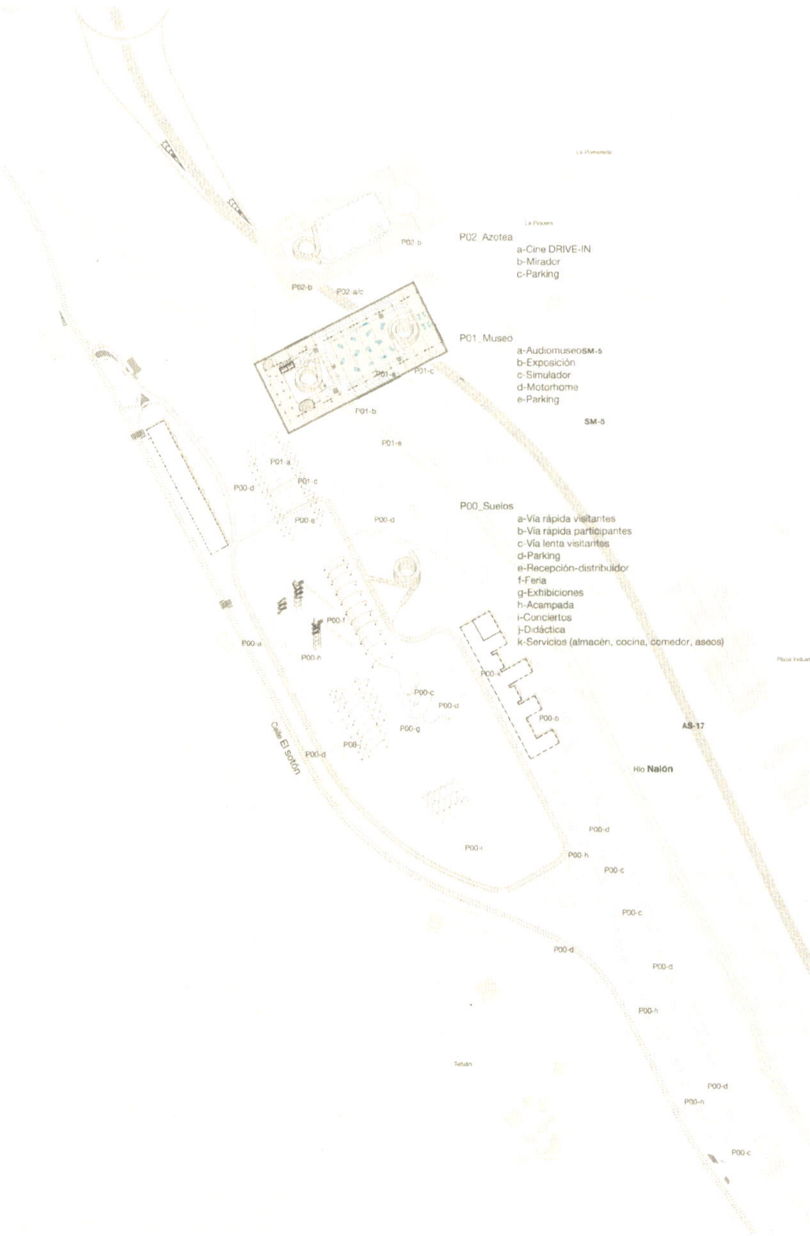

Groundfloor plan with exploded museum levels

226 — MINING LOGISTICAL CENTER

Álvaro Bravo

In this proposal, the existing mining infrastructures maintain their industrial and symbolic use. They become a geospatial reference point, bringing in visitors and introducing them into the complex. The abandoned mine is still required to maintain its infrastructure, especially the hydrology. It is used as a service station, allowing for the inclusion of large sophisticated pieces, which are only seemingly out of place in the surroundings. The project presents a collection of four types of what are called "deepenings".

These operations consist in a vertical communication between the primary and secondary galleries used in the existing mine. A courtyard serves as a transition between spaces. The largest deepening includes two buildings of different sizes, facing one another, which house the main program. Lastly, the exit in the shape of a spiral sets up the user to discover the territory.

The "inhabited" deepening is the central new added space, the most complex and receptive space in the program. It is characterized by a façade that is optimized for maximum reflection of sunlight. The entrances are located between the reflective glass skin and the interior program. The outside world comes in through the roof, which lets the rain water into the bottom of the space, creating a curtain of water.

Model of the mining infrastructure showing new "inhabited deepenings"

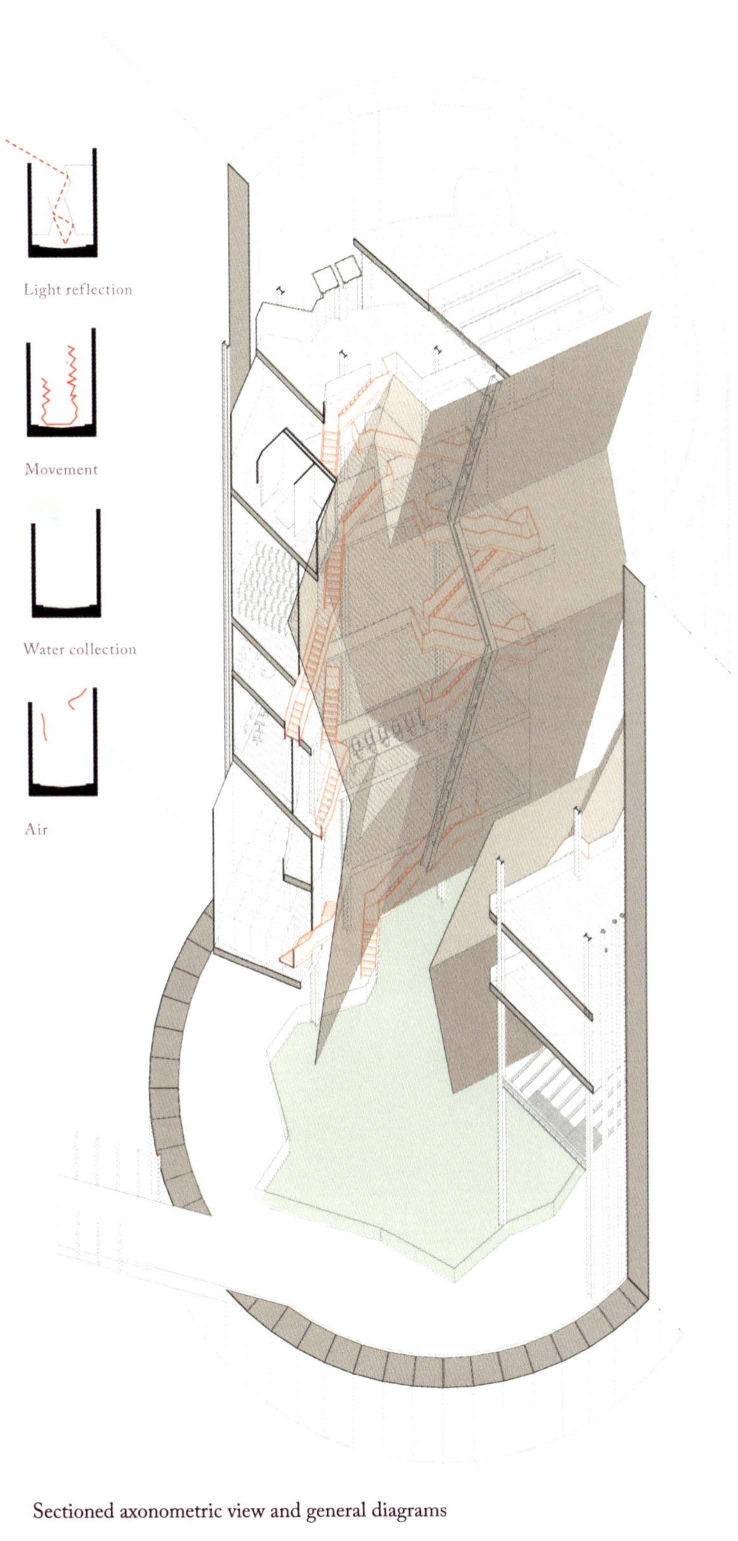

Sectioned axonometric view and general diagrams

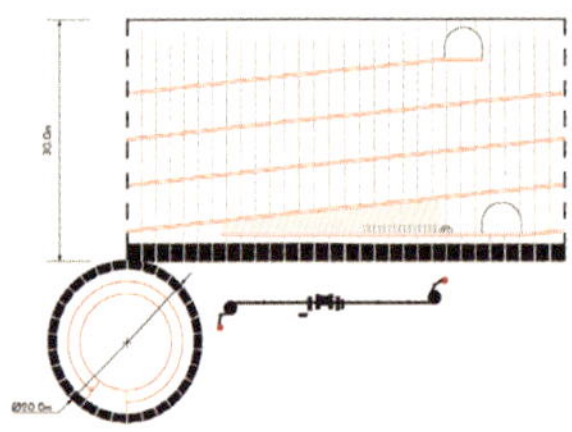

Spiral

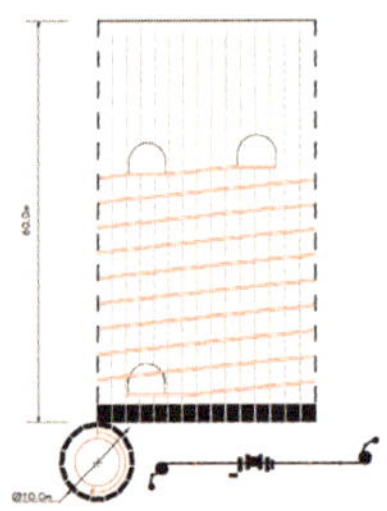

Comunication

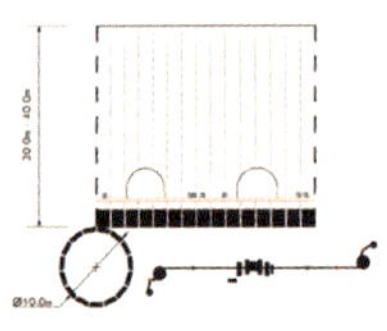

Courtyard

Three types of "deepenings". Diagrams and model

Inhabited "deepening". Horizontal sections.

227—

ORNITHOLOGICAL WALKS

Pedro de Pascual Samper

The environment around the Llumeres cove is rural. It is surrounded by hayfields and pastureland for cattle grazing. Woodlands combine with steppe and meadows of brush and shrubs.

From the Llumeres warehouses, there are three visual reference points. The first is the village of Viodo, where life is dedicated to agriculture, which represents the present. The second is the group of buildings closest to the sea, which used to belong to the mining installations, referring to the past. Finally, the future, in the area proposed for bird watching. These three visual points of reference have a connection with the project, in the visitor reception center. The complex identifies two ornithological experiences for tourists: first, the reception phase (where the existing warehouses are located) and then the areas for bird watching.

The first, the theoretical experience, is a space that introduces users into the world and the history of the birds in the area, alongside the second, the practical experience, where visitors can observe reality.

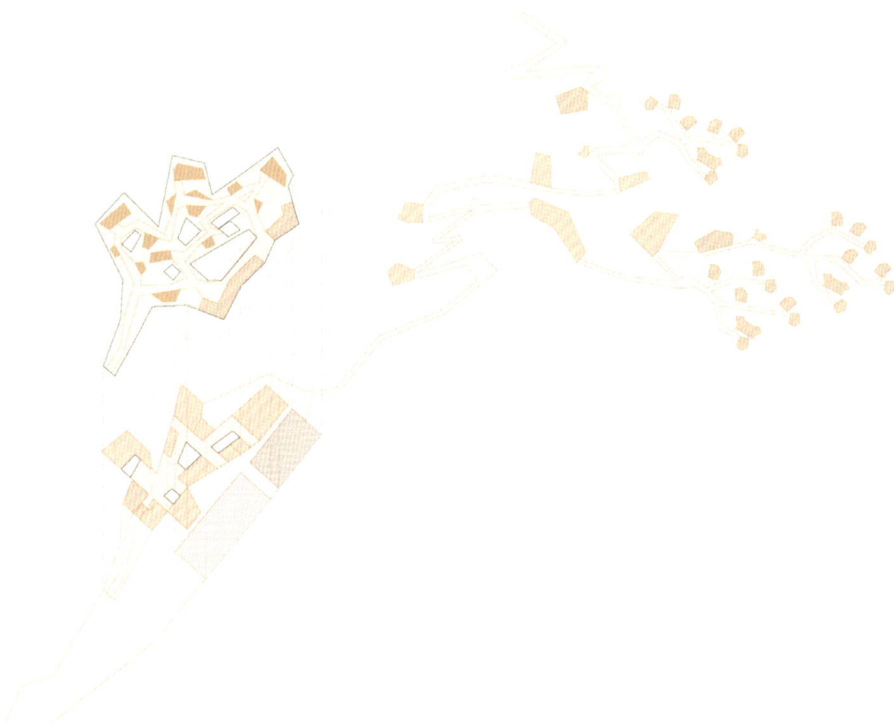

Two scales are proposed: the new building adjacent to an existing warehouse and bird watching pavillions.

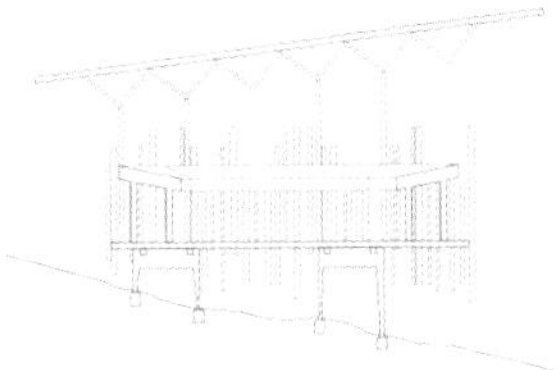

Information

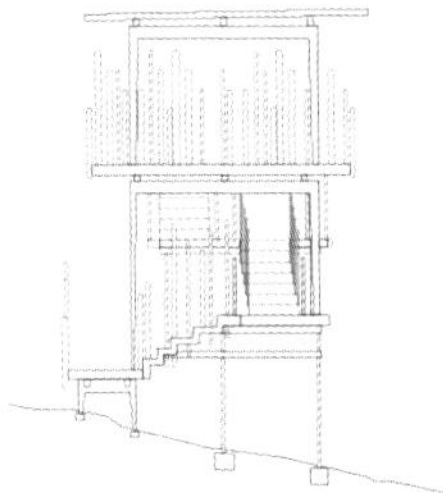

Observation tower

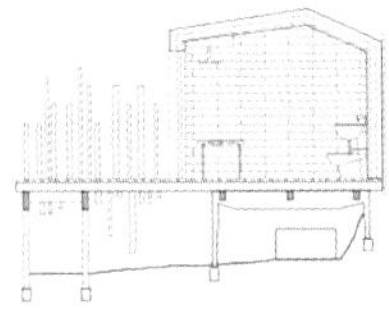

Ornithologic services

Vertical view

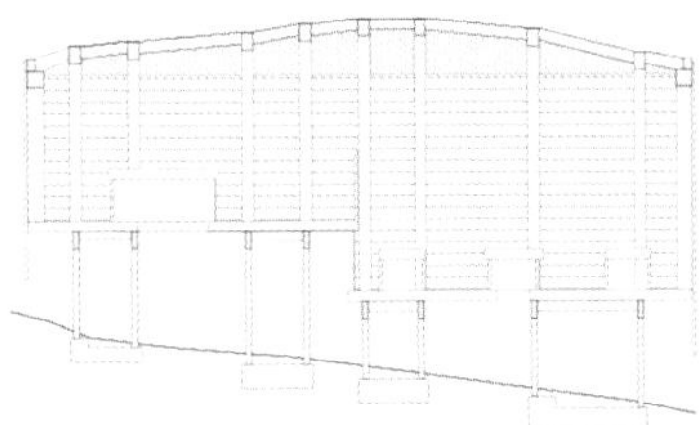

Ornithologist meetings

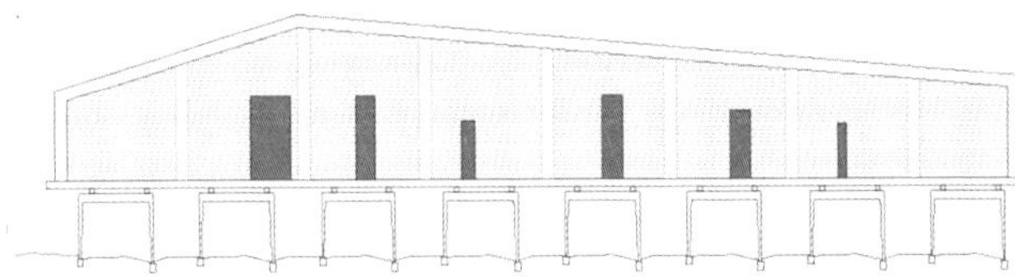

Exhibitions

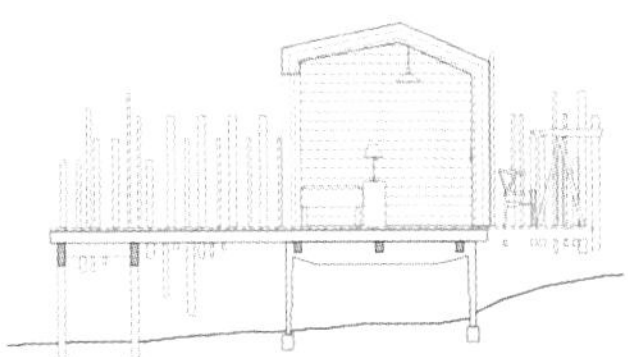

Room

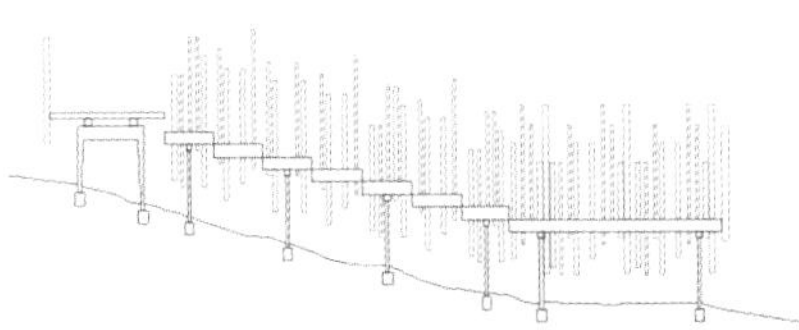

Tiered gazebo

Types of bird watching pavillions

227

S.O.S MINES

Juan Gilsanz

The project extends in small buildings connected to each other and with the natural terrain, filtered by the surrounding vegetation, seeking out locations in open spaces and avoiding aggressiveness with regard to the environment. The program responds to a dual vocation: that of assembly in a colonizing extension according to its potential, needs and future possibilities, as well as their disassembly, transfer or recycling elements, if necessary. As a succession of layers, the intervention is added to the mine, which was built on untouched terrain. The broken up volumes and the small dimensions attempt to adapt to the changing order of nature. Wood is the dominant material, creating a skin that covers the surfaces and extends into platforms, paths and walkways, connecting them together like a fold-out. Part of the glazed openings corresponds to the entrances, which are large and serve to link the exterior space with the interior in an uninterrupted spatial series, lending meaning to the shared and participatory space of the whole. The others, serving as windows, provide lighting and views to the interiors according to their placement.

Site experiences

Plans and section of the volumes

REVERSIBLE LANDSCAPES

Unveiling the Hidden by Blanca Pérez. A number of pavilions scattered in the woods and linked by a promenade, hosting yoga and meditation activities. Construction techniques aim for the maximum lightness and the use of local and reclaimed materials.

227 —

REVERSIBILITY WITHIN THE "SOLVING FOR PATTERN" CULTURE

192 — Izaskun Chinchilla

Design Critic, UTP-DSVII, TOTAL IBERIA 1.0, IE University

Often enough, commissions will encourage designers to create architecture that can be disassembled: exhibition pavilions, facilities intended for events, emergency architecture, etc. There are, however, some designers who intentionally decide to design architecture that can be disassembled and moved, even though it is not an implicit condition inherent in the commission. The reasons that may lead an architect to opt for reversible unions and portable materials are varied. This text will focus on projects where reversibility is adopted as a scaled and adapted response to the significant complexity and fragility of the preexisting context and the awareness that they contribute to generating more complexity and more fragility in the surroundings they affect.

In these cases, reversibility is part of what I call the culture of "Solving for Pattern". This expression comes from an essay of the same title by Wendel Berry. In his text,[1] and in the readings that have been done from different disciplinary perspectives,[2] he defends that the actions we affect in our surroundings should not attempt to address a single problem, but rather a synthesis of different problems. Similarly, our actions should minimize the collateral problems that derive from them. Reading these premises, it makes sense that no one should be exempt from this culture: it seems unthinkable that architects might

Ephemeral Spaces by Tamara García

170

not be responding to multiple problems and attempting to minimize the collateral harmful effects of their practice. The "Solving for Pattern" perspective is, however, a near methodological revolution in architectural design.

What has changed? The main practice that is called into question is the use of the cascade method of problem solving. The stages in the cascade method will sound familiar: data is first collected and then analyzed; a solution is proposed and then implemented.

Did you follow a similar process during your training? Most likely. What, then, is wrong with this system? The answer is that it invites the designer to adopt a partial goal that is isolated and has been deduced from a very biased analysis. The cascade method isolates specific problems from the others and allows for concluding that we are solving one of those "prefabricated" (in the sense of artificially isolated) problems. Let's look at an example: a project that is being built in a forest with enormous ecological wealth. The architect quickly analyzes one aspect of the forest: the foliage produces textures of light and color that is broken up along diagonal lines. Then he draws those textures based on pictures of the place. A more or less "prefabricated" problem appears: generic architecture (a prism shape with sharp corners) would break up the continuity

172 — *Network City* by Claudia Mannenti and Valentina Occhini

of the lines and would ruin the views of the forest. Soon enough, a solution is found: small-scale boxes with a reflective material on the façade. The stretch of forest is reflected on the façade of the invading architecture, which seems to be more visually integrated.

Did the designer consider where the water for the inhabitants will come from and whether that will change the water supply of the forest? Does he know what effect the interference will have on animal movements? How was the mirror transported through the forest; did any trees need to be cut? The list of questions the designer does not address is nearly infinite. In exchange, he has solved the "problem" that he himself constructed: the visual continuity of the forest texture.

This kind of design has led architects to propose creating enormous defects in solid mountains in the interest of a spatial metaphor: "my design is a crevice". The spatial coherence of the project takes precedence over environmental or social criteria, or a holistic vision of the territory and the context.

As a reaction to this legacy a number of intentionally reversible designs have appeared, which attempt to respond to a larger and more imprecise number of problems. Their location can be partially changed if they become an obstacle for fauna, or their surface area can be reduced in the case of drought. How are these projects designed? What changes have been made with respect

The cascade method isolates specific problems from the others and allows for concluding that we are solving one of those artificially isolated problems.

to the modern method of applying the cascade approach?

Since the 1980s,[3] a number of designs have expressed an explicit desire to become part of what Berry calls a "pattern". A series of descriptions can help us better understand Berry's intention; these designs acknowledge that they are part of a territorial pattern, a network of pre-existing conditions or a model that organizes movement through the territory. A number of designs have attempted to fit into a set of larger-scale and more durable structures. This short article is not intended to provide an exhaustive list of these designs, but rather to reflect on some of the methods they have used.

The metaphor of navigation has become relatively popular with projects that take on an awareness of their contribution to the "pattern": "What does a pilot do when he wants to maneuver his ship to enter a port? he doesn't precisely follow a pre-determined program, but modifies it constantly. The boat diverts from its route to the left, the pilot evaluates which new deviation is optimum for continuing the route toward the port (...) At all times, this deviation needs to be corrected in accordance with the purpose, the *telos* of the trip."[4]

The metaphor of navigation, reprised by Heinz von Foerster, one of the fathers of cybernetics, clarifies a design method based on the cyclical information models that are characteristic of living systems: cause-effect relationships are constantly reconsidered in a continuous system that periodically reexamines

context, modifies behavior, advancing and retreating, in order to construct a relationship between apparently incongruent emerging information and events. In the reversible landscapes of these Undergraduate Final Projects, the relationships between the parts are not derived from a general system of deductions, but from the construction of a system made from components whose relationships can be reconstructed in different ways.

This orientation continues along the lines of the philosophy laid out in Morin's texts[5] "instead of isolating the objects of study, look at them through the process of eco-organization that ties them into the cultural, social, economic, political and natural environment."

The ecological challenge generates a pedagogical, professional and methodological challenge: technical knowledge and imagination must be mobilized so that, in addition to resolving the stable situations that are traditional to the discipline, problems of complexity and uncertainty can also also tackled. The total and partial reversibility of the designs that we propose is part of a set of measures that can contribute to building a better understanding of the territorial and social models that we are contributing to generating.

Other measures such as basing designs on existing networks as much as possible, introducing varied materials or visiting sites repeatedly under different conditions, would be some of the recommendations for designers in train-

Asturian Waters by Gonzalo Merino. A set of temporary floating pavilions that propose a short-term activation of a mountain area during the warmer months of the year. Longitudinal section of the lake and programmatic diagram of the proposal. 168

ing, as a corollary to a fundamental change in criteria: the most important aspect of design is no longer the purety of the idea itself and its embodiment in a piece with great artistic value; what is most important is contributing to the vitality of an existing pattern, model or network.

1. "Solving for Pattern" by Wendell Berry. *The Gift of Good Land: Further Essays Cultural and Agricultural*, Chapter 9. North Point Press, 1981.
2. A good example of the massive following of Berry's philosophy from different disciplines is the blog www.solvingforpattern.org.
3. A good starting point would be Koolhaas's design for the *Parc de la Villette* (1982). The design refers to four layers or strata: the strips, characterized by different functions; the grids that regulated the distribution of the program, called confetti; the circulation that ensured different types of accessibility for each function; and the final layer that defined the configuration of the built spaces, the connectors and references that formed a user's interface for local residents. The design brief emphasized the fact that the creation of a weak structure that can be reexamined maintained flexibility because of the autonomy provided to each of the parts, creating a type of method that "combines architectural specificity with programmatic indeterminacy".
4. Heinz von Foerster (1998) "Die Wahrheit ist die Erfindung eines Lügners," Heidelberg.
5. Morin, Edgar (1973) "Le paradigme perdu: la nature humaine," Seuil, Paris.

229

UNVEILING THE HIDDEN

Blanca Pérez

This project is a link between the visitor and nature. The program called for some pavilions scattered in the landscape that will host activities like yoga and meditation. A promenade through the forest would link all the pavilions. It is not the same experience walking in a forest of trees which protect you, where you will easily get lost, or walking within fields of flowers and aromatic plants which will probably be easy to touch and smell.

The system of the promenade, which links the pavilions, is designed with the aim of creating these different "scenes" because it changes depending on the different landscapes and programs. Each pavilion would be different from the next—the light conditions inside, and the relationship with the surrounding nature—depending on the program.

The design shall be as light as possible with no ambition to overtake the landscape with its presence. The use of local and recycled materials and light structures will minimize the impact on the landscape.

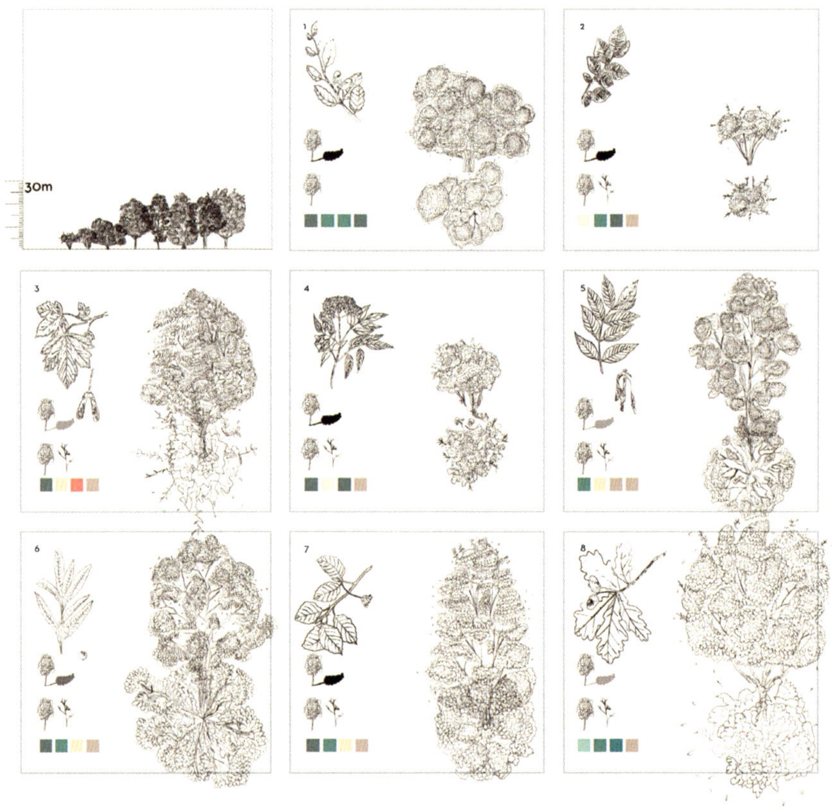

Forest taxonomy. Meditation pavillion (opposite page).

229 — ASTURIAN WATERS

Gonzalo Merino

The proposal consists of two consecutive interventions. First, since there are currently no means of accessing the selected area, the natural area is modified to encourage tourist visits during the entire year. This is achieved through a series of trails that structure the different distinctive perspectives in the area, culminating with the lake, the central feature of the design. Second, the proposal for tourist activation through temporary occupation of the lake. Because it is such a characteristic place, the proposal involves an ephemeral intervention that is not harmful to the environment. The lake is transformed from an unknown location —from its usual silence and timelessness— into a meeting point for people to enjoy and relieve the stress of day-to-day life. The proposal is based on three different spaces: one for concerts and festivals; another for water activities; and a third dedicated to a more introspective user relationship. These spaces can be activated simultaneously or separately, giving priority to one or another. As such, the lake can be occupied during the warmer months, when the access is easier, and vacated during the winter months.

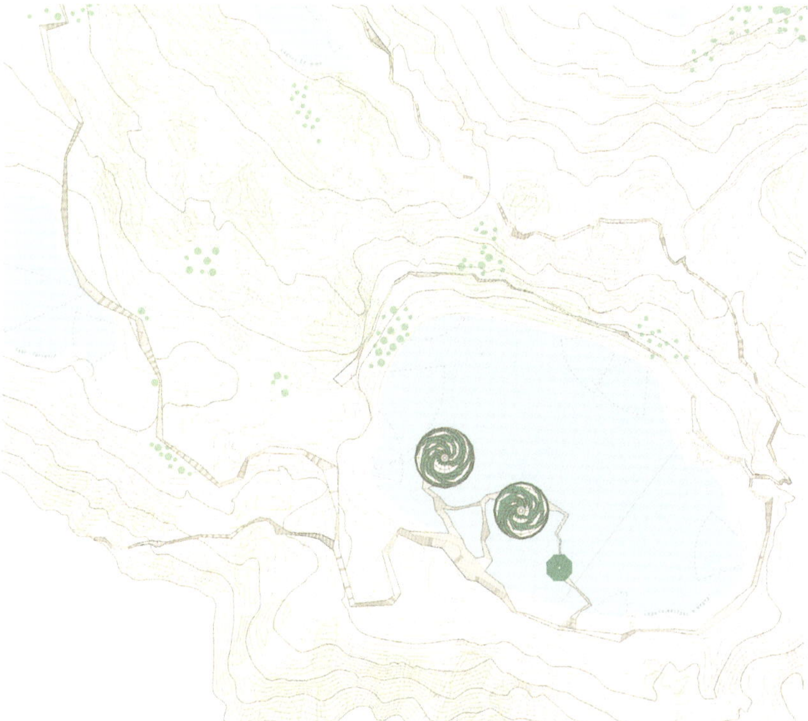

Site map. The proposed structures occupy the lake temporarily. Plans (opposite page)

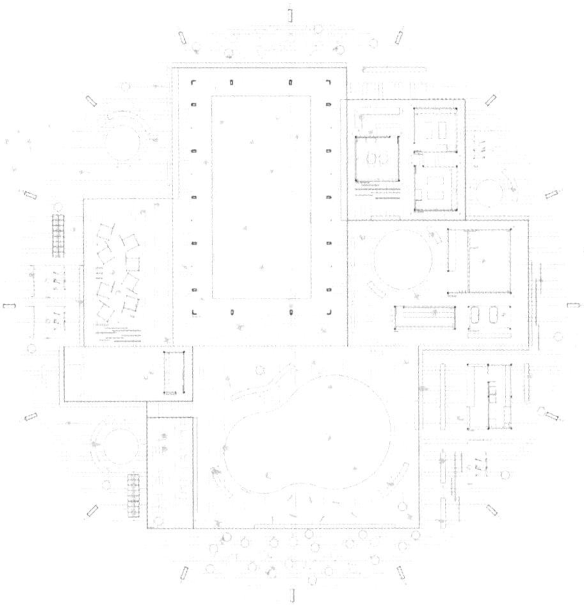

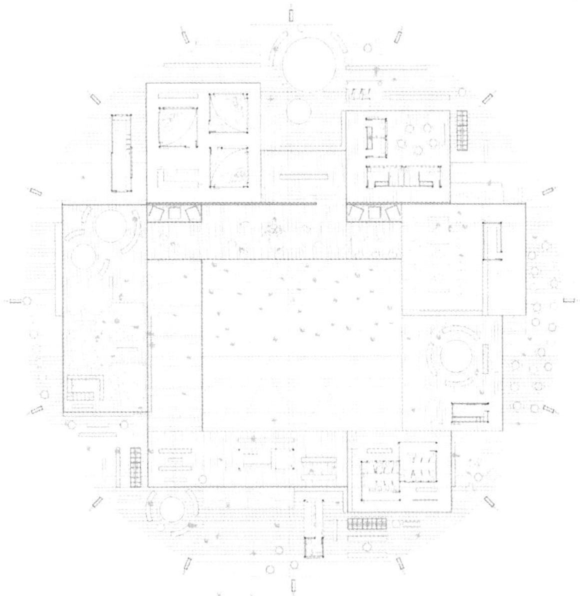

229 EPHEMERAL SPACES

Tamara García

In the Sierra del Áramo, an hour from the AP-66, we find forests that house ghost towns, reservoirs and lakes at the foot of the mountains. The whole landscape is majestic and complex at once, full of little details that make it special.

The project extends across three settings: the forest, the reservoir and the mine. In the woods, structures for spending the night are exposed to agents like the wind and the differences in temperature accentuate the feelings of mystery through the night.

Along the reservoir, a slender structure is proposed which consists of five floors, where fog, reminiscent of 19th century romantic novels, envelops the reader. Finally, near the abandoned mines of Texeo, we find the laundries and barracks where the miners lived. The historical memory of the place is what makes it the perfect setting for experimenting with mechanisms of light and shadow. Spaces where light and water are used for experimenting, a small shadow puppet theater and an element for observing the extension of LEDs that expand toward the ruins of the laundries, tracing paths and areas for relaxation.

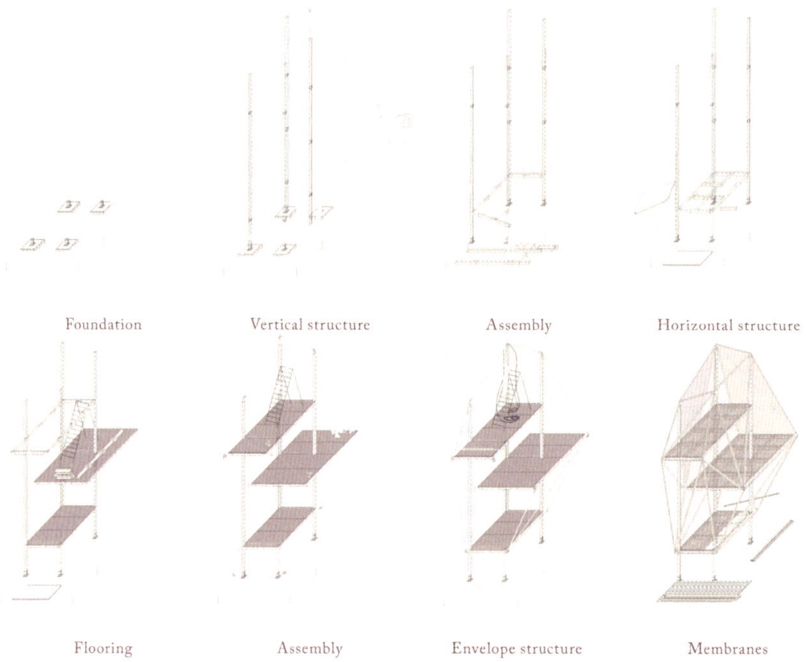

Construction process

Sections and elevations of the pavillions in the woods

229 — NETWORK CITY

Claudia Mannenti and Valentina Occhini

An interweaving of roads, paths and people is proposed. The project aims to upgrade a new urban factory whose identity has been impoverished over many decades. It has an industrial identity that was founded on an uncontaminated landscape, where the monumental La Camocha coal mine now stands, a complex intersection of ramps and paths plowed into the ground by iron rails.

The mine was the place where the metamorphosis of a natural element—coal—shaped and changed the ground. Now, human activities interact with the industry and the landscape: floods of people that move on the two main historical walking paths and pilgrimage routes, Santiago de Compostela and the Ruta de la Plata, for which La Camocha is the foundation. The area takes on life, thanks to the strategic and direct connections with the paths and the surrounding cities such as Gijón, sea port and cultural center. Spaces are designed to accommodate the flow of people, generated sequentially at certain times of the year. However, the project is not limited to these contexts, but it opens with the same enthusiasm towards the reactivation of the area from insidethanks to the dedicated service of citizens.

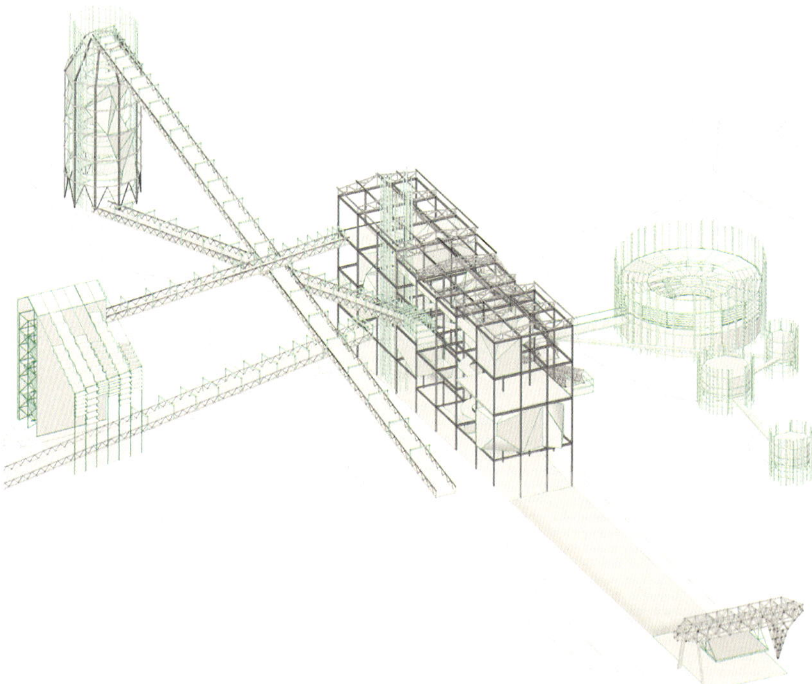

Axonometric view of the existing infrastructure and the intervention

230

THE FUNCTIONS AND LIMITATIONS OF TOURIST ARCHITECTURE

191

José Miguel Iribas

Sociologist specialized in territorial, urban and touristic diagnosis

Sixty years after the tourism boom in Spain, with the first waves of foreign clients to the Costa Brava and Mallorca, from an exacting professional perspective the architecture associated with this activity is seen as a kind of unsolvable and phantasmagoric entelechy. This is especially so since tourism – which is, after agriculture, the most expensive activity in terms of how the territory is used and the one that has generated the most buildings, some of which are unusually large– doesn't seem to fit into a discipline that is characterized by a self-sufficient, differential and conceptually recognizable language. This is not the case with other fields of architecture intended to house and develop economic functions and flows, such as industrial or railroad architecture; and the latter has many more limitations and conceptual and functional requirements than tourist architecture does.

There are certainly remnants of tourist architecture that have given rise to specific typologies: factory-hotels, cruise-ship-hotels, apartment buildings that are managed unitarily and industrially, theme parks, night clubs and the naval architecture of cruise ships. These typologies are characterized as trivializations of their original equivalents, demonstrated by the abundance of psychologically comforting style elements intended to take tourists' minds off any possible worry. In this setting of rolling curves and flamboyant decorations, in these non-places invariably painted with pastel hues and immune to any influence from the surrounding context (be it geographic, territorial, cultural, or social), any concern that threatens to disrupt the peaceful vacation atmosphere must be automatically eliminated. That is the basis for the parallelisms between cliché tourist architecture and disneyfied imagery in all its sickly sweet syrupiness. Generally speaking, tourism has steered clear of cultured architecture, sticking to the repetition of very simple formulas which invariably respond to function (requirements for efficiency in an industrial production process) and representation (formal configurations based on standardized styles, so that they are easily recognizable to clients[1]), a symbology that ties in with the idea of an "attainable paradise" offered by most tourist brochures.

TIME, THE BASIC TOURIST COMMODITY

The banality of tourist architecture has to do, of course, with the cultural weakness of the offering and the demand but, above all, with the unquestionable fact that tourism's proposals are based conceptually on the generation of activity sequences and not on the production of space, as it is commonly believed. Many of the errors committed in recent years by the Spanish administration have been the result of politicians and architects thinking that creating magnificent spaces would be enough to generate a flow of recurring visits. Gross error: the commodity of tourism is time. What tourists are really looking to buy is a sequence of activities in time, if possible providing simultaneous alternatives (except, obviously, in the case of last-minute offers). Given these conditions, space takes on an instrumental condition: it is essentially just the physical medium for time, such that it tends to lack substantive value in terms of product formation.[2]

As spectacular as tourist spaces may be, the time sequences associated with their contemplation is very limited because, as Henri Lefebvre said, "The emotion of landscape is instantaneous". This explains, on the one hand, the limited weight given to the direct contemplation of global-scale landmarks in the time distribution of organized visits[3] and, on the other, the abundance of hotel establishments located near the geological and cultural landmarks that have become tourist destinations. These successful bars and restaurants draw out the emotion of space in time; that is why they are so popular.

The failure to understand this elemental principle has led to catastrophic errors in programming, which have resulted in resounding disasters in terms of visitor numbers and profits. Perhaps the most often mentioned case is the City of Arts and Sciences in Valencia, where although Calatrava's forceful enclosures have managed to attract visitors, they haven't diverted tourists into the for-profit areas inside or kept them there long enough for them to consume, due to the insignificance and limited interest of the content. Given that the non-professional contemplation of the buildings is of short duration, this false City has become an absurd and wasteful stage set which visitors wander through, displaying contradictory emotions. Unfortunately, the numbers of paying users are a far cry from the expectations generated by the endless investment.

PROBLEMS WITH RURAL TOURISM

Rural tourism as a consistent, widespread and well-organized offering was born in France in the early post-World War period as a central part of the Ministry of Land Management's strategy to prevent the exodus of rural population toward big cities, especially the outskirts of Paris.

Encouraged by the favorable differential in the comparison between the funds required for promoting continuity in the rural world and the costs of establishing the population in the suburbs (new homes, infrastructures, facilities and services), a propagandistic action was set in motion, sustained by

Generally speaking, tourism has steered clear of cultured architecture, sticking to the repetition of very simple formulas which invariably respond to function and representation.

three principles: praise for the figure of the farmer as a bastion of the essence of Republican France;[4] glorification of agricultural products as a foundation for (what was then) the best cuisine in the world; and promotion of the consumption of agricultural products *in situ.* In Spain, however, the proposals for rural tourism don't respond to any programming at all. Decisions are made individually and spontaneously, which is not necessarily a guarantee of failure, since countries like Switzerland and Austria have developed powerful rural offerings that have not been planned from within the government. In Spain, however, the process is characterized by the limited size of the installations and their tendency toward isolation. The structural conditions of the Spanish offering –especially in terms of seasonal behavior and the resulting occupancy rates– are entirely insufficient to allow for significant investments with the potential to create qualification and specialization. Finally, the limited strictness of the legislation concerning the quality of the establishments and the services provided increases the bias of uncertainty for rural visitors, since it prevents homogenization of the lodging and dining offering. Under these conditions, there are two consequences that have had perverse effects for tourism: excessive client recurrence and a progressive reduction of the potential client base, as well as the reduction in occupation rates—down to 20% annually, a clearly insufficient figure.

The results obtained by rural tourism demonstrate the relative failure of this category of tourist activity. It is not statistically significant in the formation of general tourist revenue, nor has it become an activity that satisfactorily complements rural income, since the scarcity of the offering and its strictly individual origin, with no planning or public financing to help in its emergence, prevents

124 — *Ecological Bridges* by Clara Bueno

...in those rough places where the landscape is fragile, it is difficult to put up new buildings without creating significant ruptures in the landscape.

the effects from becoming structural.

Lastly, whereas in France, as we mentioned, there was a campaign to promote rural areas, the social portrait of farming and livestock-raising in Spain has been organized along two lines: chronicling dark tragedies associated with rural Spain and ridiculing backwoods rednecks and rural culture. Compared to the dignity and strength of French rural heroes, in Spain the rural community is represented by grotesque characters like Paco Martínez Soria, Pajares and Esteso.

Since the activities associated with rural tourism tend to be individual and generally take place in rough and mountainous settings, it is practically impossible to generate enough of an accumulation to allow for the emergence of the most elemental seasonal offerings, which also have to be organized on both ends by the clients themselves: a titanic (and frequently sterile) effort for the vast majority of potential users.

In addition, in those rough places where the landscape is fragile, it is difficult to put up new buildings without creating significant ruptures in the landscape, which become more severe in direct correlation to the volume of these new interventions. This contributes to preventing any accumulation and weakens the alternatives for the dynamic use of time. As such, and as I have demonstrated repeatedly in my research, articles and lectures, the condition for success when it comes to rural tourism is that it can't be successful. Because its success would imply the destruction of its essential argument.

The growth experienced in the rural tourism offering has been very scant: urban developments have recently been built on the Mediterranean coast that are larger than the growth of the rural offering for the entire peninsula. Some years ago, I pointed out that the accumulated offering of hotel beds in three city blocks of the Rincón de Loix in Benidorm was greater than the absolute occupation numbers for the entire hotel and rural accommodation offering for all of the sea-side provinces along the Cantabrian Sea combined, including the urban business offerings in the respective capital cities. Given that these are the basic conditions for rural tourism, architecture cannot provide effective solutions to its main problems, nor can rural tourism, due to its economic insignificance and its inevitable propensity for reduced costs, make up for the problem of reduced activity that the profession is currently suffering from.

TWO NEEDS, TWO SOLUTIONS: THE TERRITORY AND THE CITY

Although tourism has been able to do without cultured architecture without diminishing its strength, it is evident that land-use planning and urban management in terms of activities are absolutely decisive and can have very differentiated effects according to the model that is adopted. That model determines the structural composition of the lodging offering and, through it, the typology of the demand and the use of time/space. It promotes a differentiated distribution of tourist income: the more dense and dynamic the offering the better; it resolves the infrastructural and functional requirements for the activity (with different degrees of success) and defines its environmental and economic impact. It can stimulate accumulation and density (i.e., complexity and crossbreeding) or, alternatively, it can produce boring and extensive, monofunctional, abundantly green yet environmentally insane and economically burdensome suburbs. It can generate dense and concentrated spaces for the benefit of the subordinate masses or it can plan isolated enclosures for the exclusive and restrictive enjoyment of a select few.

In Spain, land-use planning for tourism has generally been carried out on a regional scale (Autonomous Communities), which is too large to allow for going into detail about how roles should be distributed among the different territorial fragments in a way that is coherent with the availability and complementary in terms of proposals. On the other hand, it has also come up against municipal resistance when it comes to transferring competencies.

As such, land-use planning for tourism has been a secret activity with respect to agents in the industry and entirely useless for the associated administrations, because it comes down from very weak and/or insufficiently legitimized departments. And it has been undertaken without much common sense, either promoting a repetition of models that were built up on the wake of specific destinations –but without ever understanding the arguments behind their success, or enshrining the oft-repeated (and inane) slogans that the Spanish political establishment and the media have associated with the success and profitability of tourism: low density, unshakeable greenery, an alleged rural or suburban vocation among the masses, or, invariably, the search for a hackneyed idea of quality– an omnipresent concept, which is absolutely empty, since it defines nothing. A redeeming mantra that is meant to be all-inclusive, but explains nothing.

For its part, urban management in tourist cities, rather than attending to how the problems of the offering and the activity itself should be resolved, has taken on tasks that correspond to Spanish urban planning, attempting to determine distribution, average exploitations and other aspects which are very

Land-use planning for tourism has been a secret activity with respect to agents in the industry and entirely useless for the associated administrations, because it comes down from very weak and/or insufficiently legitimized departments

useful from a legal standpoint to allowing for trafficking in real-estate, but of very little value when it comes to creating good cities. It is a nearly impossible task since Spanish land laws, in addition to conspiring against the city and producing very poor quality urban pieces,[5] prevent *de facto* the emergence of tourist destinations as the best and most profitable ones along our coastline.

1. The styles in question are associated with good weather, social calm and the absence of negative events that might disrupt their stay. As such, these arguments refer back to efficiency, in this case within the sphere of consumerism, understood as a satisfactory return on an investment of time/money.

2. Tourist space tends to be perceived as a shapeless mass of buildings. Spatial recognition surveys completed by tourists, based on photographic questionnaires, have demonstrated that they don't tend to perceive any distinctive characteristics in buildings. However, their recollections are very precise when it comes to recognizing certain stores and spaces for leisure and enjoyment.

3. During outings to the Grand Canyon, the contemplation of this powerfully unique feature occupies just 20 minutes out of the scheduled 3 hours, little more than 10% of the total time.

4. The roll call of the heroes of agrarian France stretches from the simple-minded intelligence of Fernandel and the congeniality of Bourvil, to the likes of Asterix and Obelix, and even the controversial figure of José Bové – similar both in appearance and disposition to those Gaulish comic-book heroes.

5. This assertion finds its justification in the analysis of the social effects of the outlying suburbs of our cities, i.e., those that promote reduced environmental costs, maximum functionality, adequate socialization and the capacity for economic dynamization. These are the goals that should really matter.

124 — *Ecological Bridges* by Clara Bueno

4

APPENDIX

PRESIDENT OF IE UNIVERSITY
Santiago Íñiguez de Onzoño

RECTOR
Salvador Carmona

DEAN OF UNDERGRADUATE STUDIES
Antonio de Castro

FACULTY DIRECTOR
Luisa Barón

DIRECTOR OF UNDERGRADUATE STUDIES IN ARCHITECTURE
David Goodman

ASSOCIATE DEAN FOR EXERNAL RELATIONS
Martha Thorne

BACHELOR OF ARCHITECTURE PROGRAM ASSISTANTS
Yolanda Cuerdo, María del Mar Vega

1

2

MATHEMATICAL FOUNDATIONS IN ARCHITECTURE I, II
Pablo Linares, María Vela, Gregorio Tirado, Karim Abbaisa, Nubia J. Mendoza, Jesús Hernández

PHYSICAL FOUNDATIONS IN ARCHITECTURE I
Juan García Monge, Carmen Herrero, Carlota Gonzalez, Javier Macías, Juan Travesí, Anna Mestre

DIGITAL IMAGE
Miguel Paredes, Anna Plá, Arantza Alvarez, Adolfo Nadal

ARCHITECTURAL GEOMETRY I, II
Roberto Molinos, Carlos de la Barrera

IDEA AND FORM I, II
Laura Martínez de Guereñu, Firat Erdim, Ignacio Moreno

ARCHITECTURAL EXPRESSION
Angela Ruiz, Firat Erdim, Jesús Garcia Herrero, Fernando Moral

IE EXPRESSION
Daniel Mayoral, Paloma Mtnez de Velasco

CONSTRUCTION SYSTEMS I, CONSTRUCTION WORKSHOP I
Julián García, Rafael Iñiguez de Onzoño

DESIGN STUDIO I, II
Isabel Collado, Ignacio Peydro, Pablo Gil, Manuel Ocaña, Ali Ganjavian, Key Portlilla-Kawamura, Jose Juan Barba, Pablo Oriol, Fernando Rodríguez, Structural Types I/ Structural Calculations I, George Fäller, Anna Mestre

I

II

ENVIRONMENTAL AND BUILDING SYSTEMS I
Andy Bäcker, Antonio Villanueva

CULTURE AND THEORY IN ARCHITECTURE I, II
Eduardo Roig, Nieves Mestre, Ivan Lopez Munuera, Roberto Gonzalez, Jose Vela

IE HUMANITIES
Rolf Strom Olsen, Julián Montaño, Julia McAnallen, José Ramón Marcaida, Fernando Dameto, Manuel Lucena, Laura Martinez de Guereñu

URBAN CULTURE / URBAN WORKSHOP I
Gonzalo Melián, Francisco Mata

EXPERIMENTATION WORKSHOP I
Daniel Canogar

INTEGRATION WORKSHOP I
Ruth Vega, Jose Mª Gª del Monte

3

ENVIRONMENTAL AND BUILDING SYSTEMS II
Juan Travesí, Javier Macías

ENVIRONMENTAL AND BUILDING SYSTEMS WORKSHOP
Lara Elbaz, Jose Mª Ortiz Cotro

CULTURE AND THEORY IN ARCHITECTURE III, IV
Ivan Lopez Munuera, Roberto Gonzalez, José Luis Luque

CONSTRUCTION SYSTEMS AND CONSTRUCTION WORKSHOP
Manuel Pérez Romero, Sara Hernández, Antonio Vaillo

STRUCTURAL TYPES AND STRUCTURAL CALCULATION II
Ramón J. Gonzalez Márquez, Jan Peter Koppitz, Adrián Sanchez Sevilla, Anna Mestre, Javier Giménez Vila

DESIGN STUDIO III, IV
III IV
Julie Kaufmann, Jesús Vassallo, Pablo Oriol, Fernando Rodríguez, Manuel Gª de Paredes, Fernando Gª Pino, Manuel Ocaña, Lina Toro, Romina Canna

URBAN CULTURE AND URBAN WORKSHOP II
Mark Dwyer, Maki Kawaguchi, Francesca Arici, Diego Barajas, Camilo Gª Barona

EXPERIMENTATION WORKSHOP II
Guzmán de Yarza, José Luis López Linares

INTEGRATION WORKSHOP II
Javier Pérez Herreras, José Mª Churtichaga, Javier Quintana

4

ORGANIZATIONAL MANAGEMENT
Fernando de la Calzada, Ignacio Urrutia, Ramiro de Cea, Jose Ignacio Arenzana, Sol Gómez de la Barreda

PROFFESIONAL ETHICS
Romina Canna, Angel Peña, Francisco Mata

CULTURE AND THEORY IN ARCHITECTURE V, VI
David Goodman, José Vela

CONSTRUCTION SYSTEMS AND CONSTRUCTION WORKSHOP III
Luis Alvarez Alfaro, Fermín Gonzalez Blanco, Ruth Vega

DESIGN STUDIO V, VI
V VI
Valerio Canals, Clara Moneo, David Casino, Bernardo Angelini, Jaume Mayol, Fernando Gª Pino, Isabel Collado, Ignacio Peydro

URBAN MANAGEMENT
Ricard Frigola

URBAN WORKSHOP III
Bárbara Pons, Christopher Marcinkoski, Javier Arpa, Juan Elvira

EXPERIMENTATION WORKSHOP III
Edgard González, Andrew Schachman, Miguel Angel Giner

INTEGRATION WORKSHOP III
Santiago Cirugeda, Odile Decq, Manuel Aires Mateus, Antonio Jiménez Torrecillas

5

ALTERNATIVE PRACTISES: DESIGN
David Díez

ALTERNATIVE PRACTISES: DIGITAL STUDIES
Sergio Irigoyen

ALTERNATIVE PRACTISES: LANDSCAPE AND ENVIRONMENT
Marta Landazábal, Ana Coello de Llobet

ALTERNATIVE PRACTISES: MANAGEMENT AND ENTREPRENEURSHIP
Daniel Mayoral

ALTERNATIVE PRACTISES: THE CITY
Romina Canna

DESIGN STUDIO VII
VII
Izaskun Chinchilla, Laura Martínez de Guereñu, Mónica García

TECHNICAL STUDIES: THESIS PROJECT
Rafael Iñiguez de Onzoño, Manuel Pérez Romero

THESIS PROJECT
UTP
Lina Toro, Fernando Rodríguez, Pablo Oriol, Laura Martínez de Guereñu, Mónica García, Andrew Varela, Izaskun Chinchilla, Pedro Iglesias, Juan Elvira, Antonio Vaillo

URBAN ISSUES: GLOBAL CITIES
Martha Thorne

DAVID GOODMAN

David Goodman is Director of Undergraduate Studies in Architecture at IE University. He received his Masters Degree in Architecture from the Harvard University Graduate School of Design, and completed degrees with honors in Government and in History of Architecture and Urbanism from Cornell University. He is co-author of the book An Introduction to Architecture Theory: 1968 to the Present, and his work has also appeared in the journals a+t and Log, in the anthology Chicago Architecture: Histories, Revisions, Alternatives, and in the book Walter Netsch: A Critical Appreciation and Sourecebook. Before co-founding the firm Roadwork Studio, he worked in the studio of Rafael Moneo in Madrid and for David Woodhouse Architects and Nagle Hartray Architects in Chicago. He has taught architecture at the Illinois Institute of Technology (IIT) in Chicago, Harvard University Graduate School of Design, and at the Boston Architectural College. The work of Roadwork Studio has been featured in the Burnham 2.0 Exhibition at the Chicago History Museum, and the office was awarded second prize in the national competition for the Reconquista Civic Center in Argentina.

PABLO ORIOL

He has served as curator of cultural activities for the General Subsection for Architecture under the Ministry of Public Works, for ETSAM, and for the Cervantes Institute between 1999 and 2002. In 2003, he was a founding partner at the Nolaster Oficina de Arquitectura in Madrid, where he pursued his professional activity until 2007. In early 2005, he established FRPO Rodríguez & Oriol Architecture Landscape together with Fernando Rodríguez. They have received the Design Vanguard 2012 Award and the Europe 40 UNDER 40 Award (2009). Their work has also been selected for the 9th Spanish Architecture and Urbanism Biennial (2007), the 9th Exhibition of Young Spanish Architects (2006), the Bauwelt Award 2007 and the Wallpaper Design Awards 2007. Along with Lina Toro and Fernando Rodriguez, he is the co-director of the Undergraduate Thesis Project at IE University and is associate professor of Architectural Design at ETSAM. He has also been a professor of Design Thinking in the Launch Program for the MBA at IE Business School and is involved in the research project "Beyond Tourism," writing articles and editing books, such as The Infrastructural Beach.

FERNANDO RODRÍGUEZ

Since 2005, he has pursued his professional work with Pablo Oriol at FRPO Rodriguez & Oriol; they have won a number of awards, including the Design Vanguard 2012 Award, the Europe 40 Under 40 Award (2009) and the Bauwelt Award (2007). Their work was also selected for the 9th Spanish Architecture and Urbanism Biennial, the 9th Exhibition of Young Spanish Architects (2006) and the Wallpaper Design Awards (2007). Their work and their designs have been published and exhibited in publications and in group exhibitions in several countries; it was recently part of the exhibition "Cut 'n'Paste" at the MoMA in New York. Along with Lina Toro and Pablo Oriol, he is co-director of Undergraduate Thesis Projects at IE University, and is an associate professor of Architectural Design at ETSAM. He is currently writing his PhD dissertation, "El Entendimiento Infraestructural del Proyecto Arquitectónico" and publishes articles in Circo, Sociedad y Utopía, Quaderns and Pasajes Diseño. He is editor of the books Ma/SP Proyectos de Arquitectura, Matterscapes and The Infrastructural Beach. He is involved in the research projects "Emergencia Creativa", "Beyond Tourism" and "TRLab".

LINA TORO

Architect graduated with honors from the UPB of Medellín, is accredited by the RIBA (2001) and holds a Spanish architecture degree fro m ETSA (2007). She has worked in Medellín, Palma de Mallorca and Rotterdam. She is a partner at LinaToro.arch and one third of the Dosmasunoarquitectos studio. Since 2003, she has won awards in 27 national and international competitions. Her built work and work in progress includes 102 dwellings in Carabanchel EMVS, 67 dwellings in Colmenar Viejo IVIMA and the Social Services Center in Móstoles. Her work has been widely published and exhibited. She is co-editor of the magazine Arquitectos for the Spanish CSCAE (2006). She curated the exhibition cycle and edited the monograph "Monoespacios", COAM (2004-2007). She is currently an architecture columnist with Ivorypress (2013). She is a professor of Architectural Design and the Undergraduate Thesis Projects workshop at ETSAM (2008), and is a member of the Research Group "Prácticas Emergentes en Arquitectura" ("Emerging Practices in Architecture") (2013-), directed by Juan Herreros. She is co-director of the UFP at IE University, where she also teaches the Design Studio (2013).

RAFAEL ÍÑIGUEZ DE ONZOÑO

Received his degree in architecture from the ETSAM (1992), where he is now preparing his PhD dissertation. He is currently a professor of Construction Systems and Technical Practices at IE University, and has taught for the Master's Program in Heritage Administration and Facility Management at UEM since its beginning. He has taught courses at ETSAM in Construction Techniques in the Construction department and Undergraduate T Projects in Interior Design. His professional activity in the studio includes building projects for the Public Administration and for the private sector in the following areas: residential, tertiary, healthcare, commercial, representational, data centers, furniture, exhibitions, etc. both in new construction and rehabilitation, based on the understanding that building architects are part of a multidisciplinary team, which allows them to take on more complex programs. In order to reconcile seemingly contradictory categories, such as global tendencies and local realities, he has worked both in Spain and abroad, with buildings in Berlin, Equatorial Guinea and Astana. During his career, he has also worked in construction and development companies.

MANUEL PÉREZ ROMERO

Ph.D. in Architecture Universidad Politécnica de Madrid (ES), B.Arch, Universidad de Las Palmas de Gran Canaria (ES). He also studied architecture in Politecnico di Torino (IT), Politecnico di Milano (IT) and Westminster University (GB). He is a Lecturer of Design Projects at E.T.S.A.G. in Alcalá de Henares since 2001, and he has been Lecturer of Design Projects at E.T.S.A. Madrid. He is also a professor of Construction Systems, Construction Workshop and Thesis Project at IE School of Architecture. He has collaborated with Soriano&Asociados (Madrid) and Foreign Office Architects, (London). He founded the partnership nodo17 architects (2002), and has received awards in many national and international competitions. He has more than 100 publications in magazines and books. Recently, the Korean editorial Damdi Publishing Co, has published a monographic "mook" about nodo17.

JOSÉ MIGUEL IRIBAS

Sociologist specialized in territory, urban planning and tourism. He was part of the team that won the March Grant in urban planning and architecture for 1972-1973 and carried out the first urban studies on new Spanish tourist cities, which were awarded First Prize in the 1st National Essay Contest on Tourism. He served as Director of Research for the Benidorm City Council for 7 years. He has undertaken more than 190 studies and collaborated on more than 40 master plans and various strategic plans for ports, and in the development of the land management guidelines for Asturias, Valencia, Extremadura and Galicia. Trustee of the Foundation "Arquitectura y Sociedad" and consultant for the Metrópoli Foundation. He has participated in several urban and tourism projects in Spain and other countries (Algeria, Morocco, Brazil, Taiwan, Italy, France, Russia, Peru, Argentina, China and Korea). He has completed 60 strategies and programs for designs by Jean Nouvel, Renzo Piano, Patxi Mangado, Jaime Lerner, Aicequip, Ben van Berkel, Rex Architects, Iñaki Ábalos, Juan Herreros and Benedetta Tagliabue, among others.

LINNA CHOI, TARIK OUALALOU

Partners and Co-Founders of KILO, based in Paris and Casablanca. Studied at Harvard University, Cambridge, MA. and Yale University, New Haven (Linna) and the École d'Architecture Paris-Malaquais, Paris and Rhode Island School of Design, Providence (Tarik). Finalists at the Grand Prix AFEX 2014, winner of Young Arab Architects. June 18, 2012, and nominated for the Aga Khan Award in 2009. Their work has been exhibited worldwide. Recetly, at the Venice Biennale 2014, Pavillon du Maroc, 2014; Arab Contemporary, Louisiana Museum of Modern Art, Cophenhagen, Denmark, 2014; Young Arab Architects. CA'ASI, Venice (Venice Biennale) 2012; Young Arab Architects. L'Institut du Monde Arabe, Paris. 2012.

Invited professors at Rice University, Rhode Island School of Design, Harvard University Graduate School of Design and Ecole d'Architecture Paris-Malaquais.

ELIA ZENGHELIS AND ELENI GIGANTES

Architects and professors of architecture. Zenghelis divides his time between Brussels, London, Rotterdam, and Athens. He studied, and later taught, at the AA in London. As one of the original founders of OMA, he worked with Rem Koolhaas until 1987, when he established Gigantes Zenghelis Architects in Athens and Brussels with Eleni Gigantes. He has been thesis tutor at the Berlage Institute for more than 10 years and professor at the Dusseldorf Academy of Fine Arts, visiting professor at the EPFL Lausanne, the ETH in Zürich, and at the Accademia di Archittetura in Mendrisio. He has also taught at Princeton, UCLA, Columbia University and other schools in the US, South America, Spain, and Japan. He was awarded the RIBA Annie Spink Award for outstanding contribution to architectural education. His current practice includes the Felmish Administration Centre in Louvain finished recently.

IZASKUN CHINCHILLA

Architect from ETSAM in 2001. Runs her own firm, Izaskun Chinchilla Arquitectos. Senior teaching fellow and senior research associate at the Bartlett School. She is a professor of Architectural Design at the École Spéciale d'Architecture (Paris) and associate professor of Architectural Design at ETSAM. She has extensive teaching experience: Geneva University of Art and Design, University of Alicante, CEU San Pablo University, IE University, the Institute of Advanced Architecture of Catalonia (IAAC) in Barcelona, and the European University (UE) in Madrid. She has received grants for research at international universities, such as Columbia University and Princeton University. More than 200 magazines and architecture publications have made reference to her work. Her submissions have received awards in numerous calls for proposals. She has participated as a lecturer or as a curator for more than 150 forums. Her work was exhibited at the 8th and 10th Venice Biennale, New Trends in Architecture Europe – Asia 2009, Fresh Madrid, or the 5th Biennial in São Paulo. Her contribution to architecture has been recognized with an honorable mention for the ArcVision Prize 2013.

JUAN ELVIRA

Architect from ETSAM, 1997. Partner and founder of Murado y Elvira Arquitectos. Architectural Design at ETSAM since 2001 and a design critic and Urban Workshop professor at IE University since 2013. He received a scholarship from the "LaCaixa" Foundation for postgraduate studies (1998) and received a Master's degree from Columbia University in New York City (AAD, 2000). He has been a visiting professor and lecturer at various national and international universities, such as NTNU in Trondheim, the International University of Catalonia or the Alicante School of Architecture. His projects have received awards in various national and international competitions and have been exhibited at Freshmadrid and at the 11th Venice Biennale, among others. Recently his student residence hall in Trondheim was nominated for Norway's National Architecture Prize (2012) and selected for the 2013 Spanish Architecture Biennial. He engages in editorial work and criticism, which he began as editor of the architecture magazine Oeste. His doctoral thesis "Ghost Architecture" is based on research into the cultural and technological practice of producing architectural atmospheric effects.

MÓNICA GARCÍA

Trained at the Valencia School of Architecture (1998). She received a Master's degree in Architecture from the Graduate School of Design, Harvard University (2002) and a Diploma in Advanced Studies from ETSAM (2004). Since 2002 she has been a professor in the Architectural Design department at the Valencia School of Architecture. She has been an associate professor at the Boston Arquitecture Center (2002), an assistant professor at the Graduate School of Design, Harvard University (2001-2002) and a visiting professor at the Paris La Villette School of Architecture (2010-2011) and the Vienna University of Technology (2011). Between 1997 and 2000 she collaborated with different architecture studios in Paris: Ateliers 234, Olivier Chaslin Architecte and Architectures Jean Nouvel. In 2003, she established her practice in Valencia, where she co-founded Garcia-Floquet Architects with Frédéric Floquet. Their work has received awards in several public tenders: social housing in Nanterre (France), a residential building in Geneva on rue Louis Favre, etc. Her work was selected for the 10th Spanish Architecture and Urbanism Biennial and was a finalist for the 11th BEAU.

PEDRO IGLESIAS

Born in 1958 in Madrid, he studied at the ETSAM and obtained a doctoral degree. His doctoral thesis was awarded a distinction from the Technical University of Madrid and served as the basis for the book La Habitación del Enfermo, published by Caja de Arquitectos in 2011.

He worked at the studio of the architect José María García de Paredes from 1983 to 1984 and subsequently founded Noriega, Iglesias, Gámez, Arquitectos S.L. with Jose Luis Rodriguez-Noriega and Silvia Gámez Carrasco. The studio has worked on unique buildings such as the Teatro Real in Madrid and the Hospital de San Pedro in Logroño. He has won several awards, including the prize for Urban Planning, Architecture and Public Works from the Madrid City Council and the Silver Medal at the Miami+Beach Bienal held by the Florida International University School of Architecture with the American Institute of Architects (AIA). Since 1985, he has remained active as a concert harpsichordist, specialized in Spanish Baroque repertoire.

LAURA MARTÍNEZ DE GUEREÑU

Graduated with distinction from the University of Navarra (1998), where she also earned her PhD in Architectural Design (2006). She graduated with distinction from the Master's program in Design Studies at Harvard University (2004) for which she was awarded a scholarship from the Rafael del Pino Foundation. Since 2008, she has been a professor and lecture series coordinator at IE University. She has taught at La Salle-Universitat Ramon Llull (2006-2008), was a Visiting Fellow at Harvard University (2004-2006) and served as an assistant professor at the University of Navarra (1998-2003). Her research has focused on exploring issues of perception, design narratives and points of intersection between architecture, technology and art. She has published more than twenty articles on architects, artists and thinkers in the Modern tradition, such as Josef Albers, Mies van der Rohe, Romano Guardini or Le Corbusier. She the editor of: Josef Albers: Una Antología (1924-1978) (2014), Rafael Moneo: Portfolio Internacional. 1985-2012 (2013) and Rafael Moneo: Apuntes sobre 21 obras (2010), each with their respective English editions.

ANDREW VARELA

Founding principal of New York based office OOAA, Inc. He is a licensed architect in the US and in Spain. Andrew holds a Masters degree in Architecture from the Graduate School of Design at Harvard University, a Masters degree in Advanced Architectural Design from the ETSAM and a Bachelor of Arts from Brown University. Andrew´s professional experience has been focused on specific building types that include cultural institutions, such as the expansion and renovation of the Juilliard School of Music and Alice Tully Hall at Lincoln Center in New York City, academic buildings like the Syracuse University Whitman School of Management at School of Management, residential projects such as the Sky House Tower in New York, retail such as the Abercrombie and Fitch Flagship store in Madrid, and infrastructure projects like the 2nd Avenue Subway Line in New York. Andrew is currently adjunct professor at the New Jersey Institute of Technology in Newark, NJ. He is also a design critic at the IE Architecture School.

INTERNSHIP MAP

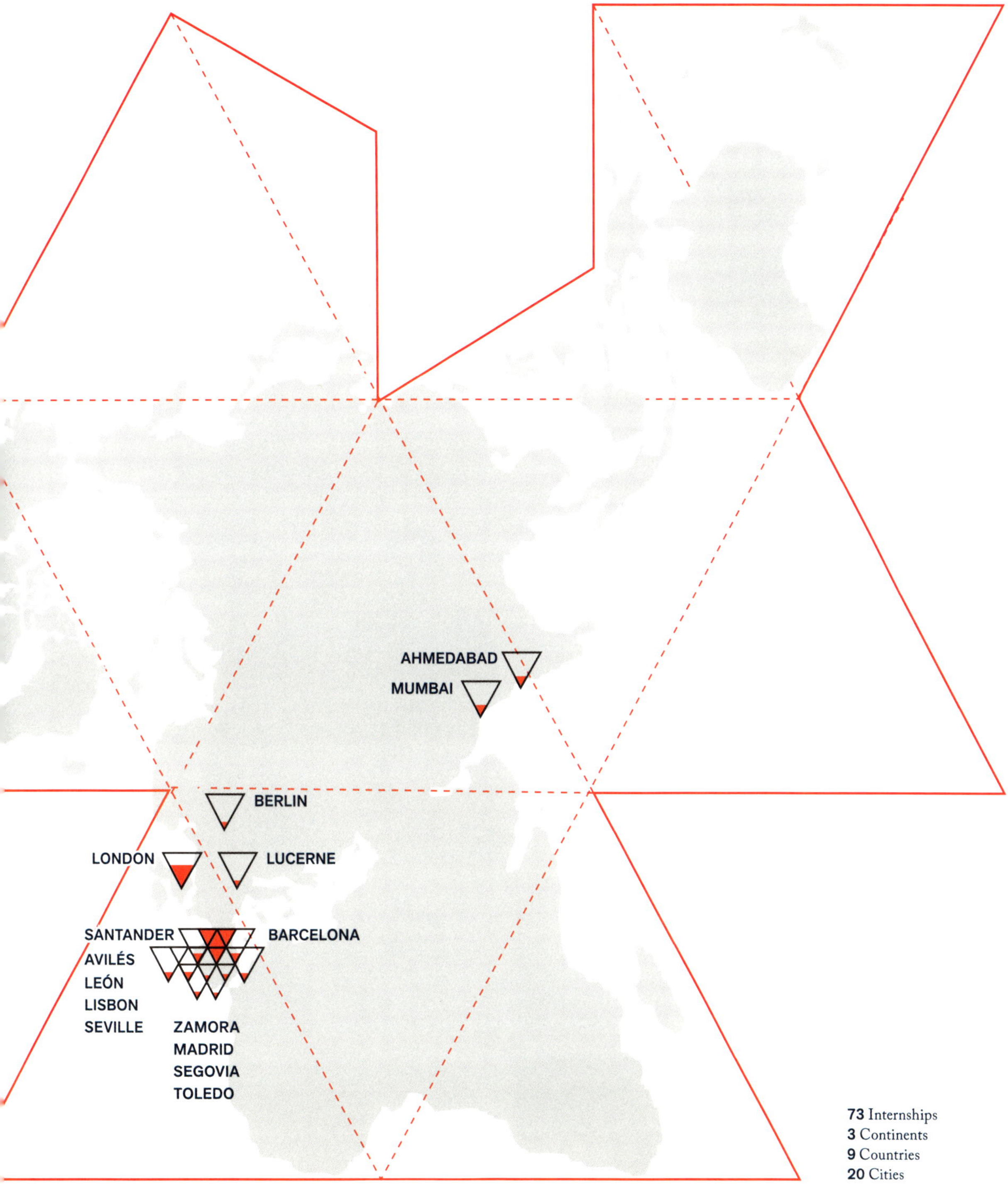

73 Internships
3 Continents
9 Countries
20 Cities

PAULA ÁLVAREZ GARCÍA
Zamora, 1986. Internships: González Ramos, Zamora; Fundación Escolá, Madrid; Francisco Somoza, Zamora; MTM, Madrid.

ÍÑIGO ARIAS DÁVILA
Bizkaia, 1990.Internships: LBT Architekten, Luzerne, Suiza; S&Aa, Madrid; Picado de Blas Arquitectos, Madrid.

ÁLVARO BRAVO ALONSO
Salamanca, 1987. Internships: MTM Arquitectos, Madrid; Rubio & Álvarez-Sala Arquitectos, Madrid; IC*, Intelligent Coast Group, Barcelona.

CLARA BUENO MORENO
Segovia, 1990. Internships: Museo Contemporáneo de León (Musac); Argesplan 2000 S.L, Madrid; Pemán y Franco, Zaragoza.

Mª ELENA CARDIEL
Segovia, 1990 Internships: Iñaki Ábalos, Madrid; Juan Navarro Baldeweg, Madrid.

MARINA CARRETERO
Segovia, 1990. Internships: Gil-Bartolomé Architecture, Madrid; Kinzo, Berlin; Studio Mumbai, India.

ETTORE DISCONZI
Cairate, 1987.

BEATRIZ FERNÁNDEZ GÓMEZ
Valladolid, 1990. Internships: Ross Barney Architects, Chicago; Broadway Malyan, London; The Beverly Willis Archtectural Foundation, New York.

TAMARA GARCÍA GARRIDO
Segovia, 1990. Internships: Picado-de Blas Arquitectos, Madrid; Producción Gráfica Future Arquitecturas, Madrid; Base Design, Madrid.

JUAN GILSANZ SÁEZ
Madrid 1990. Internships: Arup, London; Zaha Hadid Architects, London; Junquera Arquitectos, Madrid; Ecosistema Urbano, Madrid.

JUAN GONZÁLEZ
Segovia, 1990.Internships: Estudio Rubio & Álvarez -Sala, Madrid; Estudio Ruiz Larrea & Asociados, Madrid; Estudio Carlos Riaño, Madrid.

ANA GONZÁLEZ GRANJA
Vilagarcía de Arousa,1990 Internships: R. Barney, Chicago; Navarro Baldeweg, Madrid; Zaha Hadid, London; Gil Bartolomé, Madrid; A. Mateus, Lisbon.

CÉSAR GUSANO
Palencia, 1989.Internships: SSD, New York; BASE Design, Madrid; Mareines Patalano, Rio de Janeiro.

FERNANDO JIMÉNEZ SALMERÓN
Segovia, 1990. Internships: Base Design, Madrid; Gumuchdjian Architects, London; Studio Mumbai, India.

CLAUDIA MANENTI
Bergamo, 1989.

CECILIA MARINA
Segovia, 1990. Internships: SsD (Single-SpeedDesing), New York; AV Arquitectura Viva, Madrid; Estudio Miguel Ángel G. Grande, Segovia.

CARMEN MENCOS
Sevilla, 1990. Internships: Rare Architecture, London; VAMOS Architects, New York; Articam Agronomy Engineering Studio, Seville.

GONZALO MERINO
Santander, 1990. Internships: Paisajes Arquitectura y Crítica, Madrid; APIAXXI, Santander; DIA 4, Santander.

LETICIA MERINO
Cantimpalos (Segovia), 1990. Internships: Arquitectura Viva, Madrid; SsD, New York; Vastu Shilpa Consultants, Ahmedabad India.

CRISTINA MORENO
Toledo, 1990. Internships: Ayuntamiento de Madrid; ERES, Castilla la Mancha; TASH Arquitectos, Toledo.

JUAN MORENO
Segovia, 1990. Internships: Ruiz-Larrea & Asociados, Madrid; IDOM-ACXT, Madrid; FHECOR Ingenieros Consultores, Madrid.

VALENTINA OCCHINI
Milan, 1989.

CANDELA OLIVA
Madrid, 1989. Internships: C4 Coriñas, Buenos Aires; Palo Arquitectura Urbana, Buenos Aires; Diéguez Fridman, Buenos Aires.

PEDRO DE PASCUAL SAMPER
Madrid 1990.Internships: SCB, Chicago; Rare Architecture, London; David Chipperfield, London; B720, Barcelona.

VANESA PAYO
Palencia, 1989.Internships: ACXT, Madrid; Scalar Architecture, New York; Vastu Shilpa Consultants, Ahmedabad.

BLANCA PÉREZ
Madrid, 1989.Internships: Jesús Moreno y Asociados Arquitectos, Madrid; Daniel Canogar Studio, Madrid; David Chipperfield Architects, London.

TERESA RODRÍGUEZ-GIMENO
London, 1985. Internships: Caroline Wiggin Landscape, Madrid; Dosmasuno Arquitectos, Madrid; Niemeyer Center, Avilés.

TEXTS IN SPANISH

1

PRESENTACIÓN

AL SERVICIO SECRETO DE SU MAJESTAD

8

233

David Goodman

Director de Estudios de Grado de la IE University

> *Como institución estatal, tenemos obligaciones para con el Estado de Texas. Como escuela profesional, tenemos obligaciones para con los arquitectos de Texas. Nuestra obligación primera continúa siendo para con nuestros estudiantes. Por el momento, nos limitaremos a debatir nuestras obligaciones para con los estudiantes, que son dos:*
> *1. Dotar al alumno de los conocimientos necesarios para el ejercicio de su profesión y*
> *2. ayudarle a desarrollar su capacidad de selección por medio de su propio juicio.*
>
> Colin Rowe, Declaraciones de Harwell Hamilton Harris en la Facultad de Arquitectura de la Universidad de Texas, 1954.

1. ESTÁ PASANDO DE VERDAD

La práctica arquitectónica está amenazada. En consecuencia, también la formación de los futuros arquitectos. La poca probabilidad que el autor sospecha de que las dos frases anteriores causen conmoción o resulten muy controvertidas, no hace sino confirmar la precisión de dicha declaración. Parece que empieza a haber consenso sobre la idea de que la profesión del arquitecto se transformará radicalmente en los años venideros, independientemente de que los arquitectos acepten este cambio o participen activamente en él. Observaciones como estas vienen a veces acompañadas de la certeza de que el nuevo orden de las cosas, acarreará inevitablemente (y, tal vez, afortunadamente) un menor peso para el arquitecto y hará que las herramientas de la disciplina de la arquitectura, a pesar de merecer ser conservadas aunque sólo sea por razones sentimentales, en el mejor de los casos no tengan uso alguno en el nuevo entorno y, en el peor de los casos, sean antagónicas al mismo.

Una respuesta alternativa a la crisis actual en la práctica profesional ha sido la de defender el (¿imaginario?) estatus anterior del arquitecto y de la arquitectura fortaleciendo y desarrollando nuevas herramientas disciplinarias, ya sea para mantener la arquitectura con vida hasta que pase la tormenta, o para aislarla de las fuerzas económicas y sociales globales, preservando así una muestra pura de la cultura arquitectónica autónoma, no contaminada ni por las demandas del mercado ni por las condiciones actuales.

El primer planteamiento esbozado más arriba sugiere que la disciplina de la arquitectura puede permanecer más eficaz, viva y relevante disolviéndose casi por completo en la acción directa y la toma de poder por parte del ciudadano. Este tipo de acción está, por lo general, vinculada a una crítica política explícita y tiende a utilizar la arquitectura, o lo que queda de ella, como vehículo o sustituto de la actividad política, generando sucesos y episodios de activismo arquitectónico y cívico. Este trabajo invierte la exhortación de Le Corbusier en las páginas finales de *Vers une Architecture* y se vincula directamente a la Revolución concluyendo que la arquitectura puede evitarse.

El arquitecto, en la medida en la que está presente en este tipo de trabajo, es a menudo facilitador de impulsos y deseos iniciados en otros lugares. Aunque sin duda eficaces e inspiradores, los resultados descartan el valor de las herramientas disciplinarias de la arquitectura en favor de la acción directa, y tal vez lo más problemático sea que este enfoque tiende a institucionalizar la oposición y las posturas más críticas. Es decir, asume que el arquitecto siempre funciona de un modo crítico a la situación actual y, por lo tanto, con mucha frecuencia en los márgenes de las fuerzas que lo conforman.

Una postura crítica es una de las muchas posturas disponibles para arquitectos y estudiantes de arquitectura y tiene por objeto combatir, o al menos protestar, ante algunas de las más flagrantes injusticias. Sin embargo, sería un error confundir una comprensión más amplia de la práctica arquitectónica con los enfoques "emancipadores", o con el modo de actuar basado en la protesta. Y, del mismo modo, sería un error limitar el conocimiento de los estudiantes sobre las salidas profesionales disponibles a aquellas que presenta el modo crítico. En pocas palabras: nuestros estudiantes deberían tener la libertad de ir a las barricadas, pero no deberían estar obligados a hacerlo.

El segundo enfoque descrito al principio es esencialmente una versión del argumento adorniano de la autonomía y la pureza disciplinaria: negándose a participar del mercado y las fuerzas sociales más amplias que condicionan la producción arquitectónica, este argumento sostiene que los arquitectos podrán mantener su disciplina auténtica y viva, aunque, una vez más, condenada a los márgenes de la vida cotidiana.

Tal posición conduce frecuentemente a una exploración en profundidad de las herramientas disciplinarias, pero el intento por evitar la contaminación del exterior, también puede conducir a una exploración estéril de formas o procesos sin referentes a las demandas reales que se le plantean a la profesión de la arquitectura ampliamente entendida.

2. TRANSGRESIONES SISTEMÁTICAS

¿Cuál es, entonces, el papel del arquitecto o de un programa de arquitectura frente a las actuales turbulencias? Si el desafío se presenta complicado para aquellos que buscan maneras de definir su propia práctica, es aún más desalentador para aquellos de nosotros dedicados a la formación de los futuros arquitectos, ya que nuestras obligaciones son múltiples: para con el estudiante, la profesión, y la sociedad a la que ambos pertenecen. ¿Cómo, entonces, preparar al arquitecto para un futuro profesional incierto? ¿Y cuál es el papel de las herramientas disciplinarias en ese futuro? Estas han sido las preguntas centrales y principales objetivos del programa de Grado en Arquitectura de la IE University, y estas fueron también las líneas de investigación sobre las que se asentó el trabajo de tesis del presente volumen.

Nuestro enfoque ha consistido en enseñar arquitectura como emprendimiento de diseño, a partir de la exploración de las herramientas disciplinarias y la comprensión de lo que constituye el futuro de la práctica arquitectónica. Dicho sucintamente, nuestro objetivo es el siguiente: utilizar herramientas disciplinarias de arquitectura para transgredir los límites disciplinarios y convertir esta transgresión en un elemento estructural e institucionalizado en la pedagogía de la arquitectura. Perseguimos este objetivo durante nuestro programa de cinco años combinando una formación rigurosa en diseño (nuestros estudiantes reciben su licencia profesional para España inmediatamente después de graduarse) con formación en gestión y emprendimiento y tres años de prácticas profesionales en arquitectura y disciplinas afines. Pero el enfoque es, quizás, más evidente en los estudios de cinco años y en la estructura del Programa de Fin de Grado. El primer semestre del quinto y último año de nuestros estudiantes se dedica exclusivamente a una serie de talleres de “prácticas alternativas”. Cada uno de estos talleres, llevados a cabo de uno en uno en una serie de módulos de tres semanas de duración, trata una “aplicación indebida” de las herramientas disciplinarias aprendidas a lo largo de los estudios de diseño y de los talleres, enfocados a temas como Imagen y Simulación, Paisaje y Medio Ambiente, La ciudad, Gestión y Emprendimiento o Diseño y Emprendimiento Cultural. Cada taller se lleva a cabo como un breve estudio de diseño. En ellos los estudiantes participan en proyectos que van desde el diseño de directrices de planificación urbana, al de juguetes de construcción pasando por el diseño de videojuegos.

Al concluir esta serie de talleres, los alumnos de quinto año comienzan el semestre dedicado al PFG aquí documentado. El Proyecto de Fin de Grado tiene por objeto la creación de un diseño de construcción integral y una propuesta empresarial al mismo tiempo; nuestros estudiantes definen el programa y el lugar y vinculan sus proyectos individuales a un programa más amplio para la revitalización regional a través del turismo.

Con el fin de evitar la dinámica maestro-aprendiz entre estudiante y tutor de PFG reunimos a un equipo de críticos de diseño, profesores de Proyectos Arquitectónicos y otros invitados para crear un clima de debate en el que el estudiante se ve obligado a elegir entre varios puntos de vista con el fin de formar un proyecto que responda tanto a un programa o informe impuesto desde el exterior (en este caso, el turismo en las regiones mineras en declive de Asturias y León), como a un programa individual.

3. SUPRA-ARQUITECTURA

A la hora de valorar los proyectos que aparecen en este volumen en particular y en el programa de Grado en Arquitectura de la IE University en general, puede resultar productivo situar el trabajo dentro de una matriz con las variables “disciplinariedad” y “profesionalidad” (Figura 1). Para nuestro propósito, *disciplinariedad* hace referencia al grado en el que la obra está concebida y ejecutada a través del uso de herramientas específicas para la disciplina de la arquitectura, como la proyección ortográfica o mapping. Por el contrario, el término *profesionalidad* describe la amplitud de salidas profesionales a disposición del arquitecto. Una definición muy acotada de profesionalidad, por ejemplo, podría afirmar amplia podría incluir el diseño de nuevas estructuras de organización o de nuevas formas de participación ciudadana, así como las manifestacio-

11

nes físicas de este compromiso.

Sobre esta matriz, podríamos clasificar (con tan solo algo de ironía) como "buena arquitectura", los trabajos con un alto grado de disciplinariedad y una definición muy acotada de profesionalidad. Aquí nos encontramos con el trabajo altamente autoral de los maestros, catalogado en las monografías de tapa dura y reconocido con premios internacionales. Las obras de Foster, Piano, Moneo y Zumthor bien podrían estar ubicadas en este cuadrante. Obras de baja disciplinariedad y una definición acotada de profesionalidad podrían situarse en la "Arquitectura Sencilla" y describir trabajos como los del *Bjarke Ingells Group* o *Work AC*, que se sitúan en los límites tradicionales de la profesión de arquitecto, pero que adoptan algo parecido al relajado modo de producción "proyectivo" descrito por Robert Somol y Sarah Whiting en su ensayo de 2002 "El efecto Doppler", en lugar de la laboriosa y casi ostentosamente rigurosa obra del "buen" arquitecto.

El cuadrante de baja disciplinariedad y profesionalidad, que podríamos denominar "Pos-arquitectura", comprende la producción crítica y activista, en la que la eficacia política es más importante que la autoría, la forma, la lengua o la expresión y en la que los límites profesionales importan poco. El trabajo de *Spatial Agency*, EXZYT o Recetas Urbanas serían ejemplos de este cuadrante.

El cuadrante restante es el que más me interesa. Podríamos calificar de "Supra-arquitectura" a los proyectos de alta interdisciplinariedad con una concepción muy amplia de la profesionalidad. Este tipo de proyectos aplicarían las herramientas del arquitecto a los problemas no inmediatamente o exclusivamente relacionados con la arquitectura. Haría mal uso de las herramientas de arquitectura para maximizar su efecto e ignoraría las fronteras entre profesiones. El trabajo de OMA/AMO, en mi opinión mucho más integrado y dependiente de las herramientas disciplinarias que el de muchas empresas que nacieron inspiradas en esta firma, podría considerarse Supra-arquitectura, capaz de abordar el diseño de una casa, de una bandera, o de un desfile de moda con el mismo rigor disciplinario y profunda falta de respeto por los límites entre la arquitectura y todo lo demás.

Aquí es donde se situaría lo mejor del trabajo que vemos en el presente volumen y es a este cuadrante al que creo que deberíamos dedicar la mayor parte de nuestros esfuerzos en la enseñanza de la arquitectura.

4. SU MAJESTAD

Los grados de arquitectura que reciben nuestros estudiantes no los otorga formalmente el programa de grado en Arquitectura, ni la Universidad, ni el gobierno regional, ni el español, ni si quiera la Unión Europea. Se los otorga a nuestros estudiantes, una minoría de los cuales son españoles, Su Majestad el Rey de España. Oficialmente, el trabajo que hacemos en esta universidad es en su nombre, en favor del bien común.

Este ensayo comenzaba con un epígrafe escrito por Colin Rowe para Harwell Hamilton Harris, que proclamaba la triple obligación del profesor de arquitectura: con el estado, con la profesión, y con el estudiante. En el contexto sociopolítico actual, resulta cada vez menos factible separar estas obligaciones; un arquitecto formado tan solo para construir es una carga para las tres partes. Nuestra obligación de servir al bien común ya no se cumple si tan solo formamos buenos arquitectos, aunque esto sea, oficialmente, lo único que se nos demanda. Por tanto, debemos trabajar en silencio, casi en secreto, para ampliar el alcance de estas demandas, sin con ello descuidar las más básicas. Por este motivo nos centramos en nuestra disciplina y, al mismo tiempo, nos saltamos con asiduidad los límites de nuestra profesión. En la actualidad, la buena arquitectura no es suficiente.

2

MÉTODO

PFG IE: 140 DÍAS Y 140 NOCHES 16

Fernando Rodríguez, Pablo Oriol y Lina Toro 233
Directores del Proyecto Fin de Grado IE Unviersity 233

INSTRUCCIÓN 233

"Por ósmosis". Eso respondió John Hejduk en una entrevista concedida a su gran amigo y poeta David Shapiro a principios de los noventa, cuando este le preguntó cómo enseñaba arquitectura. A la respuesta Hejduk añadió: "saco de los alumnos aquello que llevan en su interior. Sigo manteniendo que esa es la única manera de poder ofrecer a la sociedad arquitectos que de verdad desempeñen una labor que pueda ser considerada arquitectura. [...] El proceso formativo de un estudiante debería ser algo más parecido al de un laboratorio, quiero decir, un proceso que, al trabajar con lo real, muere y nace constantemente... entendiendo y aceptando que no hay otra verdad misma que la posibilidad de aprender del error sin tratar de esconderlo"[1].

ACTUALIZACIÓN

Así que, en un momento de obligados cambios y plena redefinición profesional del arquitecto, parece inevitable cuestionar los métodos y procesos en los que se ha visto disuelto el *objetivo* del Proyecto Final, con el cual se culmina la carrera universitaria de arquitectura. Si la profesión se transforma y los campos de batalla para el arquitecto se multiplican, no cabe duda que la musculatura de los estudiantes deberá fortalecerse en la universidad con el fin de anticiparse a los acontecimientos venideros.

Ya podemos desconfiar de la insistente enseñanza basada en los *conocimientos adquiridos y los procesos aprendidos*. Hoy, sin duda, parece más útil y honesto *incentivar y dar concesión a los propios criterios y libertades*; hipertrofiando las destrezas y pasiones que permitirán al futuro arquitecto surfear con el máximo vigor por el surrealismo más puro que es la propia realidad.

PRODUCCIÓN-PRODUCTO

El PFG IE surge en 2013 y se desarrolla como un gran *Studio Culture* norteamericano bajo la organización de tres directores y un equipo de profesores con *target* definido. La organización es compleja y de carácter multidireccional. El equipo está moldeado por perfiles profesionales diversos y antagónicos; intencionadamente elegidos con el único fin de fortalecer el criterio de los futuros arquitectos. La mezcla siempre supone un importante factor de riesgo, pero como decía el propio Hejduk en aquella entrevista a Shapiro, "sin este tipo de desafíos, se pierde el azar de la posibilidad, el elemento de duda, el riesgo del fracaso" y por supuesto, el acierto del avance.

INTENSIDAD

Pero el máximo reto de este PFG está tan condicionado por su multi-direccionalidad como por el limitado periodo de desarrollo y conclusión. El PFG está concebido como un entrenamiento de alta intensidad programado a corto plazo.

En cada una de las veinte semanas, marcadas por ejercicios de objetivo particular según la especificidad de cada proyecto y alumno, se trabaja un tema de arquitectura con el fin de producir un *documento* potente, de alta calidad grafica y detallado formato. El objetivo, construir un proyecto-puzzle estructurado por acumulación y encaje de esa *colección de piezas y asuntos específicos de arquitectura* testados en cada proyecto.

Este método no lineal, adaptable a las necesidades particulares, permite que el alumno pueda abarcar y enfrentar el proyecto desde diferentes ángulos, estableciendo un protocolo que es más cercano al del laboratorio experimental, donde el proyecto se nutre de esos necesarios e inevitables aciertos y errores.

Son 140 días los que ofrecen la oportunidad de experimentar contenidos esenciales que van más allá del compromiso de creación de un proyecto de arquitectura. También supone el reto de explorar las tangencias vitales para concebirlo, como la organización, la transmisión y la comunicación de la idea: ¿qué clase de información es la que realmente necesitamos?, ¿qué tipo de documentos necesita cada proyecto en específico?, ¿cuáles son los documentos y formatos que permiten informar y transmitir pensamiento en diferentes ámbitos? Preguntas recurrentes en el actual debate universitario global.

Por ello incidimos en la búsqueda del lado más directo, emocionante y potente de un proyecto para hacer de cada uno de ellos un manifiesto específico, cuidadosamente editado. 18

CARDUMEN

El PFG es además un proceso creativo donde el espacio y la estrategia son determinantes. Para conseguir resultados satisfactorios en este corto periodo de tiempo adoptamos un comportamiento similar al de un banco de peces: los alumnos de PFG se mueven conjuntamente, conforman un único organismo de movimientos coordinados donde la posición define su papel y ambiciones propias.

El estudiante que va a la cabeza, hambriento y en forma, dirige los movimientos del grupo. Quien elige los arriesgados *laterales*, apuesta por una posición personal y más propositiva, susceptible de múltiples críticas que sin duda se traducen en recompensa. En el *núcleo*, las posturas más tímidas se resguardan, pero igualmente navegan. Los que van *detrás* gastan un porcentaje inferior de energía, pero aprovechan el rebufo como táctica de supervivencia.

Así, la producción individual tiene repercusión en el desarrollo colectivo y viceversa. Cada estudiante experimenta su propio límite dentro de ese organismo de gran fuerza que representa el cardumen PFG.

COMUNICACIÓN

Los alumnos se ven enfrentados a enseñar e intercambiar opiniones de su proyecto en los *juries* conjuntos junto a los *Design Critics*, en lo que interpretamos como una formación en la confrontación de las propias ideas: exponerlas, defenderlas y filtrar la información recibida. Los estudiantes también cuentan con clases especializadas de *Technical Practices*. Al igual que un proyecto profesional, cuentan con asesores que benefician y profundizan en conceptos esenciales relativos a las decisiones importantes del proyecto.

RECOMPENSA

El PFG es una apuesta que se asemeja más las experiencias reales de la propia profesión, y sin duda acerca a los alumnos a su primera experiencia real de trabajo como arquitectos profesionales en un estudio de arquitectura. Situación compleja y enriquecedora ya que ofrece diálogo en diferentes direcciones, lo que permite desarrollar un proyecto riguroso. La difusión y la proyección de este primer proyecto profesional se registra en la edición y elaboración de su propio material en un libro propio y la posterior exposición colectiva *Finish Line*, llevada a cabo a final del proceso.

La mejor carta de presentación queda editada en un formato donde además de exponer un proyecto de arquitectura, se evidencian las habilidades específicas e intereses personales que inauguran una especializada presentación de cada perfil profesional de cara al mercado laboral. El descubrimiento de esta *otra realidad* más versátil, dinámica, incluso pragmática de Proyecto Final se instala como un excitante experimento educativo configurando un portfolio a prueba de las demandas profesionales más exigentes.

ACTORES, INSTANCIAS, *DEADLINES* Y PRODUCTOS
BE WATER, MY FRIEND

22 Los números que resumen el PFG IE 2013 son los siguientes: 28 estudiantes, 14 docentes, 20 semanas de producción, 4 semanas de edición, 2 *workshops* intensivos de lanzamiento de 15 sesiones cada uno, 45 sesiones de seguimiento del proyecto, 30 sesiones de prácticas técnicas, 3 directores de PFG, 4 profesores invitados como directores de *workshop*, 2 profesores de prácticas técnicas, 5 *design critics*, 3 sesiones críticas generales (*juries*), 5 píldoras de habilidades proyectuales, 1 exposición, 1 lección magistral, 28 libros resumen, 28 maquetas finales, 28 proyectos entregados… Este elenco numérico nos permite hacernos una idea física y temporal de lo que hemos descrito más arriba: un proyecto fin de grado como entrenamiento de alta intensidad desarrollado en un ámbito colectivo en constante intercambio entre estudiantes y docentes de perfiles diversos que permite un aprendizaje osmótico como actualización de estrategias didácticas previas y experiencia pre-profesional.

La densidad de actores, instancias, *deadlines* y productos exige de los docentes un alto grado de orden y precisión y de los estudiantes un ejercicio extraordinario de ritmo, flexibilidad y adaptabilidad. Cada uno de ellos se ha convertido durante veinte semanas en un verdadero Bruce Lee del Proyecto Fin de Grado: "Don't get set into one form, adapt it and build your own, and let it grow, be like water. Empty your mind; be formless, shapeless—like water. Now you put water in a cup, it becomes the cup; you put water into a bottle it becomes the bottle; you put it in a teapot it becomes the teapot. Now water can flow, or creep, or drip, or it can crash. Be water, my friend"[2].

El grupo de 28 estudiantes está formado por las dos líneas—español e inglés—de la primera generación de arquitectos de IE University. Todos ellos han pasado por un ambicioso programa de Grado que les ha preparado para responder con éxito al ejercicio del PFG. Ahora comienzan su carrera con la seguridad de saber adaptarse a las exigencias profesionales que se presentarán en su camino.

CARRERA DE FONDO Y *SPRINT*

El trabajo se inició en enero de 2013 con dos *workshops* de lanzamiento de una semana de duración cada uno. El primero de ellos (14-18 enero) fue dirigido por Linna Choi y Tarik Oualoulou de *KILO Architectes* y el segundo (21-25 enero) por José María García del Monte y Laura Martínez de Guereñu.

El viernes 1 de febrero se iniciaron las sesiones semanales de seguimiento de proyecto conducidas por nosotros mismos, los 3 directores de PFG. Los *Design Critics* entraron en escena el 15 de febrero en la primera sesión crítica conjunta (jury). Allí estaban Izaskun Chinchilla, Juan Elvira, Mónica García, Pedro Iglesias y Andrew Varela. A partir de ese momento el ritmo semanal se densificó con las sesiones de *Technical Practices* impartidas por los profesores Rafael Iñiguez y Manuel Pérez, todos los martes hasta el final del mes de mayo. Además de las sesiones semanales de martes y viernes, los estudiantes recibieron una serie de píldoras de habilidades de proyecto –herramientas, conceptos y metodologías- preparadas por los cinco *Design Critics* durante 9 miércoles repartidos en todo el calendario.

El 22 de marzo tuvo lugar la segunda sesión crítica general con todo el equipo de profesores, que fue el inicio de la etapa final, más intensa en trabajo y número de sesiones. Finalmente, como colofón a la etapa de producción, para la sesión crítica final del 31 de mayo los estudiantes prepararon las mejores presentaciones de sus proyectos en un esfuerzo por compendiar todos los formatos trabajados

—dibujos, imágenes, maquetas, videos—y por sacar el máximo partido a las mayores fortalezas de sus propuestas.

El trabajo más difícil ya estaba realizado. El mes de junio—con una única sesión docente programada para identificar carencias y posibles mejoras—sirvió para completar los proyectos y editar toda la documentación generada. El 27 de ese mes se produjo la entrega final del Proyecto Fin de Grado, acompañada por un libro de cada proyecto editado por los propios alumnos. Al día siguiente—28 de junio—Salvador Carmona, Rector de IE University, inauguró en el claustro central del Campus de Santa Cruz la Real en Segovia la exposición *Finish Line* con todo el trabajo entregado por los estudiantes. Como guinda del pastel, en ese mismo marco tuvimos el placer de escuchar la lección magistral de Juan Herreros, Catedrático de Proyectos Arquitectónicos de la ETSAM y *Chair Professor of Architecture* en GSAPP-Columbia University, una intervención cargada de sugerencias sobre los arquitectos, las universidades, la arquitectura y el aprendizaje.

1. Texto basado en la entrevista realizada por David Shapiro para la película documental *John Hejduk. Builder of Worlds*, © 1992, Michael Blackwood Productions Inc.

2. Lee, Bruce. *A Warrior's Journey*. Warner Home Video, 2000.

¿ES LA INTEGRACIÓN UNA NUEVA METODOLOGÍA DOCENTE?

26

233

Manuel Pérez Romero

Profesor de Sistemas Constructivos y Prácticas Técnicas en el IE Unviersity

"Mientras que el pensamiento simplificador desintegra la complejidad de lo real, el pensamiento complejo integra lo más posible los modos simplificadores de pensar"[1].

Conviene aclarar que uno de los principales motivos por el cual la enseñanza de la arquitectura se encuentra fragmentada en diferentes áreas de conocimiento no es más que por una cuestión puramente metodológica. También conviene recordar que aunque el aprendizaje se realice a partir de sus partes el objetivo final tiende a ser holístico. Esta especie de paradoja es la que en cierta forma ha regido la enseñanza de la arquitectura en España: estudiamos las partes para comprender el todo, aunque sepamos que el todo es más que la suma de las partes. El actual modelo de PFG que aquí se defiende parte de un sistema complejo orientado a la integración de las distintas áreas de conocimiento que un arquitecto debe adquirir. El saber del arquitecto no debe estar parcelado, ni dividido, ni reducido, sino simplemente integrado.

Tradicionalmente el estudiante de arquitectura se ha enfrentado al PFG sin el apoyo de una clara metodología docente. De forma brusca y repentina el alumno debía integrar el conocimiento que había adquirido a lo largo de la carrera. Pero más que un sistema integrado el proyecto devenía en un sistema aditivo, resultado de la suma de las distintas áreas que el alumno debía demostrar que conocía y dominaba. Y así la dificultad de abordar una estructura compleja se suplía con mucho tiempo.

Aquí el reto se presenta doble. Por un lado transformar el PFG en un sistema integrador y por otro reducir su duración. Ambos factores están intrínsecamente relacionados. A una mejor implementación de la integración, una mayor reducción del tiempo de duración del PFG. En el caso concreto de la IE University *Undergraduate Architecture Degree* el modelo de un PFG integrado está apoyado y potenciado por su propio plan de estudios. La integración es una estrategia que está presente a lo largo de toda la carrera y que contrasta con los tradicionales planes docentes. En este sentido el PFG se puede entender como la culminación de todo un proceso que comienza durante 27
los primeros cursos de la carrera. 27

INTEGRACIÓN *"IN BOUND"* E INTEGRACIÓN *"OUT BOUND"*

De forma genérica se pueden clasificar en dos los sistemas de integración: aquellos que se producen desde el interior y aquellos otros que se importan desde el exterior. Es decir, sistemas "in-bound" y sistemas "out-bound", respectivamente. Aunque habría que añadir un tercer modelo basado en la superposición de ambos. Este último podría representar el actual PFG de la IE University.

Desde el interior del PFG dos profesores con distintos grados de especialización estructuran la integración "in-bound", uno más volcado hacia el *design* y otro más hacia la técnica, aunque con unas fronteras bastante borrosas entre ambos. Y desde el exterior un grupo de *design critics* llevan a cabo la integración "out-bound" del sistema.

De esta forma el PFG se configura como un sistema dual que evoluciona tanto desde su propio interior como desde el exterior. El PFG es el espacio intersticial entre ambos modelos de integración. Un espacio colchón que se comprime y se expande en función de las presiones internas y externas. Así el alumno deberá estar preparado para enfrentarse a un modelo no lineal de enseñanza y basado en la integración compleja del conocimiento. Quizás convendría enseñar al estudiante a "surfear" entre los movimientos "in-bound" y "out-bound"; ya que una estructura de este tipo obliga al alumno a asumir una actitud abierta y flexible.

La figura del tradicional tutor de Fin de Carrera se sustituye por un complejo sistema de interrelaciones donde los roles de cada profesor podrán ser modificados en función de las demandas del proyecto. Ya el alumno no "sabe" quién es su tutor, pero si quienes son sus *coaches*.

PROTOCOLO DE INTEGRACIÓN

El reducido tiempo que el alumno va a dedicar al PFG (en comparación con otras escuelas de arquitectura) obliga al estricto cumplimiento de un protocolo de integración. Un número elevado de "coaches" para un PFG puede generar un alto nivel de ruido que el alumno posiblemente no llegue a asimilar.

Para amortiguar este más que probable ruido y conseguir la creación espontánea de una estructura de orden, es necesario la coordinación de todos los profesores mediante un *planning* temporal que de entrada a cada uno de estos actores.

Es más, la coordinación deberá devenir en sincronización. Por ejemplo, si los "profesores técnicos" entran demasiado pronto su labor puede que sea vacua, mientras que si llegan demasiado tarde su aportación consistirá me-
28 ramente en la verificación de lo realizado.

Cuenta Cecil Balmond que cuando Rem Koolhaas le llamó para definir la estructura para una casa en Burdeos[2], los dos se acercaron al lugar y lo exploraron conjuntamente. Koolhaas quería que la casa flotará sobre la colina y que se asomara a la villa de Burdeos. Pero frente al músculo que requiere el acto de flotar, Cecil Balmond propuso una revisión de las clásicas estructuras porticadas. Un movimiento suave y matizado tanto vertical como horizontalmente. Por un lado desplazó al exterior del rectángulo que formaba el volumen de la casa los ejes de los pórticos y por otro hizo visible el comportamiento apoyado o colgado de la estructura.

Este ejemplo sirve para ilustrar la gran capacidad de cualquier sistema integrador y cómo la decisión de cuándo debe entrar el componente técnico o de cualquier otra índole es fundamental para el devenir del proyecto. La casa de Burdeos de OMA nunca sería lo que es sin aquella germinal excursión entre Balmond y Koolhaas.

La rigurosa planificación desarrollada para el PFG está enfocada a coordinar la integración de los distintos agentes que intervienen en el proceso del proyecto. Aunque, por otro lado, la evolución del proyecto de cada alumno es muy variable, lo que obliga a una organización precisa pero al mismo tiempo flexible y adaptable.

Una de las metáforas que quizás mejor ilustra la epistemología del pensamiento complejo es aquella de navegar por un mar de incertidumbre entre islotes de certeza. Los islotes bien podrían representar a los profesores (aunque no se pretende relacionar al profesor con la verdad, ya que el alumno siempre podrá abandonar una isla en busca de otra); mientras que el número de islotes, su situación y distancia estarían definidos por el método de integración.

1. Morin, Edgar. *Introducción al pensamiento complejo.* Marcelo Pakman (edición española). 10ª reimpresión. Barcelona: Gedisa Editorial. 2011. Colección Cladema. Pág. 22.

2. Balmond, Cecil. *Informal.* Prestel. 2007.

PRÁCTICAS TÉCNICAS 30

Rafael Íñiguez de Onzoño 233
Profesor de Sistemas Constructivos y Prácticas Técnicas en el IE University

> *"Los jóvenes acuden a la Universidad, quieren ser arquitectos o arquitectas, quieren averiguar si poseen las cualidades para ello. ¿Qué es lo primero que se les transmite? Lo primero que se les ha de explicar es que no se encontrarán con ningún maestro que plantee preguntas ante las cuales él sepa de antemano la respuesta.*
>
> *Hacer arquitectura significa plantearse uno mismo preguntas, significa hallar, con el apoyo de los profesores, una respuesta propia mediante una serie de aproximaciones y movimientos circulares. Una y otra vez"*[1].

FORMATO

Prácticas Técnicas forma parte de un sistema de integración definido como Proyecto Fin de Grado, junto a Proyectos VII, los 2 Talleres de inicio del PFG, así como las sesiones puntuales realizadas a lo largo del curso por un grupo de *Design Critics*. Las sesiones de PT se han desarrollado en formato de Taller, con el objetivo fundamental de integrar de forma práctica todas aquellas materias técnicas imprescindibles en el Proyecto Fin de Grado, mediante el estudio y desarrollo de los aspectos tecnológicos inherentes al trabajo propuesto. Desplegar el conocimiento acumulado hasta el momento para establecer un lenguaje propio, aglutinador de experiencias, ha permitido establecer, desde una dimensión profesional, las conexiones necesarias entre los distintos aspectos integrantes del Proyecto.

INVESTIGACIÓN

La estructura no lineal del Taller, más próxima al ejercicio profesional real que al estrictamente académico, permite realizar una reflexión incidiendo desde distintos campos en la evolución del concepto de proyecto mediante sucesivas "aproximaciones circulares", con la idea de analizar las distintas opciones en cada momento, buscando sus propias leyes. El alumno selecciona las herramientas en la toma de decisiones, desde la convicción de que el fin último de la Universidad debe ser convertir a sus estudiantes en autodidactas.

CONTENIDO

Partiendo de un marco conceptual—el turismo—y un marco físico común de actuación —La cuenca Astur-Leonesa—, se desplegaron planteamientos muy dispares. Aceptando la escasa utilidad de un perfil de contenido estricto y uniforme para todos los proyectos, las condiciones iniciales así como los requisitos exigibles en el contenido final de los proyectos fueron establecidos desde el principio en una imprescindible bodega temática:

Topos. La lectura del lugar y de los condicionantes locales como verdadero motor de la propuesta proyectual; la relación con el terreno, entendido como uno de los temas en los que la arquitectura debe desarrollar la mayor sensibilidad, ha permitido múltiples soluciones: la intervención firmemente integrada en el suelo, formando parte de él, modelándolo, excavándolo, flotando sobre él, apoyándose puntualmente, sumergido, suspendido a merced de la gravedad... demuestran la hetereogeneidad de encuentros y desencuentros con el terreno propuestos.

Energía y adecuación al ambiente. Explicar la propuesta desde su comportamiento con el entorno, la optimización de recursos y su estrategia, el empleo de sistemas pasivos de confort térmico e iluminación natural... son requisitos decisivos a la hora de definir la arquitectura en términos de coste energético, conseguidos mediante procedimientos sencillos: reflexión de la luz solar, ventilación natural por convección, emplear el terreno como aislante térmico...

Sistema estructural. Es preciso destacar el alto grado de aportación al Proyecto de la estructura en todos los ejercicios, con ideas arriesgadas alejadas de la comodidad de soluciones convencionales. Fruto de esta tensión, los Proyectos explotan el potencial de la estructura para enriquecer la experiencia arquitectónica, el esqueleto como generador de espacios, más allá de la función primaria de trasladar las cargas al terreno, como lo demuestran una vez más la diversidad de propuestas que abarcan patrones reticulares, murarios, lineales, curvos, membranas... 32

Materialidad y Sintaxis. Las diversas estrategias y escalas de intervención en el lugar han conducido a otras tantas respuestas constructivas; desde la contundencia de emplear materiales con una fuerte componente estereotómica para dialogar con el terreno y contenerlo, hasta la opción de seleccionar materiales prácticamente ingrávidos que flotan en el aire, subrayan la necesidad de establecer para cada trabajo un escenario material y discurso proyectual específico. El análisis de las uniones entre distintos materiales y elementos se convierte en una ocasión para ensayar la propia validez del Proyecto.

Obsolescencia y Caducidad. Permanencia. Trabajar sobre arquitecturas preexistentes o marcos físicos sensibles ha determinado el carácter permanente de algunas propuestas, y temporal o efímero de otras, y se convierte en un factor especialmente decisivo a la hora de explicar algunos de los trabajos, propuestos desde la escalabilidad del edificio o su reversibilidad total.

Proceso constructivo. Planificar una estrategia acertada de ejecución del ejercicio como una reflexión que analiza y detecta las posibles dificultades que pueden aparecer en el desarrollo y conclusión del Proyecto, si fuera ejecutado.

Finalmente, es necesario reconocer la intensidad y compromiso de los alumnos con el desafío propuesto, compartidos sin duda por todos los profesores que hemos participado en el curso. A pesar de la incertidumbre inicial, por tratarse del primer grupo de estudiantes que afrontaba el nuevo formato del PFG, su respuesta ha sido muy positiva, con una actitud innovadora desde múltiples ángulos (programa, uso, viabilidad, idoneidad...) y 35
que podríamos interpretar como parte de la "responsabilidad" del arquitecto: la apertura a nuevos entornos y disciplinas.

1. Zumthor, Peter. *Architektur Lehren*, Architektur lernen. Conferencia pronunciada en la Accademia di Architettura, Mendrisio, Suiza. 1996.

LA REALIDAD LO VUELVE TODO FANTÁSTICO

38 234 233

Eleni Gigantes y Elia Zenghelis conversan con David Goodman

Me reúno con Eleni Gigantes y Elia Zenghelis en la inevitablemente espectacular neblina dorada de las últimas horas de la tarde en Atenas. Mis anfitriones me están esperando en la terraza de un bar enfrente del *Athens Hilton*, y yo llego sin apenas aliento después de haber caminado demasiado rápido desde Plaka, cruzando la Plaza Syntagma—donde la Policía Nacional Griega al completo parecía estar reunida esperando (¿o provocando?) a los protestantes anti Troika—, pasando por el palacio presidencial y los restos de los Juegos Olímpicos de 1896, bajando por un ajetreado bulevar atragantado de humo y coches franceses de cinco puertas, y atravesando un barrio tranquilo con robustos y solemnes bloques de pisos neomodernistas de la década de los sesenta, donde casi la mitad de los escaparates a pie de calle están vacíos y en alquiler. Me dan la bienvenida con una amabilidad y una familiaridad sinceras, que resultan por un lado completamente naturales y, de algún modo, sorprendentes, ya que no conozco a Eleni y solo he coincidido con Elia una vez, hace un par de meses, en una conferencia en Segovia. Llegados a cierto punto de nuestra conversación, saco de mi bolso un micrófono absurdamente grande, lo enciendo, y empezamos a hablar sobre la primera de las muchas preguntas que había preparado. Esta es la única de esas preguntas que acabaríamos tratando, ya que la conversación va dando giros fascinantes que yo no había previsto, llena de breves referencias a la sanación psíquica, los comunistas, serpientes y montañas que explotan. Durante toda la conversación, nos concentramos en el turismo, el territorio, la infraestructura y la posibilidad de una planificación inteligente. Ya se ha hecho de noche y estamos hambrientos para cuando vuelvo a guardar el micrófono.

DAVID GOODMAN: Me gustaría empezar hablando sobre el Movimiento Moderno y el turismo, porque podría decirse que surgieron a la vez. Es decir, creo que podría afirmarse que un nuevo modelo de turismo apareció más o menos al mismo tiempo que el Movimiento Moderno y, hasta cierto punto, ambos provienen del mismo tipo de conducta higienista. Durante un tiempo, los mismos impulsos que condujeron a la edificación masiva, llevarían al fenómeno del ocio masivo, la habilidad de tener tiempo libre e incluso de considerar la posibilidad de ir a algún lugar a disfrutarlo. Todo esto evoluciona a la par que se desarrolla la arquitectura moderna y, hasta cierto punto, las mismas motivaciones sociales impulsaron el desarrollo de ambos. De hecho, muchos de los primeros modernistas, como André Lurçat o incluso Le Corbusier, son los responsables de algunos proyectos muy interesantes relacionados con el turismo. Pero algo ocurrió durante el trayecto. Creo que es acertado afirmar que hoy en día, o en el siglo que ha pasado desde que nació la arquitectura moderna, ya no existe un vínculo tan claro entre el turismo y una arquitectura de cierta ambición. ¿Qué ocurrió? Es decir, si se produjo un divorcio—y, por supuesto, mi pregunta presupone que lo hubo—, ¿cómo y por qué se alejó la corriente central de la Arquitectura Moderna del turismo?

ELIA ZENGHELIS: ¿Te refieres al divorcio entre modernismo y turismo? Bueno, lo interesante es que, por lo menos en Grecia, ocurrió todo lo contrario. Lo que quiero decir es que el modernismo y la arquitectura moderna pasaron a formar parte del día a día. Es decir, puedes ver que toda Atenas está basada en el típico bloque de apartamentos que tienes a tu alrededor. Es un producto derivado del modernismo. De hecho, uno de los primeros bloques de apartamentos arquetípicos del centro de Atenas fue admirado por Le Corbusier. Pero, mientras que el modernismo adoptó estas cosas de las que está hecha Atenas, esta especie de píxel de Atenas, el turismo adoptó el modernismo, es decir, el modernismo de calidad. La mayoría de los proyectos realizados para el turismo en Grecia, al menos históricamente, fueron modernistas de alta calidad. Hay un arquitecto en particular, aunque también hay otros, que ejemplifica ese movimiento: Aris Konstantinidis. Es muy interesante que no existiera ningún divorcio, al menos en Grecia. Al contrario, se reforzó lo mejor de la arquitectura griega moderna con el turismo. Fue un matrimonio.

GOODMAN: Entonces, ¿estás diciendo que el turismo es uno de los ámbitos en los que todavía se puede observar una ética modernista?

ELENI GIGANTES: No necesariamente ahora mismo, no. Eso fue en el primer período de turismo en Grecia, que empezó en la década de los cincuenta, y fue un programa muy específico. Lo que pasó fue que, inmediatamente después de la Segunda Guerra Mundial, Grecia se vio inmersa en una guerra civil que terminó finalmente en 1949, y lo hizo de forma decisiva. Fue básicamente una lucha para decidir si Grecia se iba a volver comunista o no.

Pero lo que pasó en realidad fue que, durante la ocupación alemana, el verdadero gobierno de Grecia se había exiliado a El Cairo, y aquí teníamos un gobierno que colaboraba con los alemanes. La mayoría de los griegos no estaban de acuerdo, así que huyeron y formaron unidades de resistencia, se hicieron bandoleros. Pero Grecia casi no tiene llanuras. Hay islas y montañas. Algunas partes son bastante impenetrables, y los griegos conocían esos territorios, pero los alemanes, por supuesto, no. Los bandoleros se dividían entre los que se habían quedado atrás, que no eran comunistas, y los más eficientes, que se organizaron como unidades comunistas. Pero lo más importante es que fueron a las ciudades y se organizaron allí, y le dieron comida a la gente, porque los alemanes se estaban llevando la comida y la estaban enviando a Alemania; 300.000 personas murieron en Atenas solo en un invierno, en 1942. Hubo una hambruna terrible. Así que, mientras el gobierno propiamente dicho estaba en El Cairo, los comunistas básicamente hicieron funcionar la sociedad.

ELIA ZENGHELIS: En el campo todo iba muy bien, porque era inaccesible para los alemanes. Las cosas funcionaban de un modo muy justo y podría decirse incluso que democrático. Era comunista. El tema de si las cosas habrían seguido siendo así o no si el Partido Comunista hubiera llegado al poder, y si hubiéramos formado parte del Bloque del Este, ya es otra cuestión.

GIGANTES: Pero, básicamente, lo que pasó es que después de la guerra los comunistas habían conseguido que el Estado sobreviviera, que los griegos sobrevivieran, y los griegos les estaban muy agradecidos. El gobierno volvió y en Yalta tuvo lugar un milagro: Grecia formaría parte del bloque capitalista.

ZENGHELIS: Los tratos fueron muy... crueles políticamente.

GIGANTES: En realidad, en un principio, los británicos eran los que iban a controlar Grecia, no los estadounidenses. Sin embargo, Gran Bretaña estaba en bancarrota, no tenía fondos. Durante el primer año de la guerra civil los británicos estuvieron aquí, pero después básicamente les cedieron el control a los estadounidenses. Entonces, ¿qué hicieron estos? Ellos fueron los que apoyaron y ayudaron a las fuerzas no comunistas, porque Grecia estaba destinada a formar parte de occidente. La cosa es que algunos comunistas sí que practicaban el comunismo de Stalin y toda su ideología, pero otros solo eran personas que se habían unido porque era lo que se hacía en su pueblo o su grupo de pueblos, y así era como habían sobrevivido. Ellos les suministraban pan, comida, etc. De todos modos, fue bastante horrible y, al final, los primeros jets que se desarrollaron se emplearon en la Guerra Civil de Grecia. Te vamos a enseñar dónde, en Vasilis Konstantinou. Ese lado era el de las filas no comunistas, y este lado era el de las filas comunistas.

ZENGHELIS: Vasilis Konstantinou antes era un río, y había una división clara. Una parte del río era comunista, y la otra parte era británica.

GIGANTES: Y después estadounidense. Total, que los británicos habían desarrollado este modelo de jet.

ZENGHELIS: El *Meteor*.

GIGANTES: Y los probaron aquí en Grecia. Los probaron bombardeando esa colina verde que está junto al estadio olímpico, porque ahí era donde los comunistas tenían enterrado su arsenal. Y Elia, en realidad, vivió al otro lado.

ZENGHELIS: Solían caer enfrente de nuestro apartamento. Yo veía el fuego, la metralla, salir de la parte frontal de los jets, y venían así. Nunca habíamos visto nada parecido: ¡un jet!

GIGANTES: Nadie lo había visto. Era la primera vez que se veían jets en Grecia.

ZENGHELIS: Un día le dieron al arsenal.

GIGANTES: La colina explotó.

ZENGHELIS: La colina estalló en pedazos. Nosotros vivíamos en un bloque moderno de apartamentos bastante sólido. Todo se rompió. Todo lo que había dentro se rompió. Todas nuestras estanterías, la vajilla, los cuadros. Todo.

GOODMAN: Habéis dicho algo que quiero volver a unir con el tema del turismo. Hubo un momento en el que—y esto no está relacionado con el turismo específicamente en el caso que habéis mencionado—habitar un territorio otorgaba una especie de identidad. Los griegos conocían su tierra y los alemanes no. Los griegos podían desaparecer en medio del campo, pero los alemanes no podían seguirlos. Es ese paisaje lo que permitió a la nación sobrevivir, en cierto modo. Desde luego, en términos de turismo de interior, se ha utilizado la identidad y el paisaje para crear ese sentimiento de nación, la idea de una identidad nacional, cuando puede que nunca hubiera existido realmente. Así que, definitivamente, en términos de mercado interior, creo que el turismo se ha utilizado de ese modo. Sin embargo, la relación es más complicada cuando se trata del turismo entrante o externo. Es una relación muy complicada porque depende de una especie de caricatura súper definida de una identidad, ¿verdad? Los turistas alemanes o británicos quieren ver una cierta visión de España, por ejemplo, cuando vienen de visita, y esa visión puede o no corresponder realmente con la auténtica España. Aún así, hay que proporcionársela de todos modos, para que estén satisfechos y sigan viniendo.

ZENGHELIS: Bueno, los primeros años, el turismo griego era más que nada algo cultural. Se trataba de visitar lugares importantes de la antigüedad, y combinar eso con el buen tiempo y el cálido mar azul.

GOODMAN: Eso es bastante distinto, desde luego, de lo que vemos hoy en día. Esta mañana estaba leyendo la revista que te dan en los aviones de *Aegan Air*, y lo que aparece en todos y cada uno de los anuncios de la revista es una imagen del horizonte, la costa y una piscina infinita. No hay ni una sola foto de nada relacionado con la antigüedad.

GIGANTES: Lo sé. Me dan ganas de vomitar. En primer lugar, ningún auténtico amante del Mediterráneo quiere una piscina. Eso es para los turistas del norte. Es decir, tienes el mar ahí mismo. ¿Para qué quieres la piscina?

ZENGHELIS: Sin embargo, el último número de "Blue" es muy interesante, porque no aparece Atenas, ni la Acrópolis, ¿vale? Pero sí que habla mucho de las islas.

GOODMAN: Es verdad. Me baso en una muestra muy limitada, por supuesto, pero me parece que las islas están bastante presentes en la conciencia de los griegos. Solo llevo aquí ocho horas. El taxista, los recepcionistas del hotel, la mujer que limpia mi habitación en el hotel, todos me han dicho a los 60 segundos de conocerme: "Atenas es bonita, pero tienes que ver las islas". Así que, a primera vista, me parece que las islas están muy presentes, incluso en la ciudad.

GIGANTES: Sí. Lo cierto es que hay otra cosa que está muy presente, pero que los veraneantes no visitan, y me refiero a las montañas. Lo más auténtico, el gran itinerario turístico de Grecia, es venir a Atenas, ir a Delfos, después a Meteora y, por último, ir al Peloponeso; y allí es donde está todo.

Pero me gustaría volver a lo que has dicho al principio, y que ya hemos respondido antes hablando de Grecia. He pasado toda mi carrera trabajando en este tema, y me gustaría señalar que el ocio de masas nació con la industria de masas. Los dos fueron de la mano, y esto se remonta al siglo XIX. Hasta los Juegos Olímpicos surgieron a partir de esto. Por primera vez había exposiciones universales, eso era algo espectacular. Fíjate en la Exposición Universal de Chicago. Los ingleses también tuvieron la suya, con el Palacio de Cristal de 1851. De repente, se celebraban estos eventos de masas a gran escala, y la gente cruzaba el océano en transatlánticos para visitar esas enormes exposiciones. Era algo colosal. Al mismo tiempo, el deporte se estaba convirtiendo en una actividad de masas. Eso fue muy importante para el movimiento olímpico. Empezamos a ver estos eventos deportivos de masas, como los de boxeo o de ciclismo, pero estaban todos amañados. Entonces llegó el barón de Coubertin, un francés profundamente protestante que se sentía ofendido porque el dinero estuviera destruyendo la belleza y la integridad del deporte. Esa fue una de las fuerzas que motivaron el surgimiento de los Juegos Olímpicos, que en realidad fueron creados por todas las familias reales de Europa. Los crearon desde arriba, y la idea era restituir el antiguo concepto griego de las Olimpiadas en tiempos de paz, y también el de cuerpo sano y mente sana que los ingleses habían desarrollado, la verdad.

La cuestión es que el turismo es algo bastante diferente al ocio de masas, y el turismo siempre fue algo muy caro. El ocio de masas consistía en vivir en Manhattan y poder ir a la playa en Far Rockaway en tren para pasar el día, y luego volver. Eso era el ocio de masas. Pero el turismo de masas no existió literalmente hasta 1970. ¿Por qué 1970? Porque ese fue el año en el que apareció el avión Jumbo. Literalmente, no había turismo de masas antes de aquello. La idea de turismo hasta entonces era la de turismo cultural.

ZENGHELIS: La década de los setenta también fue la apoteosis del florecimiento económico del capitalismo, tras los cincuenta en occidente, y después de eso empezó a haber una serie de crisis económicas que condujeron a la situación actual.

GIGANTES: Te voy a explicar el caso de Grecia. Después de que terminara la guerra civil en 1949, Estados Unidos se dio cuenta de que Grecia era el límite sudeste de su hegemonía en el Mediterráneo, Grecia y Turquía. Grecia había sido literalmente destruida por los alemanes. Antes de marcharse, lo volaron todo por los aires. Todo. Todos los puertos, todas las carreteras, todos los puentes. Y tampoco era un país tan avanzado antes de eso, así que la guerra civil se luchó en medio de las ruinas. Los estadounidenses habían desarrollado, antes del Plan Marshall, la Doctrina Truman, que en parte significaba que Estados Unidos le enviaría dinero a Grecia y a Turquía. Era distinta del Plan Marshall, que estaba más orientado al préstamo y arriendo, ya sabes, a la venta de productos estadounidenses. Esta doctrina se trataba, literalmente, de reconstruir estos países, especialmente Grecia, para que pudieran funcionar. Turquía es otra cuestión, pero Grecia, por ejemplo, tenía grandes puertos. Las bases navales estadounidenses estaban aquí, así que destinaron grandes sumas de dinero para reconstruir las infraestructuras griegas. Los gobernantes que teníamos por aquel entonces, que eran muy listos, dijeron: "vale, vamos a hacer eso, pero además vamos a usar este dinero para un plan de turismo". En realidad, no era algo tan extravagante. No es que estuvieran engañando a los estadounidenses. Por ejemplo, en los lugares más importantes, como Epidauro y Meteora, construyeron autopistas y carreteras, de modo que crearon caminos pavimentados para llegar a una zona turística.

GOODMAN: ¿El plan era solo construir la infraestructura, o añadir infraestructura turística a otra que se estaba construyendo?

ZENGHELIS: Verás, el primer ministro por aquel entonces estaba obsesionado con la infraestructura. Solo construyó carreteras.

GIGANTES: Construyó carreteras, construyó puertos, construyó centrales eléctricas...

ZENGHELIS: Eso está relacionado con la idea de la que ha hablado Eleni del el turismo. Este estaba vinculado, extrañamente, a una compañía de seguros, Astir, que había sido creada para eso y que era una rama del Banco de Atenas por aquel entonces. Astir empezó a construir una serie de complejos turísticos en la playa.

GIGANTES: Lo que pasó en realidad es que no solo propiciaron que las instalaciones eléctricas, las instalaciones de agua y las carreteras se establecieran en los lugares que los turistas visitaban, sino que se dieron cuenta de que no tenían infraestructuras como hoteles ni nada parecido, así que hicieron algo maravilloso. Mil novecientos cincuenta, cuando llegó por primera vez el dinero de Estados Unidos, fue un año clave. Lo que hicieron fue crear el Ministerio de Cultura. Ese ministerio tenía dos ramas: la rama de arqueología y el departamento de turismo. Por supuesto, los dos estaban estrechamente relacionados. Lo habían concebido de manera que los principales yacimientos arqueológicos tuvieran cerca un bonito hotel, con el equipamiento más moderno, y carreteras modernas para que los turistas accedieran hasta allí. Nada de esto existía. Antes, si querías ir a esos sitios, tenías que dormir en tiendas y beber de un arroyo, o de un pozo, si tenías suerte.

Así que tuvieron que crear esas infraestructuras. Para hacerlo se fijaron en España, porque en los años treinta España había empezado a desarrollar la idea de los paradores y necesitaba turismo. España miró lo que tenía a su alrededor y, por supuesto, España tiene toda esta magnífica arquitectura medieval, que Grecia no tiene. No tenemos nada. Somos de la época clásica y la moderna. Ya está. No tenemos nada de la época intermedia. Tenemos unas pocas iglesias bizantinas y las ruinas de algunas edificaciones bizantinas, pero no es mucho. No teníamos lo que tenía España. De modo que se fijaron en España e hicieron básicamente lo mismo, excepto porque no tenían los castillos, las fortificaciones y esas cosas que los españoles habían convertido en Paradores. Entonces, dijeron: "vale, no tenemos nada de eso, pero construiremos las infraestructuras y pondremos electricidad, igual que en España, y realizaremos un programa arquitectónico para tener la arquitectura más hermosa y moderna, de los mejores arquitectos, e iremos a todos esos lugares y elegiremos el emplazamiento ideal para poner los hoteles".

ZENGHELIS: Esa era la diferencia con España. Seleccionamos puntos específicos en vez de toda la línea de costa. Después, se creó una legislación, una legislación extremadamente dura, que hizo imposible construir nada a lo largo de la costa. Eso fue lo que salvo las costas griegas.

GIGANTES: Y salvó Grecia.

ZENGHELIS: Salvó a las costas griegas de convertirse en...

GOODMAN: ¿De acabar como Valencia?

ZENGHELIS: Exacto. Y ahora han aprobado una legislación...

GIGANTES: Bueno, eso es un escándalo. Es la Troika. Luego volveremos a ese tema. En realidad, en Grecia todo el mundo tiene acceso a la costa por ley. Creo que es una ley europea. No puedes tener una costa privada, como en Estados Unidos. Todos los edificios tienen que estar a un mínimo de 50 metros de la costa, y si está a solo 50 metros de la costa, solo puede medir nueve metros de alto. A medida que te alejas de la costa, puedes construir edificios más altos.

ZENGHELIS: Aún así... Aunque esté a 50 metros, tiene que estar en una zona en la que se permita edificar. Si no es en una zona en la que esté permitido edificar, no se puede construir nada.

GIGANTES: Ni siquiera una choza. Puedes montar una estructura temporal en la playa. Puedes tener un par de cables eléctricos conectados a una nevera, pero todo eso tiene que desaparecer al final del verano.

En cualquier caso, sobre esa época se creó toda la infraestructura del gobierno, y una de las ramas estaba dedicada a la arqueología. A partir de ahí crearon la escuela de arqueología, para los guías. Me refiero a que entrenaban a los guías. Era un curso de dos años. Muy, muy intensivo. Además, obligaron a los miembros de todas las universidades extranjeras que estaban trabajando aquí, como los estadounidenses que estaban trabajando en las *stoa* y demás, que estaban trabajando de manera aleatoria (eran arqueólogos privados de distintos países), a trabajar en escuelas. Estaba la escuela estadounidense, la escuela canadiense, la escuela danesa de arqueología – así es como las llamamos aquí. No quiere decir que sean realmente escuelas. En realidad significa "instituto". Tenían que trabajar con el Estado griego. Todos y cada uno de los yacimientos arqueológicos pertenecen, por supuesto, a Grecia, y tienen sus arqueólogos griegos, pero se los entregan a los estadounidenses o a quien sea para que excaven, bajo la supervisión de los arqueólogos griegos. La verdad es que funciona muy bien, nunca ha habido ningún problema.

Desde el punto de vista arqueológico, construyeron infraestructuras en los yacimientos, los limpiaron, y organizaron todas las obras y los accesos a los yacimientos. Aparte de todo eso, desde el punto de vista del turismo lo que hicieron fue crear dos cadenas hoteleras: Astir y Xenia. Astir es de cinco estrellas, y Xenia es de tres a cuatro estrellas.

ZENGHELIS: Xenia también estaba financiada por Astir y, como ha dicho Eleni, pensaron: "vale, vamos a contratar a buenos arquitectos".

GIGANTES: Los mejores. Pusieron al mando de la oficina de arquitectura a este gran arquitecto, Konstantinidis, y él fue el que eligió a los que consideraba que eran los mejores arquitectos.

GOODMAN: ¿Y esto fue para el turismo entrante, principalmente?

ZENGHELIS: Bueno, el nombre de Xenia viene de *philoxenia*, que significa "hospitalidad".

GIGANTES: Y *xenos* significa "desconocido" o "extranjero", y *philo* es "amigo", así que sería la amistad del extranjero, o del desconocido. ¿Y quién era la gente que venía? Por aquel entonces, vivir en Inglaterra y pensar en ir a Grecia era como vivir en Brasil hoy en día y pensar en ir a Camboya. Es un viaje muy largo y tienes que tener mucho dinero. Lo cierto es que solo la gente realmente rica viajaba, y los que venían a Grecia eran los que estaban interesados en la cultura antigua. Esto era perfecto para ellos.

GOODMAN: Entonces, era el tipo de gente que podría haber hecho el *Grand Tour*.

GIGANTES: Sí, era como el *Grand Tour* moderno. Venían en cruceros, normalmente.

En cualquier caso, Konstantinidis contrató a grandes arquitectos para esos yacimientos. Algunos de esos sitios no eran tan interesantes, pero siempre estaban bien. Otros eran verdaderamente espectaculares. Eran tan hermosos. El mismo Konstantinidis trabajó en muchos de ellos. Tal vez Epidauro fuera el gran teatro. ¿Sabes? Hay una cosa que yo no sabía hasta que me la contó mi tía, que es guía turística. Yo siempre había visto Epidauro solo como un teatro, pero ella me dijo: "no, Eleni, en realidad, desde los tiempos de la Antigüedad ha sido un balneario". Era un centro médico, porque allí estaban los pozos de Asclepio. ¿Sabes la imagen del médico con las serpientes? Ese es él. Hipócrates, el del juramento de los médicos, se formó en la tradición de Asclepio. Lo cierto es que, incluso antes de la época clásica, los griegos venían desde todos los rincones hasta este sitio, hasta Epidauro, para beber de sus aguas y curarse. De hecho, es un yacimiento enorme, y la parte antigua tiene una especie de lugar de sanación impresionante, donde la gente se quedaba a pasar la noche.

Al principio, se lavaban y se quedaban a pasar la noche, y ocurría algo muy misterioso con las serpientes, pero parece ser que era sanación psíquica. Y se curaban. Pero hay hoteles, o algo parecido a moteles, alrededor de todo el yacimiento. Más tarde, pensaron que la sanación psíquica podría acelerarse con el teatro. Esto coincidió con el auge de los grandes dramaturgos trágicos. No sé si conoces alguna de las grandes tragedias griegas. Terribles. Espeluznantes. Una madre devorando a sus hijos, ya sabes. Total, que construyeron el teatro. La idea era que te quedaras allí, pongamos, durante dos meses. Ibas al teatro y volvías a casa, solo. Siempre dormías solo, eso era parte del proceso de curación, y tenías unos sueños purificadores para tu psicología, y eso te sanaba. Estas situaciones extremadamente dramáticas provocaban tu propio drama, y así podías curarte psíquicamente. De este modo, el teatro estaba ligado, en un principio, a la medicina como una especie de catarsis psíquica, una curación.

GOODMAN: ¿Y había un lugar físico real donde pasaba todo esto?

GIGANTES: Sí, en Epidauro. Tú vas allí y hay un yacimiento enorme, y la gente solo conoce el teatro, pero puedes ver los hoteles y el balneario de sanación y después, cerca del mar, está el teatro. Las estancias especiales de Epidauro las construyó el propio Konstantinidis. Fue un gran arquitecto, y lo que hace fascinantes a esas estancias es la manera en que las diseñó. Cada habitación estaba hecha para dos personas. Pero no era una habitación a la que fueras cuando salieras del teatro para emborracharte y practicar sexo. No. Era como si tuvieras esta profunda experiencia en el teatro. Konstantinidis replicó esas habitaciones catárticas de sanación en esta serie de preciosas estancias construidas en medio del paisaje. Cada habitación mide aproximadamente dos metros y medio de ancho y cinco metros de largo. Estas estancias tienen dos camas, muy estrechas, una detrás de la otra, y un espacio muy reducido para colgar la ropa, y fueron diseñadas especialmente para esto. No fueron populares entre los turistas, y ahora solo las usan las compañías de teatro y la gente que trabaja en el yacimiento arqueológico. Konstantinidis siempre usaba materiales naturales y le gustaban las estructuras tranquilas, siempre dejaba a la vista el hormigón. Precioso. Es algo muy griego.

Y lo interesante de Kalambaka, cuando vas a Meteora, es ese paisaje tan peculiar. Hay esas extrañas cumbres que sobresalen, y en la cima están los monasterios. La ciudad de Meteora están debajo, y los monasterios están ahí encima. Lo que hizo Konstantinidis fue inclinar el tejado del vestíbulo principal del hotel, de manera que tuvieses ante ti a toda Meteora, como una postal: el peculiar paisaje y los extraños monasterios en las cimas.

Lo que conseguimos con todo esto, básicamente con la Doctrina Truman de los estadounidenses, fue una edad de oro de la arquitectura en Grecia. En realidad, produjeron esta impresionante arquitectura moderna en Grecia, que luego se trasladó a las ciudades. Pero, básicamente, todo esto llegó a su fin con la Junta.

ZENGHELIS: Mira, ese es el Hilton [señala al otro lado de la plaza]. Es muy bonito. Se ha deteriorado, pero tiene un vestíbulo precioso.

GOODMAN: Es de Saarinen, ¿no?

GIGANTES: Saarinen hizo los bocetos, y lo construyeron unos arquitectos griegos bien intencionados. Pero tiene esa maravillosa generosidad con los espacios amplios típica de los 60. Ya sabes, tienes espacio para respirar.

GOODMAN: Claro. ¿Conocéis el Hotel Fontainebleau original en Miami Beach, de Morris Lapidus? Tiene un entresuelo que solo existe para que te puedan ver mientras bajas por las escaleras desde él. Hay un ascensor en el vestíbulo que sube hasta una pequeña plataforma con una gran escalera por la que te pueden ver bajar. Y ya está. Esa es la única razón por la que existen la escalera y el entresuelo: para que te vean.

GIGANTES: Bueno, ¡me gusta pensar que esto es un poco mejor que eso! La belleza y la generosidad de los años sesenta. Tenía carácter. Y vino acompañada de esa especie de espléndida facilidad para el espacio, y el espacio interior/exterior. Entonces, llegó Saarinen y diseñó el antiguo aeropuerto, y le invitaron a dar ideas para el nuevo Hilton. Se las arregló para hacerlo en la parte de atrás de un sobre o algo así, sabe Dios, y se le ocurrió esa primera idea de un bumerán contemplando todo el paisaje, y detrás todas las montañas de Atenas. Es espectacular.

GOODMAN: Entonces... Esa forma, ese bumerán, en tu trabajo parece que lo tenías en mente. Puede que no te dieras cuenta de ello o puede que sí, pero ahora que veo este hotel, lo veo en tu trabajo, por todas partes. El Hilton está ahí, de algún modo.

GIGANTES: Sí, desde luego. Es verdad, pero, por raro que parezca, no fue por él. Lo cierto es que inicialmente estudié bioquímica. Adoraba la naturaleza y los jardines, y me encantaba la arquitectura, pero el que me hizo enamorarme de la arquitectura fue Saarinen. Eso fue justo cuando él acababa de construir el maravilloso aeropuerto de Washington, Dulles. Creo que, aproximadamente un mes después de que lo abrieran, mis padres volvieron de un viaje al Caribe. Yo tenía unos seis años y recuerdo que íbamos conduciendo por una carretera recta y lo vimos en la distancia, lo único que se veía era la azotea. ¡Y podías ver a través de él! Pensé que era precioso. ¡Los aviones estaban aterrizando por detrás del edificio y podías verlos! Ese día, de algún modo, la luz brillaba y podías verlo. Fue un momento importante para mí. Estaba en plan "¡vaya!". Así que esa fue mi idea de arquitectura desde el principio.

Cuando dejé la bioquímica, no sabía si debía tirar por el paisajismo o por la arquitectura. Decidí que la arquitectura me proporcionaría más herramientas, y siempre podía hacer paisajismo. La gente que me gustaba de verdad durante el tiempo que estuve estudiando no estaba nada de moda. Saarinen, por supuesto. Roberto Burle Marx, y eso fue antes de que se pusiera tan de moda. Geddes. Affonso Reidy. Estaba obsesionado con Reidy. Más que con Niemeyer, porque Niemeyer a veces tiene demasiada dejadez, pero también es genial. Reidy solo realizó un par de proyectos.

GOODMAN: La verdad es que iba a sacar ese tema. Creo que también hay mucho del casino de Niemeyer, el Casino Pampulha, en tu trabajo.

GIGANTES: Bueno, lo gracioso es que hice ese trabajo antes de conocer el casino. En realidad, Reidy fue la persona que me enseñó geometría. Y Elia también. Reidy es increíble con la geometría. Yo dibujaba algo y decía "quiero que quede así", y él, literalmente, se sentaba ahí con un compás. Compases largos y compases cortos. Los dibujos que le daba eran muy precisos, pero él los volvía perfectamente precisos, con todos los puntos centrales y los puntos de unión, de modo que pudiéramos dibujar una segunda línea, el espesor, para que hubiera una plantilla, porque, por supuesto, estaba dibujando con tinta. Era un genio.

GOODMAN: Esas son las cosas que tienen un aspecto libre y suelto, y que imita la gente que no pertenece necesariamente a esa disciplina.

GIGANTES: Bueno, la cuestión es que la arquitectura solo funciona con la geometría. No sé si has visto lo que hice en Ashikita. Es un complejo turístico japonés. Bueno, todas las prefecturas japonesas tienen una "casa de la juventud" en un lugar privilegiado, lejos de las ciudades. Tienen dormitorios y otro edificio donde pueden celebrarse conferencias y proyectos de arte, proyectos de construcción y otras actividades. Nuestra casa de la juventud estaba en Ashikita, en el sur de Japón, y había un clima semitropical. Está en Kysushu.

Cuando empecé el proyecto, tuve eso en mente. Quería que se sintieran como si estuvieran de acampada bajo el cielo. Es como una tienda de campaña. Al principio empecé a diseñarlo al estilo de Frei Otto, pero con curvas más precisas, con un sistema tridimensional de la tienda. Por supuesto, cuando fui a presentar el proyecto a Japón resulta que solo había constructores locales, así que me dije: "olvídalo". Me di cuenta de que tenía que hacer algo en dos dimensiones y, desde luego, fue algo fantástico. La realidad siempre lo vuelve todo fantástico.

Sin embargo, lo fascinante fue que no sabían cómo empezar a construirlo. Podían entender la disposición de los puntos en el suelo. Eso era algo estándar. Pero, ¿cómo calculamos el techo? Teníamos este dibujo extraordinario del techo, y la distancia hasta la que bajaba el techo y la altura de cada viga la calculábamos desde el suelo: "esta viga está a 6,73 metros del suelo, esta otra está a 8,51 metros del suelo". Así es como lo construimos, literalmente. Así que ahora que veo estos programas de ordenador para crear cosas tridimensionales, creo que es bastante interesante, porque la geometría realmente hace que las cosas sean hermosas. Es decir, no sé si lo puedes considerar hermoso, pero es extraño. Tiene un impacto.

GOODMAN: Hoy, mientras venía en avión hacia aquí, estaba leyendo un artículo en el New York Times sobre cómo, a medida que los Estados Unidos retiran a sus tropas de Iraq y Afganistán, todo ese equipamiento militar sobrante está apareciendo en los departamentos de policía locales. De repente, un pueblo de Wisconsin tiene, por ejemplo, un tanque o un vehículo blindado de transporte de personal que nunca solicitaron. Y, por supuesto, tienen que usarlo, porque lo tienen. O, en vez de equipamiento antidisturbios, tienen trajes blindados que fueron diseñados para el combate. Todo este equipamiento diseñado para la ocupación en el extranjero está, básicamente, volviendo a casa. Y no fue diseñado para eso, pero acaba siendo utilizado contra la población local. Esa es la versión negativa, tal vez, de lo que se puede hacer con el turismo. Es decir, las infraestructuras turísticas están pensadas, posiblemente, solo en menor medida para la población local. Pero, ¿es posible desviar los beneficios? Creamos estos pequeños microcosmos de un mundo ideal. Un hotel es una visión extremadamente idealizada de una vivienda, hasta cierto punto. Del mismo modo que la maquinaria de guerra puede tener una cierta filtración en la vida diaria, ¿puede el turismo conducir hacia esa visión idealizada y aplicarse eventualmente a nuestro día a día?

GIGANTES: Vale, tengo que contestarte a dos cosas. La otra cosa que no he mencionado es algo de lo que mi padre se encargaba específicamente, como ministro de cultura: las islas. Teníamos esta arquitectura moderna de alta gama, que en realidad es extremadamente modesta, y la idea de la generosidad del espacio, como en el Hilton. Los espacios interiores suelen ser bastante pequeños, pero los espacios de interior/exterior tienen una arquitectura preciosa. Eso caló básicamente en las cafeterías de los barrios buenos, en las casas privadas y este tipo de sitios, pero no afectó al pensamiento arquitectónico principal. Lo que sí lo afectó fue que las islas estaban, desde el principio, muy controladas arquitectónicamente. Allí, cada año tenían que repintarlo todo de blanco, por ley, y nadie podía construir cosas modernas. Todos los edificios nuevos de las islas tenían que ser como falsos edificios antiguos. De este modo, en el Jónico, donde hay tejados a dos aguas y tejas rojas, todas las construcciones nuevas tienen que tener estos elementos. En el Egeo, donde hay cubos blancos, todos los edificios nuevos tienen que tener forma de cubo blanco, y no pueden superar una cierta altura. En realidad, lo interesante es que a lo largo del tiempo, las islas han ido adquiriendo montones y montones de viviendas que se quedan vacías en invierno. Algunas islas tienen una población de hasta 10.000 personas en verano, que vuelve a bajar a las 500 personas en invierno. Y no solo eso, sino que también tiene que haber toda una infraestructura en las islas. Además, han creado una policía turística, policías que hablan inglés y que se encargan de los turistas.

ZENGHELIS: Y ahora están aprendiendo ruso, y están impartiendo clases de ruso a los propietarios de los restaurantes y a los tenderos.

GIGANTES: Pero hay otro problema, porque estaban estás islitas que tenían, en cierto modo, su propia economía autosuficiente, pero muy básica, ¿de acuerdo? Y de repente llegaron estos turistas tan sofisticados. De manera que hubo que construir líneas eléctricas bajo el mar hasta cada isla, pero de las potentes, porque, por supuesto, todos los hoteles tenían que tener aire acondicionado. Los griegos no necesitan aire acondicionado en las islas en verano, pero los ingleses o los alemanes entran en sus habitaciones y tienen que encender el aire acondicionado. Y lo peor de todo es que se pasan fuera todo el día y dejan el aire acondicionado puesto. Es horrible, ¿sabes?

Y la otra cuestión era el agua. Muchas de estas islas no tienen agua suficiente, y eso siempre ha limitado la población. De hecho, algunas islas, como Hidra, tienen muy poca agua. Es una isla seca. Pero a todas y cada una de estas islas llegan barcos que transportaban agua dos veces por semana. Así que tenemos una infraestructura a la que le suministran la electricidad, a donde llevan agua en barco, a donde llevan comida en barco, y a donde envían pescado congelado desde España y desde el Atlántico, por supuesto, en avión.

¿Y qué pasa si se produce algún accidente? Hay toda una infraestructura de helicópteros de emergencia, porque todas las islas están a media hora en helicóptero del hospital principal de Atenas. Por eso, desde siempre, cada isla o grupo de islas ha tenido un helicóptero de emergencia para llevar a las víctimas de accidentes en menos de media hora hasta el tejado del hospital principal. Hay toda una infraestructura invisible bajo la superficie de estás preciosas islas supuestamente minimalistas y ajenas a la mano del hombre. Increíble.

Además, vas a las islas y ves tiendas por todas partes. Hay un montón de griegos que se ganan la vida estando en las islas desde principios de mayo hasta finales de octubre, con las tiendas. Y todo lo que ganan en esos seis meses les tiene que durar todo el invierno. Luego vuelven a Atenas con sus cosas. Las tiendas están cerradas durante el invierno. Estas personas pagan sus facturas durante el invierno, y después vuelven y trabajan como locos, de la mañana a la noche, vendiendo cosas.

Hay toda una vida extraña detrás de la realidad de las islas. En temporada de turismo, llegas y es una delicia: hay aire acondicionado, hay agua, te puedes dar duchas, tienes todas estas tiendas encantadoras que abren hasta medianoche, puedes dar un paseo por las calles después de comer... Pero todo esto cierra y desaparece. En realidad, la versión invernal de las islas es completamente diferente. En algunas de las islas más pequeñas, y también en las montañas, en los pueblos remotos, los niños pasan los días entre semana fuera. Los de las islas, se van en ferry a una isla más grande, y los de las montañas se van en bus a una ciudad más grande. Durante la semana viven en residencias y van al colegio, y los fines de semana vuelven de nuevo a sus casas en ferry o en bus.

Grecia es uno de los países con más aeropuertos de Europa. No hay manera de ir desde Atenas a Ioánina excepto conducir durante 14 horas por las montañas. O puedes tomar un vuelo de 20 minutos hasta Ioánina. Las principales islas tienen aeropuertos, y algunas tienen pistas prolongadas, de modo que pueden recibir vuelos directos desde Londres o desde Berlín. Tenemos aproximadamente 35 aeropuertos. ¿Y cuántos puertos? Cada isla tiene un puerto. A lo largo de toda la costa hay puertos mantenidos por la guardia costera y los prácticos de puerto. La verdad es que tenemos una necesidad excepcional de funcionarios.

Al final, Grecia tiene una infraestructura increíble, que es distinta del resto de Europa. Una infraestructura increíble. ¡Por supuesto! Tenemos que tenerla.

PROYECTOS

3

LOS CINCO PAISAJES 58 DEL TURISMO

233 Fernando Rodríguez, Pablo Oriol y Lina Toro
Directores del Proyecto Fin de Grado IE University

233

233 El Proyecto Fin de Grado propone una lectura del proyecto arquitectónico como herramienta capaz de generar un urgente y necesario progreso, frente al estigma adquirido durante la última década como elemento demostrativo de unos logros económicos. La arquitectura pasa a ser un medio indispensable para ordenar la realidad, de la misma manera que las infraestructuras lo son para el desarrollo de un territorio. Esta naturaleza *infraestructural* del proyecto de arquitectura confiere a la capacidad propositiva del arquitecto la *saludable ambición* de transformar un territorio en un paisaje de nuevas oportunidades.

Para que todo este planteamiento pedagógico pueda tener lugar, es necesario articular el PFG como una hipótesis territorial completa, que ha de ser defendida, desarrollada y contrastada. Para que esta hipótesis tenga oportunidades de éxito, ha de insertarse en un *debate contemporáneo* existente, referirse a un *contexto amplio* y formalizarse en un *escenario concreto* que permita trabajar con variables reales.

ARQUITECTURA, TURISMO Y ACCIÓN

En el debate sobre la actualización de los modelos de desarrollo turístico que tantas alegrías han proporcionado a la economía nacional, el proyecto de investigación *Architecture & Tourism* nace con el objetivo de potenciar el valor de las estrategias proyectuales en el proceso de reformulación de la oferta turística española, constituyéndose en el marco teórico y de investigación en el que desarrollar el PFG. Los autores de los proyectos que aquí presentamos son invitados a trabajar en el ámbito de las complejas relaciones entre arquitectura, territorio y turismo, una cuestión de actualidad, cercana geográficamente, políticamente pertinente y capaz de generar progreso económico sostenible y necesario. En el fondo de este debate sobre el papel del profesional de la arquitectura en la formación de oferta y demanda turística reside la convicción de que es deseable una nueva interpretación del territorio, y que los aciertos de este renovado pensamiento han de ser transferidos a la oferta turística existente mediante unos formatos de comunicación adecuados, complementando la conocida y exitosa fórmula de sol y playa con programas y estrategias inesperadas.

Estas nuevas arquitecturas se narran con nuevos léxicos—paisajes extremos, arquitecturas reversibles, belleza industrial—y con otros ya incorporados a nuestra disciplina—intercambio, acontecimiento, oferta de tiempo, patrimonio, paisaje humano y natural—. De este modo, el proyecto se transforma en una herramienta de gestión económica, política y administrativa, fomentando que toda intervención-acción propuesta gratifique tanto al nuevo usuario como al local, y garantizando la creación de entornos con identidad propia que sean germen de una arquitectura capaz de convivir con el paisaje pre-existente, bien sea natural, arquitectónico o urbano.

IBERIA TOTAL

Esta nueva mirada sobre el binomio *Architecture & Tourism* desvela un reciente cambio de escala que opera a dos niveles. Por un lado cambian los tiempos de desplazamiento y se reduce, por tanto, la relación espacio-temporal del conjunto. Por otro lado la dimensión del territorio al alcance de cada quien se modifica: se universaliza el acceso a lo remoto y se aumenta el radio de lo potencialmente visitable. Ante este nuevo horizonte dimensional planteamos un marco de actuación que llamamos *Iberia Total*: la Península Ibérica entendida como un destino turístico unitario con potencial de incidencia global, visitable desde sus *hubs* aeroportuarios y ferroviarios, accesible por sus redes de carreteras y capaz de sintetizar una clara identidad ibérica—que se consolida como tópico internacional—con las identidades específicas de los distintos destinos. Se pretende así reconfigurar, imaginar y consolidar una red de turismo única y especial que se articula de manera estratégica a escala territorial y que trasciende la escala del *destino singular*. Los proyectos realizados en el marco de este PFG responden por tanto a esta doble condición: su pertenencia a las redes que los trascienden y su pertinencia como catalizadores de una puesta en valor de lo específico. 60

NORTH BY NORTHWEST

El escenario propuesto para desarrollar este primer Proyecto Fin de Grado es el corredor que discurre a lo largo de la autopista AP-66, y que une la ciudad de León con el mar Cantábrico. Históricamente parte de la Ruta de la Plata—vía romana queconectaba Astorga con Mérida—, este tramo en estudio es una de las primeras autopistas que se construyeron en España, siendo definitivo en el desarrollo industrial del norte y el noroeste peninsular, a lo largo del cual se han dispuesto desde hace siglos núcleos de población—administrativos y productivos—de relevancia.

El desmantelamiento industrial de los años 80 inició un declive económico que aún prosigue; los conflictos socioeconómicos derivados del cierre de minas son portada en la prensa internacional y ponen de relevancia la necesidad de aportar un futuro posible a este corredor.

Como si de un *Paisaje Infraestructural*[1] de enorme tamaño se tratara, este escenario presenta una serie de naturalezas superpuestas que dibujan un territorio en el que la exploración proyectual encuentra diversas áreas de oportunidad.

Lo metropolitano, lo rural, lo infraestructural, lo patrimonial y lo natural se expresan con fuerza en este fragmento de Iberia Total: el Área Metropolitana de Asturias aglutina a más de un millón de personas en un sistema de poblaciones con un índice de concentración relativamente bajo, cuasi rural. La red viaria, extraordinariamente densa, se teje a partir de ferrocarriles convencionales y otros de vía estrecha, autovías y autopistas, carreteras secundarias y rutas mineras comarcales que aseguran unos ratios de accesibilidad altos. Existe una alta concentración de bienes de interés histórico-artístico y un ingente patrimonio industrial, así como un patrimonio natural formado por costas, valles y montes, y un Parque Nacional, el de los Picos de Europa.

LOS CINCO PAISAJES DEL TURISMO

A partir de este entendimiento compartido del territorio como escenario conjunto de proyecto, los alumnos de PFG fueron invitados a seleccionar un lugar, un programa, un usuario y una imagen arquitectónica para construir una propuesta de intervención en el marco de esta relación entre Arquitectura y Turismo.

La reflexión sobre esta relación y el análisis del contexto territorial desvelaron áreas de oportunidad que de manera natural se agrupaban en torno a temáticas similares. Este proceso de trabajo conjunto de los 28 estudiantes y los directores de PFG resultó en una taxonomía básica de las maneras de generar nuevos e inesperados escenarios turísticos, que bautizamos como Paisajes Productivos, Paisajes Urbanos, Paisajes Extremos, Paisajes Industriales y Paisajes Reversibles.

Los Paisajes Productivos persiguen activar comunidades enteras a través de la comunicación pedagógico-experiencial de los procesos de producción que constituyen la base de su economía local: el auge del turismo ecológico y gastronómico y el atractivo de la vuelta al consumo responsable de productos sin intermediación son los activos principales de unas propuestas con un alto grado de viabilidad.

Los Paisajes Urbanos son escenarios de reactivación de centros densos, a partir de programas de ocio de carácter metropolitano que pueden insertarse en circuitos culturales, deportivos o de creación artística de carácter internacional. Habitualmente ligados a la recuperación del patrimonio, suponen una apuesta decidida por el turismo urbano.

Los Paisajes Extremos aprovechan el enorme potencial paisajístico del medio natural astur-leonés y proponen infraestructuras de distinto carácter para su aprovechamiento. La exclusividad de las experiencias y los escenarios propuestos justifican propuestas, como su nombre ya anticipa, extremas.

Los Paisajes Industriales se miran en el espejo de tantas experiencias que, como en el Ruhr alemán, buscan aprovechar el patrimonio minero para cambiar de modelo económico. La enorme riqueza de los ejemplos que encontramos en la zona permite la aparición de propuestas diversas, todas ellas de gran intensidad.

Los Paisajes Reversibles muestran una especial sensibilidad frente a la posibilidad de intervenir en contextos naturales sensibles que demandan propuestas arquitectónicas temporales que permitan un uso intenso de sus valores paisajísticos.

Así, sin apartar la mirada de una realidad socioeconómica específica, estos Paisajes Turísticos desarrollados en este curso PFG buscan tejer una red de potenciales escenarios turísticos que articulen una nueva visión del territorio. Proponen estrategias que vislumbren proyectos inéditos para comunidades enteras. Buscan, en definitiva, hipótesis de realidades complejas.

1. Bélanger, Pierre. "Redefining Infrastructure". En *Ecological Urbanism*, editado por M. Mostafavi and G. Doherty: Harvard University GSD. Lars Müller Publishers, 2010.

TALLER 1: TURISMO. IDENTIDAD, DESTRUCCIÓN Y DESEO 64

234

Linna Choy y Tarik Oualalou
KILO Architectes

En el marco del estudio de arquitectura *Iberia Total*, este taller de una semana exploró los márgenes de las percepciones establecidas en el turismo e investigó por qué las cuestiones relacionadas con en el turismo han quedado fuera del discurso contemporáneo en arquitectura. El taller intentó redefinir el turismo no en términos de política, sino a través de medios arquitectónicos y urbanísticos. A través de la exploración de varios temas y cuatro estudios de caso, los estudiantes trabajaron en proyectos de investigación colectiva cuyo objetivo era ampliar los límites del papel de la arquitectura en la transformación del turismo en el siglo XXI.

TEMA 1: TURISMO E IDENTIDAD

Este taller examinó el modo en que la arquitectura del turismo intenta crear ambientes únicos y específicos para sus locales al tiempo que crea entornos genéricos para cubrir las necesidades identificadas en cuanto a conveniencia y confort. El taller exploró el modo en que el sentido de la identidad y del destino pueden crearse a través de medios arquitectónicos que se salgan del modelo de parque temático.

TEMA 2: EL TURISMO DE LA DESTRUCCIÓN

Este taller investigó turismos nacidos de la destrucción y la catástrofe y el papel de la arquitectura en la definición de estas nuevas áreas del turismo. Algunos de los ejemplos estudiados fueron los siguientes:

Chernobyl: Descrito por la revista Forbes como uno de los "lugares en el mundo de visita obligada", Chernobyl recibió el pasado año a miles de turistas interesados en un turismo de la catástrofe.

Muro de Berlín: Prácticamente la totalidad de los 160 km del muro de Berlín que rodeaban el Berlín Occidental fueron derribados o destruidos tras su caída en 1989. Sin embargo, cuando los turistas empezaron a preguntar "¿Dónde está el muro?", la ciudad optó por reconstruir algunos segmentos. Parte de la sección reconstruida contiene fragmentos auténticos del muro, algunos comprados a coleccionistas privados por 1.000 €.

DZM: En el paralelo 38, esta zona de 250 km de largo y 4 de ancho es la frontera más militarizada del mundo. También es una popular atracción turística, con "aldeas de paz" con fines propagandísticos en ambos lados que presentan dos versiones muy diferentes de un mismo conflicto.

TEMA 3: EL DESEO EN EL TURISMO

El taller examinó la necesidad de elementos icónicos del turismo y el rol de la arquitectura en transformar lo intangible (el deseo) en tangible. Investigamos ejemplos del rol de la arquitectura en la creación de un sentimiento de deseo en territorios en blanco (Dubai, Perla de Las Dunas, etc.) y regiones deprimidas (Bilbao, Lens). Los estudiantes trabajaron en cuatro estudios de caso:

Estudio de caso 1: La Zona Desmilitarizada entre Corea del Norte y Corea del Sur (DMZ).

Dos grupos de estudiantes trabajaron en escenarios opuestos: el primero tomaba como base la continuidad de la existencia de la DMZ y el segundo, la reunificación de las dos Coreas. El primer grupo exploró la naturaleza de las fronteras en el mundo y sus implicaciones espaciales. Las investigaciones del segundo grupo llevaron a propuestas como la transformación de la zona desmilitarizada (DMZ) en una reserva natural o en un nuevo conglomerado urbano. 66

Estudio de caso 2: Las Vegas.

Otro grupo de estudiantes trató de conciliar el corazón turístico de Las Vegas con la proliferación de tejido suburbano a su alrededor. Ya no se trata de una isla de turismo en medio del desierto, Las Vegas sufre un crecimiento incontrolado y de los típicos espacios sobrantes indeseados consecuencia de tan rápido crecimiento. Este grupo investigó los posibles escenarios de aplicación de programas adecuados para estos espacios sobrantes que beneficiarían tanto a turistas como a residentes. El segundo grupo de alumnos examinó las complejas relaciones entre las distintas áreas de la franja de *Las Vegas Boulevard* ("The Strip") y propuso transformaciones para unificar ambos lados del *Strip* y convertirlos en un tejido urbano más accesible. 68

Estudio de caso 3: Seaside, Florida. Turismo de nostalgia.

El litoral marítimo es un ejemplo del éxito del turismo en la creación de deseo por un lugar basado en la nostalgia, el deseo de un lugar y un tiempo ideales. Basado en la concepción del típico pueblo de playa, el éxito del *Seaside* se debe a su sentido de pequeña comunidad que se crea mediante códigos urbanos cuida- 69 dosamente diseñados y su arquitectura vernácula muy informada. Víctima de su propio éxito, el *Seaside* ha sufrido una expansión más allá de sus límites de diseño originales. Los dos grupos de estudiantes exploraron las ramificaciones de tal expansión: ¿Existen los límites de una fantasía? ¿Desaparece el paisaje soñado cuando alcanza una cierta escala?

Estudio de caso 4: Marfa, Texas - Turismo de peregrinación.

70 Este grupo ha explorado los turismos de peregrinación, desde las históricas peregrinaciones religiosas a Santiago de Compostela hasta las de hoy en día a las mecas del arte y la arquitectura, como Marfa, Texas, casa-estudio de Donald Judd y centro de arte minimalista. Uno de los grupos investigó el viaje a Marfa como "etapas" de una experiencia de peregrinación en el tiempo y en el espacio. El segundo grupo examinó el desarrollo de la trama urbana de esta pequeña ciudad en respuesta a las presiones del turismo y sus consecuencias en la cohesión social y arquitectónica de la ciudad.

TALLER 2: LA INVESTIGACIÓN COMO PROYECTO. VISLUMBRAR LA 72 IDENTIDAD

235 Laura Martínez de Guereñu
Profesora de Taller de Proyectos del IE Unviersity

El *workshop* "Research as Design: Framing Identity" fue el primer encuentro de los alumnos con el marco territorial del área de centralidad Astur-Leonesa (ACTAL). A lo largo de cinco días consecutivos de trabajo se trataba de conseguir vislumbrar la identidad de este marco territorial—reconocer sus mayores diferencias respecto a otros lugares—, para poder identificar posibles estrategias de intervención con capacidad para atraer turismo.

La definición del turismo de la que se partió fue la del sociólogo británico John Urry, principalmente conocido por su libro "The Tourist Gaze" (1990), según el que el turismo es una actividad de ocio que presupone su opuesto, es decir, el trabajo regulado y organizado. Y por ello, el turismo es una "manifestación de cómo el trabajo y el ocio están organizados como dos esferas diferentes de la práctica social"[1]. Una diferencia que hace que los turistas solo se fijen en aquellos aspectos del paisaje y del entorno construido que suponen un "contraste respecto a su experiencia cotidiana". Tanto es así que el principal objetivo para garantizar el consumo en el turismo es conseguir "capturar la mirada" del turista. Una mirada basada en la diferencia, que intensifica otros elementos de la experiencia perceptiva, y que la arquitectura, como disciplina que enmarca nuestras vidas, puede sin duda realzar. El *workshop* entendía por tanto el proyecto arquitectónico como herramienta capaz de subrayar esas diferencias, necesarias para garantizar el consumo del turismo.

Desde el principio se otorgó un carácter colectivo a la investigación. El objetivo principal era llegar a una idea de territorio que se entendiese como sumatorio de lugares cargados de potencial de transformación. Unos lugares donde se pudieran implementar diferentes estrategias de intervención, que aseguraran la "captura de la mirada" del turista y consiguieran convertirse más tarde en propuestas individuales de proyecto. Por tanto, los análisis que realizaran los alumnos individualmente durante el transcurso del *workshop* se irían acumulando y compartiendo hasta que cada uno pudiera, al final, vislumbrar su propia idea de la identidad del lugar.

Eran muchas las preguntas que se planteaban: ¿Cuáles son los aspectos básicos que construyen la idiosincrasia de un lugar? ¿ Cuántos elementos diferenciales es necesario encontrar? ¿Cuáles de ellos convierten un territorio en un lugar atractivo para el tursimo? Para conseguir responderlas se pensó en cuatro categorías de análisis, suficientemente genéricas y a la vez con potencial de captar aquellas particularidades que habían llevado a la selección del marco territorial de ACTAL. "Cronología: signos a lo largo de la historia", "Entorno Construido: taxonomías de la desindustrialización", "Paisaje/Infraestructura" y "Eventos" fueron las categorías escogidas. Se asignó una cateogría a cada uno de los cuatro días de trabajo colectivo, dejando un último día de síntesis para la presentación de resultados individuales.

Como paso previo al documento gráfico sintético final, los alumnos analizaron la información latente dentro de cada una de las categorías y las mapearon junto a las potencialidades de intervención que identificaron en el área. Se dividió cada día de trabajo en una sesión teórica, una sesión práctica de trabajo y a partir del segundo día, una sesión de corrección del trabajo de la categoría anterior.

El primer día, dedicado a la "Cronología", se realizó una presentación del desarrollo del marco territorial de ACTAL desde el punto de vista económico, político, social y cultural. Igualmente, se analizó el impacto que el turismo había tenido en el área históricamente. El objetivo del análisis a realizar y a mapear era identificar “los signos a lo largo de la historia”, los años de cambio que habían sido claves en la historia del marco territorial de ACTAL. El cambio podía entenderse de manera completamente libre, para identificar colectivamente aquellos signos que mostraran la idiosincrasia del lugar.

El segundo día, dedicado al “Entorno Construido”, consistió en una presentación de las posibles actitudes a adoptar respecto al legado industrial existente en el área. El abandono de los yacimientos de carbón y el conflicto minero que había ocurrido en el área no eran hechos aislados. Si bien representaban una de las áreas más deprimidas, también ofrecían muy buenas oportunidades para el desarrollo de modelos urbanos alternativos. Los espacios interiores de algunos de los edificios industriales como los paisajes exteriores de otros presentaban un potencial único para crear nuevos modelos de asentamiento. El objetivo del análisis a realizar era mapear las “taxonomías de la industrialización” y determinar las condiciones y las oportunidades del paisaje industrial existente como paso previo al entendimiento global del patrimonio construido existente.

El tercer día, denominado “Paisaje/Infraestructura”, se realizó una presentación que distinguía las categorías de lo vernáculo, lo pintoresco y lo sublime en diferentes casos de estudio. El objetivo a cumplir era analizar el entorno natural y el encuentro entre el paisaje natural, el paisaje industrial y las infraestructuras. Se trataba de llegar a entender el paisaje como producto material del trabajo humano y a la vez como objeto de apropiación estética. Si en el mapa anterior había quedado clara la herencia patrimonial, en este caso se trataba de analizar el potencial existente en el paisaje cultural. Las infraestructuras y los itinerarios de diferente carácter deberían quedar plasmados gráficamente.

El cuarto día, denominado “Eventos”, consistió en la presentación de oportunidades para posicionar regiones en el mercado del turismo, como es el caso de la competición que se produce entre ciudades para conseguir la capitalidad europea de la cultura. Se ofreció un caso de estudio de costa y otro de interior, para entender las distintas dificultades con las que se enfrentan las ciudades para hacerse legibles y consumibles. Se estudiaron casos de edificios e infraestructuras que es necesario crear para asegurar el flujo continuo e ininterrumpido de usuarios. También se estudiaron algunos de los lemas de las últimas capitalidades europeas para entender la fuerza de un slogan, cómo se puede pasar de un mito a una marca y se consigue vislumbrar una identidad que pueda atraer turistas.

El registro conjunto y mapeo de las preexis- 74
tencias y de las potencialidades para cada una de las categorías ofreció cuatro aproximaciones complementarias que contribuyeron a la aproximación del proyecto colectivamente. Para la entrega final, el quinto día consecutivo de trabajo, los alumnos produjeron un mapa sintético individual que mostraba su particular visión de la identidad del marco territorial de ACTAL. En estos mapas mostraron ya una preferencia por fomentar un potencial particular y, de algún modo, apuntaban a posibles programas de intervención con capacidad de atraer turismo. Un diagrama DAFO en el que identificaban las debilidades, fortalezas, amenazas y oportunidades del territorio complementaba de manera escrita la síntesis a la que habían llegado de manera gráfica. Empezaron a verse distintos tipos de proyecto. Algunos iban a tratar de intervenir en el patrimonio minero, otros iban a tratar de activar los paisajes naturales, otros tratarían de crear nuevas oportunidades culturales en los núcleos urbanos.

Los alumnos esperaron a concluir el *workshop* para visitar el lugar. Así, su primer encuentro con el territorio ocurrió de una ma- 76
nera más pautada, cuando existía ya una idea más clara de aquellos elementos que querían 77
potenciar. El tránsito del *workshop* del territorio al PFG se realizó a través de un cambio de 78
medio de representación. Un video-*storyboard*, compuesto con fotogramas extraídos de los mapas individuales y de la visita al lugar, sirvió de arranque del PFG.

1 John Urry, “The ‘Consumption’ of Tourism”, en *Sociology*, vol. 24, no. 1, Febrero 1990, pp. 23-35. (Versión on-line http://soc.sagepub.com/content/24/1/23).

PAISAJES PRODUCTIVOS 80

LA PUESTA EN ESCENA DEL PAISAJE AGRÍCOLA PRODUCTIVO COMO EXPERIENCIA TURÍSTICA 82

Andrew Varela
Design Critic del IE Unviersity 235

Los paisajes productivos revelan cómo hacemos uso de la tierra como sociedad, ya sea para cubrir las necesidades básicas de supervivencia, tales como la producción de alimentos, o en favor de los sistemas económicos y culturales que estructuran nuestra sociedad, como la producción de energía. La importancia de los paisajes productivos ha aumentado en los últimos años debido a la incorporación de la sostenibilidad en todos los aspectos de nuestra vida cotidiana, lo que se ha traducido, en muchos casos, en la promoción de la proximidad geográfica como algo bueno, sobre todo en lo que se refiere a la producción de alimentos.

La producción agrícola es tan especializada y tan eficiente como la mayoría de otros sistemas de producción de nuestra sociedad capitalista contemporánea. La comida se produce en cantidades industriales y ya lista para ser exportada a los mercados globales para un mayor beneficio económico. Que la producción local de alimentos ocupe algo más que una pequeña porción de mercado no es una opción viable, dadas las restricciones a las que debería enfrentarse en términos de variedad de alimentos, coste y uso de la tierra y del suministro de agua.

En el ACTAL, un territorio que ha sufrido la devastación económica, social y material debido al cierre de la industria de la minería, la producción agrícola a pequeña escala se utiliza como estrategia para la creación de destinos turísticos capaces de convertirse en centros de la reactivación y regeneración de la región. La producción agrícola a pequeña escala se emplea aquí no como alternativa a la organización de la producción agrícola global, sino como parte de la puesta en escena que define la actividad turística.

En una región cuya identidad está tan ligada a lo más profundo de la tierra y a la extracción de combustibles fósiles, estos proyectos buscan su regeneración a través de la reactivación de su capa más superficial, su suelo y el potencial que alberga. El éxito de estas iniciativas como propuestas de actividad turística se basa en su capacidad de crear un nuevo ambiente físico que es distintivo y que puede "significar una experiencia que contraste con la del día a día"[1].

En la búsqueda de ese ambiente diferente, los proyectos reconfiguran la capacidad productiva del paisaje y su estructura de edificio asociado en un nuevo entorno agrícola. Las configuraciones de construcciones que respondían a los sistemas de producción relacionados con la minería se transforman en nuevas organizaciones productivas relacionadas con la agricultura y, al hacerlo, crean un nuevo paisaje que impregna la región de una nueva identidad con fuerza suficiente como para convertirse en un catalizador para su regeneración.

Los proyectos son resultado de la aplicación de una estrategia turística regional más amplia y, por tanto, se conciben como nodos pertenecientes a una red más amplia de propuestas que, en conjunto, tienen el potencial para la transformación de una región particular dentro de la ACTAL. Este enfoque de la red no sólo proporciona una estrategia económicamente más sostenible, sino que ofrece la posibilidad de vincularse a otras rutas turísticas a nivel nacional e internacional.

En su programación, estos proyectos rodean la producción agrícola de experiencias de consumo complementarias, no sólo para hacer que las propuestas sean económicamente viables, sino, lo que es más importante, para crear la experiencia turística deseada en la que "todos los elementos forman parte de un todo"[2]. Restaurantes, procesado artesano de alimentos, establecimientos donde ofrecer degustaciones, hoteles y exposiciones, entre otros, están concebidos para promover y mejorar la experiencia de un estilo de vida diferente.

La experiencia que aquí se vende podría 84
formar parte de lo que se conoce como "vida lenta", "comida lenta" o "de la granja a la mesa". En una época en la que la mayoría de los alimentos que consumimos están procesados y envasados, en la que estamos debatiendo sobre si deberíamos etiquetar los alimentos que identifiquen los OGM (organismos genéticamente modificados), en un tiempo en el que los alimentos se venden y distribuyen por cada vez menos conglomerados globales, estas propuestas muestran la experiencia de los productos agrícolas cultivados localmente, procesados de formas no industriales y consumidos con todo el placer en el lugar de cultivo. El valor turístico de este tipo de experiencias se basa en la falta de conexión que actualmente tenemos con los alimentos que consumimos y su procesamiento. Es la activación de los sentidos que se experimenta en estos entornos lo que los convierte en extraordinarios y, en consecuencia, en una experiencia turística deseable. ¡Aquí el tomate sabe mejor! Uno puede cultivar, recoger, preparar, oler y degustar la comida de maneras que normalmente no hace.

En un mundo sin experiencias turísticas auténticas y en el que la producción local de alimentos como solución universal es inviable, estos proyectos representan la "puesta en escena de la autenticidad", que supone que la cooperativa productora de bayas, la granja, el centro de cosmética, o el museo micológico no puedan existir sin los ingresos proporcionados por el turista que come en el restaurante, hace la mermelada, prueba los hongos, se aloja en el hotel y se deja mimar en el spa[3].

1. J. Urry, "The Consumption of Tourism", *Sociology*, vol. 24, No. 1, February 1990, p. 26. (Versión on-line http://soc.sagepub.com/content/24/1/23)
2. J. Culler, "Semiotics of Tourism", *American Journal of Semiotics* 1:127-40, 1981. Cited by J. Urry, "The Consumption of Tourism". *Sociology*, vol. 24, No. 1, February 1990, p. 27.
3. D. MacCannell, *The Tourist. A New Theory of Leisure Class.* London: Macmillan, 1976. Citado por J. Urry, "The Consumption of Tourism" *Sociology*, vol. 24, No. 1, February 1990, p. 34.

PROYECTOS

Fernando Jiménez

86 **Cooperativa de frutos del bosque**

Este proyecto es la respuesta a la situación sociopolítica derivada del éxodo rural que se dio después de la clausura de las empresas mineras de los alrededores de Langreo. Su objetivo es encontrar una solución viable que revitalice el sector y salve a sus pueblos de la desaparición. El proyecto se centra en el pueblo de La Cruz, que cuenta con una cooperativa dedicada al cultivo de bayas y con capacidad para albergar a 30 personas, y tiene por objetivo atraer a un turismo cíclico y generar actividad económica. La intención es que esta idea prolifere en los pueblos del entorno. Aunque el concepto se haya materializado de un modo contemporáneo, el proyecto se inspira en la labor llevada a cabo en retiro, como ocurría en los antiguos monasterios. La propuesta consta de cuatro acciones:

1. En primer lugar, la localización de un lugar tranquilo en un entorno natural con fuerte identidad.
2. Protección exterior con vallado de madera.
3. Programa de distribución con anillos permeables.
4. Sostenibilidad autónoma ideal mediante la captación de niebla y cultivo durante todo el año.

Carmen Mencos

88 **Etc.**

La economía del turismo mediante cosméticos (*Economy behind Tourism through Cosmetics*, E.T.C.) consiste en la rehabilitación y reactivación de una mina abandonada a través de un mercado específico: el de los cosméticos. Además de ser una nueva atracción turística para el sector, el proyecto aspira a crear empleo utilizando los materiales minerales brutos existentes en la zona, teniendo en mente un mercado nuevo y específico. El binomio turismo-ocupación atrae a tres tipos distintos de turista: internacional, nacional y local. Todos dependen del tiempo que el turista desee permanecer allí, desde una semana hasta una experiencia de un día. Se fomenta una relación cercana entre el trabajador y el visitante y entre el local y el extranjero. Existen muchas diferencias entre el proceso minero y el de la elaboración de cosméticos. Uno lo componen y determinan los distintos pasos de extracción, clasificación, producción, almacenamiento, transporte y venta; el otro se basa en la conservación, producción, investigación y experimentación. El proyecto mezcla ambos procesos y pretende utilizar los edificios existentes para la fabricación de los nuevos cosméticos. La secuencia conservación-investigación-experimentación también está pensada para que los turistas participen y disfruten del proyecto.

Candela Oliva

90 **Work-Folk-Place**

Este proyecto es la respuesta a la situación social actual en la región rural de Asturias, desolada desde que empezó la decadencia de la industria minera. Se trata de una granja cooperativa dedicada al cultivo de bayas junto al río, a los pies del valle del Nalón. ¿Cómo trabajar en un paisaje para lograr un proceso productivo eficaz? Esta es una propuesta para conseguir una industria humanizada y participativa que, a su vez, no pierda el contacto con la naturaleza. Desde su cosecha en las colinas, pasando por el proceso esencial de cocción, hasta el momento de probar las confituras y jaleas junto al río... El espacio interior se organiza en una secuencia de distintas chimeneas, estructuras ligeras que cobijan las distintas actividades y que nunca descansan en el suelo. Existen, por lo tanto, dos mundos en esta fábrica de jaleas: tierra y aire. La tierra está "conformada" por plataformas de cemento que elevan la actividad a un nivel superior.

Teresa Rodríguez-Gimeno

Llumeres Yum! 94

Este proyecto no es (solo) arquitectónico, sino que pretende crear un sistema sostenible y autónomo. Se trata de un ecosistema creado por el hombre cuya filosofía pretende integrar el diseño con la jardinería, la horticultura, la ecología, la economía doméstica, el diseño comunitario y, por último, si bien no menos importante (ni más), la arquitectura. Con este proyecto queremos revitalizar y cambiar el uso que se hace del terreno, que se ha ido degradando con el tiempo debido a la explotación minera del hierro, así como a su posterior abandono y al cultivo industrial de eucaliptos. A través de distintos elementos (vergeles, pastizales, establos, arboledas) un sitio en ruinas se convierte en un paisaje con buenas condiciones ambientales. Para llevar a cabo este proyecto es indispensable tener conocimiento del entorno —agricultura de subsistencia, arquitectura autóctona—, así como la capacidad de transmitir al resto del mundo estos rasgos que conforman la identidad del lugar mediante la parte del programa enfocada al turismo.

Desde su creación, este proyecto nunca ha pretendido acercarse al terreno de una manera ingenua o condescendiente; lo que queremos es aprender al máximo. Así que, ¿no os parece que es hora de ponerse manos a la obra y ensuciarse las manos?

Paula Álvarez

Escuela micológica 96

El objetivo de esta arquitectura es atraer al turismo micológico de Tabanedo, León, un lugar idóneo para recogida de hongos. Se propone un método de construcción rápido y eficaz, que responde a la irregularidad del terreno y a su orientación. Para que estas construcciones existentes mantengan la importancia que merecen se emplea un sistema constructivo y el uso de materiales tradicionales de la zona. Sobre ellas se depositan unas cáscaras trianguladas que dejen cierta libertad para cubrir las necesidades del programa y proporcionen transparencia suficiente para intuir que es lo que ocurre dentro.

La envolvente de las edificaciones existentes se resuelve mediante vigas de madera laminada y membranas de EFTE. Se proponen membranas translúcidas en colores suaves para la orientación sur, como estrategia medioambiental para reducir la insolación directa en verano. Esta solución contrasta con la rigidez de las edificaciones tradicionales, mediante una mezcla de efectos y volúmenes que mantienen la composición dinámica del interior. Se ha pretendido sacar partido a la libertad que proporciona el entorno natural y aprovechar la mayor cantidad de luz posible, así como disfrutar de las vistas del paisaje.

PAISAJES URBANOS 98

CANALIZAR LA VELOCIDAD DEL CAMBIO 100

Pedro Iglesias 235

Design Critic del IE Unviersity

101 Luis Moreno Mansilla hablaba de la arquitectura en su precioso libro "Apuntes de viaje al interior del tiempo" como de "la vida que se finge naturaleza"[1]. Hablaba de viajes, historias, arquitectos y paisajes. Paisajes donde "merodea la arquitectura", donde la vida ha ido depositando una capa tras otra de información, dejando constancia así de los afanes y aspiraciones de innumerables generaciones en su intento de emular a la naturaleza a través de la arquitectura. Luís utilizaba su viaje por Italia como pretexto para dar vueltas al proyecto arquitectónico y ya desde el título nos anunciaba que iba a estar unido a la gran invención humana que es el tiempo. El tiempo estaba presente siempre en la conversación de Luís sobre arquitectura. El tiempo, necesario para que la vida consiga producir la arquitectura, es difícil de comprender o incluso de describir, pero va dejando poco a poco sus huellas en los paisajes urbanos.

103 Los artistas del renacimiento y del barroco se servían de la arquitectura como una metáfora del tiempo. En el siglo XV pintores como Vittore Carpaccio pintaban paisajes con edificios de una perfección desconocida en su concepción, en sus detalles y en sus acabados para representar la utopía del tiempo futuro, mientras que en el siglo XVIII pintores como Canaletto enmarcaban sus paisajes con edificios en ruinas para evocar la nostalgia del tiempo pasado de esplendor.

Hoy en día paisajes y arquitecturas están asociados principalmente al movimiento. Desde que el viaje se ha democratizado y se ha convertido casi en un derecho en los países industrializados, un número cada vez más alto de paisajes ha ido pasando a formar parte del imaginario de generaciones de viajeros ocasionales o habituales. Diferentes miradas han ido tejiendo una red de lugares en constante transformación, interconectada no necesariamente por su proximidad física, y han ido conformando visiones múltiples de una realidad que cambia a un ritmo cada vez mayor.

El enfoque del proyecto arquitectónico desde el paisaje ha permitido a los alumnos abordar con más facilidad la naturaleza escurridiza del tiempo y les han hecho ver que el primer paso para imaginar una nueva arquitectura es situarse en un tiempo diferente, que una nueva arquitectura no se puede producir ni con las herramientas del pasado ni con los del presente. Necesita estar atenta a los cambios vertiginosos de nuestra sociedad si no quiere caer en la irrelevancia.

Un primer grupo de proyectos ha elegido la antigua factoría Nitrastur en el barrio de La Felguera de la localidad asturiana de Langreo, conocida popularmente como "el Nitrógeno". Allí el tiempo cambió bruscamente de velocidad a finales del siglo pasado cuando la producción de productos sintéticos empezó a languidecer. Desde su abandono en 1997 las grandes naves industriales que construyera Fernández Casado se han ido deteriorando progresivamente y lo que había sido una ciudad dentro de la ciudad pasó a ser un gran vacío, una barrera que divide Langreo en dos, cuya escala industrial contrasta de forma muy violenta con el menudo tejido residencial circundante.

Las propuestas comienzan por imaginar nuevas actividades para esa ciudad muerta como paso previo para poder proyectar arquitecturas que tengan una incidencia real sobre la realidad social y económica de la región. Con planteamientos muy diferentes, los proyectos emplean una estrategia similar. Deciden mantener las ruinas como tales, como vestigios del pasado, y explotan la potencialidad de contraponer una nueva arquitectura —un nuevo tiempo— a las viejas estructuras industriales, de forma que no se borren las huellas de la historia, jugando con las posibilidades de diálogo entre pasado y futuro. De esta forma los proyectos transciende lo que podría haber sido un ejercicio meramente disciplinar para ofrecer soluciones a problemas sociales urgentes, con claras referencias a experiencias europeas similares. Otro grupo de proyectos se sitúa en un paisaje muy diferente: el centro de Oviedo. Si Langreo estaba fatalmente ligado a su actividad industrial, la identidad de Oviedo se ha ido conformando por el lento goteo de innumerables biografías, muchas de las cuales permanecen en el anonimato y solo se manifiestan a través de las huellas que han ido dejando en el tejido urbano. Los proyectos buscan hacer resonar sus ecos para añadir nuevas capas a la estructura compleja del paisaje e intensificar el juego de resonancias, con el objetivo de canalizar la velocidad y la intensidad de los cambios, abriendo cada uno de ellos un campo nuevo de desarrollo económico y social ligado a actividades artísticas de alto valor añadido. Si en Langreo el objetivo era dar solución a problemas urgentes, en Oviedo la estrategia ha sido explorar un mundo rico de sugerencias y posibilidades. El entendimiento del proyecto arquitectónico como el mecanismo necesario para modelar el paisaje urbano ha permitido descubrir una serie de espacios ocultos o infrautilizados donde poder realizar la labor de intensificación que ha supuesto la introducción de los nuevos programas.

Cada uno de los trabajos que se presentan aquí entra en diálogo con los diferentes tiempos de paisajes urbanos de la cuenca minera y todos traspasan los límites convencionales del proyecto arquitectónico para buscar nuevas formas en que ha de desarrollarse la profesión.

Todos hacen un uso consciente de la capacidad de la arquitectura para desplegarse en el tiempo, uniendo pasado presente y futuro, y proyectan actividades e instalaciones para un tiempo imaginado pero posible, donde se da forma a las aspiraciones e inquietudes de sus habitantes. Entre todos modelan un conjunto de miradas que nos permite además acercarnos de forma diferente a sus respectivos pasados.

1. Luis Moreno Mansilla, *Apuntes de viaje al interior del tiempo.* Fundación Caja de Arquitectos, Barcelona, 2002.

PROYECTOS

Elena Cardiel

104 Escuela de calor

Este proyecto se sitúa en un área urbana central de Asturias, donde se encuentra un elemento clave del patrimonio industrial contemporáneo de la zona astur-leonesa. La propuesta pretende reactivar y reconfigurar la ruina industrial de Nitrastur mediante un programa provocador y cosmopolita: un centro de sexualidad ligado a un jardín aromático. Y todo ello inmerso en una estrategia turística basada en la pertenencia a una red europea territorial consolidada.

En primer lugar, el proyecto se relaciona con las naves proyectadas por Fernández Casado, de estilo moderno, que hoy en día tienen un carácter monumental y de ruina. En segundo lugar se proponen el jardín aromático y los dos grandes volúmenes.

La implantación de este paisaje, urbano y público, incorpora un nuevo uso al municipio y reactiva el vacío de Nitrastur cubriendo toda la parcela y conectando los dos barrios colindantes. Los nuevos volúmenes adquieren una geometría totalmente distinta a la que presentan los edificios existentes, dotando así de carácter personal a ambas edificaciones al contraponerlas de forma clara y contundente. Estos nuevos volúmenes conectan las naves industriales y nos permiten tener un paseo/jardín semi-interior de carácter privado.

Ana González

106 Escenarios prohibidos

¿Dónde está el límite entre prohibición y deseo? Para atraer al turismo, un espacio debe tener identidad y despertar el deseo, ser limitado en el tiempo y estar sujeto al contexto. *Escenarios Prohibidos* busca un encuentro singular y una identidad concreta para Oviedo. Pretende hacer visible lo invisible: llegar a nuestras emociones a través de una experiencia que aúna gastronomía y danza. ¿Cuál es el límite, si es que existe, entre los elementos físicos y los incorpóreos de una ciudad? Las "preexistencias", entendidas como espacios potenciales, nos permiten crear arquitectura dentro de la arquitectura, un vínculo entre el público, el interior-exterior, el contexto y la experiencia.

En la ciudad de Oviedo, el proyecto invade seis espacios inaccesibles cuyos límites dejan huecos llenos de recuerdos. En su interior el placer está servido. Una experiencia que combina gastronomía y danza, en la que tres situaciones se vinculan a tres lugares de degustación. El espacio, concebido como una coreografía arquitectónica continua, refiere a un contexto rebosante de carácter y memoria. Una *performance* urbana nos desvela los puntos secretos de lo que estaba escondido.

César Gusano

Centro de tecnificación deportiva 110

Los principales motivos del desarrollo de este proyecto son el creciente interés por el turismo deportivo y la escasez de instalaciones para ciertas disciplinas de reciente creación. Deportes como el *skate, roller, BMX, parkour,* etc son habitualmente practicados en entornos urbanos no adaptados para ello, por lo que el proyecto pretende dar respuesta a esa necesidad. Imaginar un lugar para la práctica de estos deportes es sinónimo de imaginar nuevas topografías. Por otra parte, la práctica de estos deportes requiere de un espacio seco y cubierto.

Así, la operación más importante del Centro de tecnificación es la introducción de una gran cubierta sobre los edificios existentes, junto con el espacio que se genera entre ellos. Con ello se consigue una gran plaza pública exterior en la que tienen cabida las actividades deportivas mencionadas, así como la construcción de una nueva protección para los espacios interiores. Como complemento de esta gran cobertura se introduce una serie de variaciones topográficas en el terreno para generar cavidades o protuberancias, una superficie en la que se desarrolla la parte fundamental del programa.

Beatriz Fernández

Oviedo de cine 112

La creación de este proyecto tiene lugar en un momento en que Oviedo goza de un crecimiento del turismo urbano. No se refiere solamente a la población, sino también a su legado, topografía y límites (naturales y artificiales), que albergan un gran número de posibilidades para convertir una ciudad en un gran lugar no solo para sus habitantes sino también para los turistas. Mediante este proyecto se pretende transformar los espacios vacíos de la ciudad en puntos de encuentro a través de lo cinematográfico.

El mundo del cine se crea con escenografías. De este modo, para configurar estos espacios se han utilizado varios recursos escenográficos habituales del cine. Las distintas técnicas que se usan en el cine para agrandar espacios se concentran en los reflejos de un espejo, mediante una fachada de leds movible, espacios estroboscópicos y efectos de espejos en la entrada principal, orientada hacia la plaza de la Catedral. Esta entrada engrandece el espacio y muestra las diversas actividades que se llevan a cabo, desde puntos de información hasta las escaleras que conducen al auditorio/cine, pasando por la cafetería, que está destinada a un uso principalmente turístico.

Cristina Moreno

Ciudad de la moda 114

Mediante una pasarela que conecta dos naves, la propuesta parte de la idea de rehabilitar algunos de los edificios del polígono Nitrastur de una manera "no convencional". Conceptos como efímero, perdurable, temporal, atemporal, estático, móvil o adaptable son propios del lenguaje arquitectónico del siglo XXI. Del mismo modo, tales conceptos también aparecen en los diccionarios históricos de la moda. A lo largo de los siglos, moda y arquitectura han compartido un escenario estético que transcurre en paralelo y que se aproxima cada vez más. Se plantea un artefacto que sea capaz de dar uso a las naves existentes. Sin su presencia, la utilidad de las mismas no sería posible. Una idea tan simple como instalar una pasarela nos conecta con el mundo de la moda. Este espacio, transformable en el tiempo, con programa fijo y programa variable, se añadirá a los puntos clave de la zona creando áreas de visión destacadas. Un ente ligero y articulado se infiltra en los edificios, y permite una amplia capacidad de transformación. Una pasarela nos conduce directamente al mundo de la moda.

PAISAJES
116 EXTREMOS

118 MEDIO Y PLASTICIDAD

Juan Elvira
234 Profesor de Taller Urbano y Design Critic del IE Unviersity

Para hacer una aproximación a la arquitectura de los paisajes extremos en primer lugar es necesario acotar el sentido de esta categoría de lo natural. El paisaje extremo no es sólo el lecho de un río o el lago en lo alto de una cordillera montañosa. Como el cortado de una montaña, el interior de una masa de agua o el corazón pétreo de una formación geológica, es aquel lugar donde la arquitectura no parece concebible. El paisaje extremo es la naturaleza percibida como una extensión indefinida, donde la arquitectura no solo está ausente sino olvidada.

La principal cualidad del proyecto que opera en estos lugares es su dimensión paisajística. Por dos razones: una, porque interviene en un entorno natural y su presencia tiene sentido a escala territorial. La segunda, porque reproduce en su interior las características de estos espacios naturales. Los paisajes extremos propician la creación de paisajes dentro de la propia arquitectura que, independientemente de su escala, ha de combinar lo arquitectónico con lo infraestructural. De este modo, el proyecto de arquitectura ha de adoptar ciertas cualidades de la infraestructura territorial, y además incorporar una capacidad de reprogramación funcional propia de lo arquitectónico. Son flexibles, están abiertas al cambio. En esto reside uno de sus mayores potenciales, ya que plantea apropiaciones e intervenciones abiertas a diferentes usos, condición que normalmente no cumplen las infraestructuras en un sentido estricto, sorteando así una obsolescencia de otro modo inevitable.

119 Otra de sus cualidades es la ambigüedad. La arquitectura del paisaje extremo equidis-
120 ta tanto de lo invasivo como de lo mimético. Despliega sin ambages todos los recursos artificiales que le son propios, y a la vez convive sin conflictos con su entorno natural, lo que genera hábitats en un fascinante estado intermedio. Frente a ellas uno se pregunta si está delante de una ruina proyectada para ser inmediatamente invadida por la vegetación, el agua y la tierra, o si, por el contrario, están concebidas como invasiones arquitectónicas de la naturaleza.

En este sentido es destacable que, lejos de ser nostálgicas, estas intervenciones evidencian la capacidad de manipulación de lo natural, la plasticidad de su medio. Son proyectos que, aunque no se mimetizan ni adoptan una retórica de la preservación y la ausencia de impacto, evitan la negación de lo natural. No escenifican lo sostenible y lo ecológico, pero en ellos es evidente cierta naturalización de la organización arquitectónica. Las arquitecturas que podríamos denominar a partir de ahora 'extremas' deben esta ambigüedad a su voluntad de articular los conflictos presentes en el medio en que operan, trabajando con los potenciales de su entorno. En ellas es fundamental la preparación de un conocimiento analítico del contexto y de una sensibilidad natural. Cada agente, fuerza y proceso está presente. Más que proyectar, podemos afirmar que cultivan acciones en el paisaje cuya lógica se entrelaza con la del medio donde se desenvuelven. Aquí radica su aproximación a la sostenibilidad medioambiental.

Lejos de ser autónoma y autorreferencial, esta arquitectura es estrictamente cultural (en el sentido de 'aquello que se cultiva') porque asume su plena artificialidad en relación con el medio, y exhibe esta cualidad de manera deliberada. Son 'segundas naturalezas' en una doble acepción. La primera se refiere a aquello que se despliega con una facilidad innata, sólo aparente porque procede de un conocimiento profundo del medio. La segunda alude a la construcción de una naturaleza alternativa donde la acción arquitectónica se disuelve en el medio en que opera, amplificándolo.

La arquitectura del paisaje extremo emplea lógicas de ocupación propias de la naturaleza. Con frecuencia recurre a patrones para definir las leyes de ocupación del territorio. Sus límites son imprecisos o bien el resultado de recortar un perímetro regular sobre la textura abstracta de la organización, que sin él podría extenderse indefinidamente.

La arquitectura del paisaje extremo cortocircuita las relaciones topológicas preexistentes, modificándolas. Construye condiciones naturales alteradas. Reproduce experiencias 'extremas' en la naturaleza, como el alpinismo, la espeleología o el submarinismo, lo que condiciona el modo en que deben ser experimentadas. Proyecta entornos inéditos que deben descubrirse, explorarse y colonizarse. Recorrerlos significa realizar incursiones en lugares cuyas reglas no siguen los códigos habituales del proyecto arquitectónico. Son arquitecturas para escalar, sumergirse, en las que perderse. Son espacios indómitos, paisajes impredecibles que es necesario explorar.

Nos encontramos ante una arquitectura que, finalmente, podríamos calificar de salvaje. Sin duda la naturaleza inexplorada es un bien cada vez más escaso, y aquella que aún existe debe ser objeto de protección y preservación. Lo salvaje, lejos de producir temor y de ser el escenario de lo monstruoso, hoy necesita amparo, el favor de aquellos que lo temían por encima de cualquier otra cosa. Quizá por esta razón necesitamos más que nunca una arquitectura bestial e indomable, que se identifique con los paisajes extremos, que asimile las cualidades de las experiencias en la naturaleza. Una arquitectura que quiera ser montaña, cueva, río, lago.

PROYECTOS

Íñigo Arias

122 Centro de meditación y desarrollo hipersensorial

Transitar por este edificio nos acerca a la historia oculta de los pueblos que yacen bajo las oscuras aguas del Embalse de Barrios de Luna. El proyecto se materializa a partir de las tensiones que emanan del propio entorno. La colina en la que se instala contiene un pronunciado desnivel, lo que permite dominar visualmente el entorno limítrofe y el horizonte de los campos leoneses. Estas tensiones se concretan mediante gruesos muros de hormigón. La organización en planta presenta un espacio complejo que se ha de ir descubriendo a medida que se recorre.

El proyecto se plantea como una macla de espacios diversos, donde la necesidad de llegar al siguiente emplazamiento produce una visión nueva y diferente que a su vez se concatena con otro espacio, y vuelta a empezar. La Espina Vegetal es el elemento clave que recorre el edificio, compuesta de una serie de espacios que se van articulando de manera quebrada. A lo largo de ella los patios se suceden como puntos de actividad condensada. Proporciona un tránsito fluido, donde la sencillez de sus geometrías ayuda a descifrar el lugar en el que nos encontramos inmersos.

Clara Bueno

122 Los puentes de Somiedo

Nos encontramos en el Valle del Lago, muy cerca de Pola de Somiedo. En él predominan una serie de caminos y sendas de animales que son el punto de partida de esta propuesta. El proyecto es un Eco-Puente que prolonga estos caminos en el valle para facilitar el paso de un lado al otro del valle, y para que la fauna y flora autóctonos encuentren nuevas rutas de expansión. Sobre este nuevo paso se crean unas plataformas que cuelgan de la estructura principal, cada una con distinto programa.

La primera es la plataforma del conocimiento, donde se dan todas aquellas actividades para mejorar el rendimiento del turista y ampliar sus conocimientos de la zona y del deporte que vaya a realizar. La segunda es la de la alimentación, donde se encuentran el restaurante y el bar. Por último, la tercera plataforma es la del descanso, en la que se sitúan las habitaciones donde los turistas pueden alojarse. Con todo, se crea un punto en el que se concentra el turismo del Parque Natural de Somiedo.

Ettore Disconzi

Excavación entre dos paisajes 128

El concepto principal de este proyecto es la organización de una secuencia de acciones sobre el paisaje natural. Su implementación temporal responde a tres etapas. La primera es la excavación de la roca. La segunda, la colocación de el hormigón postesado. Finalmente, la tercera etapa consiste en la reutilización de la roca excavada. Globalmente, su objetivo es diseñar un paisaje artificial donde los materiales naturales se reordenan, incorporando nuevas cualidades arquitectónicas. La organización general combina dos tipos de límites: uno es preciso y estricto, el otro, frente al mar, es suave y orgánico. Entre ambos se disponen una serie de usos colectivos. Las habitaciones están diseñadas para captar la máxima iluminación a lo largo del día.

Juan González

Pendiendo de un hilo 130

A veces nos asomamos al precipicio y no nos atrevemos a saltar. La arquitectura es ese gran precipicio, donde la fórmula para conseguir un buen resultado rara vez esta en asomarnos con cautela al abismo. Aunque en ocasiones pendamos de un hilo, tenemos que asumir el riesgo. El proyecto parte de la idea de habitar diferentes paredes verticales mediante un sistema temporal de colonización, con el objetivo de potenciar distintos parajes naturales, utilizando los deportes extremos como herramienta para disfrutar de todas sus posibilidades. El edificio es un centro de alto rendimiento para la práctica y el entrenamiento de deportes extremos. Es una estrategia para colonizar temporalmente diferentes paredes verticales del límite entre las provincias de León y Asturias. El programa de proyecto no se puede encerrar en un edificio. No es un programa estático, la temporalidad y la estacionalidad son fundamentales en él, y varía dependiendo de la época del año. La propuesta toma como referencia, entre otras, los sistemas que utilizan los alpinistas para habitar temporalmente la alta montaña.

Cecilia Marina

Camino de sensaciones 134

El jardín de los paisajes astur-leoneses de la isla Erbosa es un entorno natural donde los visitantes conectan con la esencia de unos parajes dotados de una fuerte identidad. Trata de concentrar las esencias perceptivas del paisaje de Asturias y León en un lugar concreto. Frente a la inmovilidad y rotundidad del emplazamiento, estos espacios de conexión sensorial utilizan el clima del entorno para establecer un nuevo dinamismo interior. Si el clima es de gran relevancia en el proyecto, el agua también juega un papel fundamental.

El proyecto es una máquina natural en la que el clima propio del lugar se introduce en el jardín, lo modifica y lo convierte en un espacio dinámico, un espacio neutro, robusto, vacío, capaz de albergar en su interior diferentes sensaciones sin quitar protagonismo a ningún aspecto del programa. El interior de la roca granítica se convierte en un espacio neutro pero cargado de sentido, donde se propone la intervención de diferentes artistas relacionados con el mundo de la escultura, cuyas obras cargarán de sentido los vacíos de forma puntual.

Vanesa Payo

Hidden underwater 136

El agua decide cuándo mostrar los tesoros que oculta. La construcción de embalses fue en España una operación de gran relevancia, repetida en un total de 356 ocasiones por toda la península. La aparición de estas infraestructuras generó cierta polémica, pues con su construcción se dio prioridad a grandes extensiones de regadío en detrimento de numerosas poblaciones de pequeño tamaño que quedaron sumergidas, obligando a sus habitantes a buscar un nuevo hogar. En concreto, el embalse de Barrios de Luna esconde bajo sus aguas las ruinas de doce pueblos que fueron anegados. Este edificio también se sumerge en el embalse, con lo que construye una experiencia turística identificable y atractiva. Al encerrar una porción de agua en un cubo poroso se crea un espacio alrededor de la ruina de la iglesia del pueblo inundado, Miñera. La fachada actúa como mecanismo de filtrado del agua, para que se apta para el buceo y permita la visibilidad de la ruina. El proyecto contiene y hace visible parte de la memoria del embalse de Barrios de Luna.

Marina Carretero

138 **Desvelar lo oculto**

Este proyecto se emplaza en una veta de pizarra, una zanja geológica cercana a un río. Pretende investigar diferentes vías de aproximarse a la zona así como hacer posible un uso turístico y placentero. El proyecto, situado en la parte interior de la veta, acerca al visitante a esta parte inhabitada, como un retiro espiritual donde se nos desvela la naturaleza más recóndita. En este proyecto el terreno se concibe como una serie de espacios únicos que invitan al usuario a encontrarse a sí mismo en la naturaleza. Desde la forma de la veta hasta la manera de apilar las rocas de las paredes, el trabajo arquitectónico nos enseña todo lo que la naturaleza puede ofrecernos y nos permite vivir la soledad de una manera única: aquí naturaleza y arquitectura son una misma cosa. La estrategia del proyecto divide el programa completo en volúmenes diferentes, de tal modo que propone una ruta coherente a través de ellos, mezclando visitantes recién llegados con otros no tan recientes. Esta propuesta de ruta, que no es obligatoria, da paso a cuatro programas distintos en el campus, amplía el repertorio de turistas (excursionistas, trabajadores...) y da al lugar un nuevo uso más respetuoso del lugar.

PAISAJES
140 INDUSTRIALES

142 LA MEMORIA COMO MATERIAL ARQUITECTÓNICO

235 Mónica García
Design Critic del IE Unviersity

143 El concepto de paisaje industrial se inscribe en el marco teórico más amplio de *paisaje cultural,* sucesión histórica de valores naturales y valores resultantes de la acción humana. La posibilidad de vincular los términos "paisaje" e "industrial", en principio excluyentes uno a otro, es relativamente reciente.

El desplazamiento del concepto de paisaje desde la imagen pictórica fija de la naturaleza a todo producto de la actividad del hombre, rural, urbano y también industrial, ha posibilitado esta alianza. John Brinckerhoff Jackson en *Discovering Vernacular Lanscape* (1984) aporta la siguiente fórmula de *paisaje: composición de espacios hechos por el hombre sobre la Tierra*[1]. El paisaje, *paisaje cultural,* es por tanto un espacio sintético, un sistema artificial de espacios superpuestos, funcionando, evolucionando, no solo según leyes naturales sino para servir a una comunidad.

El paisaje industrial en el área de centralidad turística Astur-Leonesa (ACTAL) excede al conjunto de las construcciones fabriles, mineras, depósitos... objetos patrimoniales, morfologías inertes. Tiene la capacidad de representar la naturaleza del territorio, las materias primas y su transformación, el cómo se vinculan los hechos industriales a los sistemas organizativos sociales, en definitiva la vida. Estos paisajes están impregnados de la memoria del trabajo y de la historia reciente de las comunidades industriales que los albergan.

El trabajo sobre los paisajes industriales se alinea con un enunciado de urgencia propuesto por la joven disciplina de la *arqueología industrial*: la recuperación y revalorización del patrimonio industrial, que resulta ser de una gran fragilidad. Si bien el patrimonio industrial constituye la forma más elaborada y compleja de ocupación del territorio, es a su vez una de las estructuras más efímeras. Frente a la colonización rural, los paisajes nacidos del desarrollo de la actividad industrial son mucho más recientes, más localizados, en definitiva más vulnerables, porque están enraizados de un modo más superficial. Sus trazas desaparecen en algunos casos con gran velocidad convirtiéndose en una especie amenazada.

La necesidad de recuperación del patrimonio industrial conecta con nuestra sociedad actual con más fuerza que otros legados, debido al cúmulo de sentimientos colectivos que perviven en los territorios de una tradición industrial en extinción. La coincidencia temporal y el conocimiento directo de las estructuras territoriales heredadas de la industrialización, que han marcado el paisaje vivido, confieren un valor añadido que da vigor y dinamismo a su revalorización.

Las propuestas presentadas hacen converger dos intereses, por una parte la recupera- 145
ción de la memoria colectiva del trabajo en el territorio y de la autoestima, afirmando las señas de identidad de los ciudadanos en este área, y por otra el impulso de nuevas actividades vinculadas al turismo a fin de reactivar la economía local. El patrimonio industrial de ACTAL ofrece grandes recursos al desarrollo del turismo, no solo por la calidad de sus construcciones singulares y el sistema de relaciones que éstas establecen con el territorio, sino por su potencial de re-semantización y de inyectar

nuevos programas que conecten con el significado real del área.

Desde la industria del turismo se mira a los paisajes con avidez. Viajar en el tiempo y el espacio son premisas fundamentales en la demanda turística. La clientela exige más que nunca una des-contextualización (o re-contextualización). El manejo de la especificidad cultural o histórica se convierte en un instrumento necesario en la reconstrucción de un escenario capaz de suscitar la emoción, de albergar un "genius loci".

En el área ACTAL no se precisa recrear un decorado, generar ficciones, a modo de parques temáticos a los que nos enfrentamos habitualmente, se trata de interpretar el paisaje, reconstruir su identidad. Lejos de utilizar simples "regionalismos" formales, las intervenciones propuestas se apoyan en el legado industrial existente para dar "sentido" al corpus total de actividades turísticas. Operan haciendo una lectura atenta del lugar que permite conectar la historia con el presente y construir una tradición viva, una narrativa en progreso.

Los proyectos se convierten en herramientas de profundización en el territorio, atendiendo a las capas superpuestas del tiempo y considerando la memoria como un elemento activo. Tal como sugería Sébastien Marot en *Suburbanismo y el arte de la memoria* (1999), se establece un proceso en que se considera el lugar, la exploración de los "estratos espacio-temporales" del territorio, como matriz del proyecto arquitectónico: *la arquitectura es un instrumento de la memoria y la memoria materia de la arquitectura*[2].

La capacidad activadora de los nuevos programas que se inyectan en el lugar, culturales y docentes, depende en buena medida de la convivencia con el hecho industrial y su grado de conectividad con el territorio en general. Se actúa sobre arquitecturas significativas, nodos en el paisaje industrial, sin olvidar que éstas han surgido junto a las infraestructuras pertinentes que las vinculan a una red territorial. Los nuevos modelos de turismo desarrollan el concepto de *itinerancia*, que se apoya en la regeneración de senderos o vías de comunicación de diferentes tipos. Esta red de movilidad variada conecta las diferentes ofertas turísticas entre si en un sistema global.

Las propuestas de activación del paisaje industrial heredado deben tener una concepción globalizadora, ser capaces de generar sinergias entre si y de fomentar el desarrollo sostenible a escala regional, máxime cuando la industria es consecuencia directa del uso que la sociedad hace del medio natural en su totalidad. Lejos de posiciones nostálgicas deberíamos aprender del hecho industrial su modo estratégico de ocupación del territorio. Actuando de este modo daremos continuidad a la propia historia la región, así como a todo su patrimonio, que está conectado por su desarrollo funcional histórico y abarca ámbitos supralocales, regionales e internacionales.

1. Jackson, John Brinckerhoff. *Discovering the Vernacular Lanscape*, Ed. Yale University Press, New Haven y Londres, 1984 (*A la découverte du paysage vernaculaire*, trad. Françés Xavier Carrère. Ed. Actes Sud / ENSP, París, 2003).

2. Marot, Sébastien. "L´art de la mémoire, le territoire et l´architecture". En *Le visiteur*, nº 4, junio 1999 (Suburbanismo y el arte de la memoria, trad. español Maurici Pla. Ed. Gustavo Gili, Barcelona, 2006).

PROYECTOS

Leticia Merino

El altavoz de Asturias 146

El programa de proyecto tiene como objeto la experimentación sonora, potenciada por medio de la arquitectura. Se disponen seis espacios, contenidos en seis burbujas, dedicados a la investigación y un gran espacio abierto en el que se proyectará música con alto nivel decibélico. La calidad de la onda sonora, el modo de difusión de esta, o la trayectoria que seguirá se han estudiado a fondo para que el proyecto funcione correctamente y potencie la situación deseada. Por ello cada burbuja ha sido tratada de una forma diferente, tanto en la geometría como en el material. Su situación obedece al tipo de sonido perseguido, pero también tiene que ver con el uso y tamaño. Las burbujas se suspenden en el aire mediante unos cables de acero de 20mm de diámetro. La disposición de los cables va regida a una rejilla inferior preexistente duplicada en la zona superior y reforzada mediante una subestructura ligera de tubos de acero. De esta manera tenemos una red de puntos desde la que se descolgarán los cables. La estructura superior es la que resiste todo el peso, mientras que la interior sirve para darle estabilidad.

Juan Moreno

Museo del motor en El Sotón 148

El propósito de este museo es alojar y potenciar el turismo del motor de la zona. El Museo del Motor de El Sotón se apoya en las preexistencias singulares, modificando y absorbiendo el flujo de circulación de vehículos y ofreciendo la posibilidad de recorrer y vivir todas las actividades desde el propio vehículo. Puesto que se pretende que el turista (el piloto) viva este proyecto al volante de su coche, se propone una distribución de programas en superficie. La distribución final atiende a diversos criterios. Uno de ellos es trazar unas circulaciones basadas en las existentes en la propia parcela, pero redefiniéndolas, vertebrándolas y jerarquizándolas. Otro, separar la circulación de los visitantes de la circulación de quien acampará, privatizando así la zona de acampada. Y por último, crear una "mancha" de actividades relacionadas entre sí. La zona de acampada se asoma al río, quedando separada de la zona pública a través de la vía rápida destinada a quienes acamparán. Los programas más públicos se ordenan dentro del circuito cerrado para visitantes.

Álvaro Bravo

Centro logístico minero 150

Las infraestructuras mineras existentes mantienen en esta propuesta su uso industrial y simbólico. Se convierten en un punto de referencia geoespacial, recogiendo al visitante e introduciéndolo en el complejo. La mina, aún abandonada, tiene la obligación de mantener la infraestructura, en especial la hidrológica. Se utiliza así como estación de servicio, haciendo posible la ubicación de grandes piezas, sofisticadas y sólo en apariencia desubicadas en el entorno. Se presentan una colección de cuatro tipos de lo que en el proyecto se denominan 'profundizaciones'. Estas operaciones consisten en la comunicación vertical entre las galerías de uso de la mina existente, primera y segunda. Un patio aquí es anécdota en el recorrido y transición entre espacios. En la profundización mayor se desarrollan dos edificaciones enfrentadas de distinto tamaño, las cuales recogen el programa principal. Por último, una salida en espiral equipa al usuario para descubrir el territorio. Finalmente, la "profundización habitada" es el espacio principal de nueva incorporación, el más complejo y que contiene el programa fundamental. Se caracteriza por una fachada optimizada para la máxima reflexión de la luz solar. Los accesos se originan entre la piel de vidrio reflectante y el programa interior. El mundo exterior entra por la parte superior dejando llegar al fondo del espacio el agua de lluvia, formándose una lámina de agua.

Pedro Pascual

154 Conjunto de itinerarios ornitológicos

El entorno de la ensenada de Llumeres es eminentemente rural. Está rodeado por campos de cosecha de heno y campos de ganado. Tiene una vegetación arbórea combinada con estepas y pastizales de matorrales y montanos. Desde las naves de Llumeres destacan tres puntos de referencia visual. El primero es el pueblo de Viodo, con una vida dedicada al campo, que representa el presente. El segundo es el conjunto de edificios más cercanos al mar que pertenecieron al conjunto minero, referidos al pasado. Por último, el futuro, en el área propuesta de observación de aves. Estos tres puntos de referencia visual tienen una conexión con el proyecto, en el centro de recepción de visitantes. El complejo se identifica en dos experiencias para los turistas ornitológicos: en primer lugar la fase de recepción (donde se sitúan las naves existentes) y a continuación las piezas de observación de aves. La primera, lo teórico, es un espacio que introduce al usuario en el mundo y la historia de las aves de la zona, frente a la segunda, lo práctico, donde observa la realidad.

Juan Gilsanz

156 SOS minas

El proyecto se organiza en pequeñas edificaciones conectadas entre sí y con el terreno natural, filtradas por la vegetación que las rodea. Busca su implantación en espacios libres y evita la agresión al medio en el maoyor grado posible. Su programa nace con doble vocación: el montaje en extensión colonizadora según su potencialidad, necesidades y posibilidades futuras, así como el desmontaje, traslado o reciclado de sus elementos, si fuera preciso. Como una sucesión de capas, la intervención se suma a la de la mina que a su vez fue implantada sobre el terreno virgen. La volumetrías quebradas y de pequeñas dimensiones buscan adaptarse al orden cambiante de la naturaleza. La madera domina en ellas, formando una piel que cubre sus paramentos y se extiende en plataformas, caminos y pasarelas conectándolos entre si como un desplegable. Parte de los huecos acristalados corresponde a los accesos. De generosas dimensiones, vinculan el espacio exterior y el interior en una secuencia espacial sin interrupción, dando sentido al espacio compartido y participativo del conjunto. El resto de perforaciones dota de iluminación y vistas a los interiores ubicandose de manera estratégica en los volúmenes construidos.

PAISAJES REVERSIBLES 158

LA REVERSIBILIDAD EN LA CULTURA 'SOLVING FOR PATTERN' 160

Izaskun Chinchilla 234
Design Critic del IE Unviersity

Hay muchos encargos que instan a un proyectista a hacer arquitectura desmontable: pa- 161
bellones expositivos, instalaciones vinculadas 162
a eventos, arquitecturas de emergencia (...). Hay, sin embargo, proyectistas que toman la decisión de hacer su arquitectura intencionadamente desmontable y relocalizable sin que esta condición fuera implícita al encargo. Los motivos que pueden llevar a un arquitecto a optar por uniones reversibles y materiales portátiles son variados. Este texto prestará atención a aquellos proyectos en los que la reversibilidad se adopta como una respuesta escalada y adaptada a la notable complejidad y fragilidad del contexto que existía antes de que llegaran y a la conciencia de que contribuyen a crear más complejidad y más fragilidad en el entorno que afectan.

La reversibilidad es, en estos casos, parte de lo que yo llamo la cultura 'Solving for Pattern'. Esta expresión procede del ensayo de Wendel Berry del mismo título. En este texto[1], y en la lectura que se ha hecho de él desde diferentes disciplinas[2], se defiende que las acciones que llevemos a cabo en nuestro entorno deben tratar de responder no a un problema único, si no a una síntesis de problemas variados. Así mismo, nuestras acciones deben minimizar los problemas colaterales que de ellas se derivan. Leyendo estas premisas parece que nadie debiera estar fuera de esta cultura: parece imposible que nuestras arquitecturas no respondan a problemas múltiples y que no traten de minimizar sus efectos colaterales nocivos. La perspectiva 'Solving for Pattern' es, sin embargo, casi una revolución metodológica en la forma de proyectar arquitectura.

¿Qué es lo que ha cambiado? La principal práctica que se pone en tela de juicio es el empleo de los métodos de resolución de problemas en cascada. Las etapas del método de la cascada les van a sonar a muchos: se recopilan unos cuantos datos, se analizan esos datos, se propone una solución y se implementa. ¿Hicieron algo parecido en sus escuelas? Seguramente sí. Pero, ¿qué tiene de malo este sistema? La repuesta es que invita al proyectista a un objetivo parcial, aislado y deducido de un análisis muy sesgado. El método de la cascada aísla unos problemas de otros y permite concluir que se está resolviendo uno de esos problemas 'prefabricados', en el sentido de artificialmente aislados. Usemos un ejemplo. Un proyecto que se construye en un bosque de gran riqueza ecológica. El arquitecto rápidamente analiza un aspecto del bosque: la frondosidad produce una textura de luz y color muy abigarrada en diagonales. Dibuja las texturas a partir de fotos del lugar. Aparece el problema más o menos 'prefabricado': una arquitectura al uso (forma paralelepipédica y aristas rectas) rompería la continuidad de la trama y estropearía la vista del bosque. En seguida, se encuentra la solución: pequeñas cajitas con un material reflectante en fachada. La trama del bosque se refleja en la fachada de la arquitectura invasora y esta parece mejor integrada visualmente. ¿Ha tenido el proyectista en cuenta de donde vendrá el agua que usarán los habitantes y si esto cambiará el abastecimiento del bosque?, ¿sabe qué efecto tendrá el trampantojo en los movimientos de los animales?, ¿por qué camino del bosque llegó el espejo, hubo algún árbol que cortar? La lista de preguntas a las que el proyectista no responde es casi infinita. A cambio, él ha solucionado el 'problema' que el mismo construyó: la continuidad visual de la textura del bosque.

Esta forma de proyectar ha llevado a los arquitectos a proponer la realización de enormes desperfectos en sólidas montañas en aras de la metáfora espacial: 'mi proyecto es una grieta'. La coherencia espacial del propio proyecto ha estado por encima de los criterios medioambientales, sociales o de cualquier visión holística del territorio y el contexto.

Como reacción a esta herencia aparecen ciertos proyectos intencionadamente reversibles que buscan reaccionar ante un número mayor y más impreciso de problemas. Estos proyectos pueden cambiar su ubicación parcialmente si la fauna hallara en ellos un obstáculo o pueden disminuir su superficie en caso de sequía. ¿Cómo se diseñan estos proyectos?, ¿qué cambia respecto al método moderno de aplicación del esquema en cascada?

Desde los años 80[3], varios proyectos han expresado un deseo explícito de formar parte de lo que en inglés Berry denomina 'pattern' y que, desgraciadamente, tiene una difícil traducción al castellano.

Usando varias palabras podemos acercarnos a la intención de Berry: son arquitecturas que reconocen formar parte de un patrón territorial, de una red de preexistencias o de un modelo de desplazamiento por el territorio. Varios proyectos han tratado de integrarse en un conjunto de estructuras superiores en escala y en durabilidad. No es la intención de este breve artículo proporcionar un listado exhaustivo de esos proyectos sino, más bien, reflexionar sobre algunos de los métodos de proyectación que han seguido.

Desde que los proyectos quisieron ser conscientes de su contribución al 'pattern', la metáfora de la navegación ha sido relativamente popular: "¿qué hace un piloto cuando quiere maniobrar su barco para llevarlo a un puerto?, no sigue puntualmente un programa determinado sino que lo modifica constantemente. El barco se desvía de su ruta a la izquierda, se evalúa qué desviación qué nueva desviación es optima para continuar su ruta hacia el puerto (…). En todo momento, la desviación debe ser corregida a tenor del propósito, del telos del viaje"[4].

La metáfora del navegante, retomada por Heinz von Foerster, uno de los padres de la cibernética, clarifica un método de diseño basado en modelos cíclicos de información típicos de sistemas vivos: las relaciones causa efecto son constantemente reconsideradas en un sistema continuo que vuelve a explorar el contexto en varias ocasiones, que modifica las acciones y que va marcha adelante y marcha atrás, para conseguir poner en relación datos y hechos emergentes aparentemente no congruentes. En los paisajes reversibles de estos Proyectos de Fin de Grado, la interrelación entre las partes no viene de un sistema general de deducciones, sino de la construcción de un sistema de componentes cuyas relaciones pueden reconstruirse de varias maneras. Esta orientación es continuista de la filosofía de los textos de Morin[5] "en lugar de aislar los objetos estudiados, considérenlos a través y con su proceso propio de eco-organización que les relaciona con el entorno cultural, social, económico, político y natural".

El reto ecológico genera un reto docente, profesional y metodológico: hay que movilizar el conocimiento y la imaginación técnicas para que, además de solventar las situaciones estables a las que la disciplina se había acostumbrado, se afronten los problemas de complejidad e incertidumbre. La reversibilidad total y parcial de la arquitectura que proponemos forma parte de una batería de medidas que pueden contribuir a construir un mejor entendimiento de lo modelos territoriales y sociales que contribuimos a generar. Otras muchas medidas como apoyar los proyectos lo más posible en redes existentes, introducir materialidades variadas o visitar de forma repetida y en diferentes momentos en contexto, completarían las recomendaciones que se pueden proporcionar a diseñadores en formación como corolario a un gran cambio de criterio: lo importante ya no es la pureza de la idea propia y su plasmación en una pieza de gran valor plástico, lo importante es contribuir a la vitalidad de un patrón, modelo o red que ya existe.

1. "Solving for Pattern" de Wendell Berry. Capítulo 9 de *The Gift of Good Land: Further Essays Cultural &Agricultural*, North Point Press, 1981.
2. Una buena muestra el seguimiento masivo de la filosofía de Berry desde varias disciplinas es el blog www.solvingforpattern.org
3. Un buen punto de partida puede ser el diseño de Koolhaas para el Parque de la Villette en 1982. En él se hacia alusión a cuatro capas o estratos: las bandas, caracterizadas por diferentes funciones, la malla que regulaba la distribución de las funciones puntuales denominadas confeti, la circulación que aseguraba distintos tipos de accesibilidad a cada función, el estrato final que definía la configuración de los espacios construidos, los conectores y localizadores que disponían una interfaz de uso para el vecindario. La memoria enfatizaba el hecho de que la creación de una estructura débil y revisable permanecía la flexibilidad por la autonomía que cobraban cada una de las partes, creando una especie de método que "combina la especificidad arquitectónica con la indeterminación del programa .
4. Heinz von Foerster (1998) *Die Wahrheit ist die Erfindung eines Lügners*, Heidelberg.
5. Morin, Edgar (1973) *Le paradigme perdu: la nature humaine*, Seuil, París.

PROYECTOS

Blanca Pérez

166 Pabellones de meditación

Este proyecto busca una conexión entre el usuario y la naturaleza a través de la arquitectura. El programa consta de una serie de pabellones repartidos por el paisaje donde se realizarán actividades como yoga o meditación. Todos los pabellones convergen en un paseo que discurre por el bosque.No es lo mismo adentrarse en un bosque donde los árboles te protegen, donde no es difícil perderse, que caminar por campos de flores y plantas aromáticas que puedes oler y tocar con las manos, o hacerlo por un paisaje pedregoso en lo alto de una montaña donde las marcas de ruta son indispensables. El sistema del paseo que une los pabellones, que varía en función de los diversos paisajes y programas, está justamente diseñado para que incluya todas esas "escenas". Cada pabellón será distinto a los demás: la iluminación y la relación del espacio con la naturaleza dependerá del uso que se le de. La construcción debería ser lo más ligera posible y su presencia no debería interferir en el paisaje. Se utilizarán materiales autóctonos y reciclados que, junto con la estructura ligera de la construcción, reducirán al mínimo el impacto en el medio.

Gonzalo Merino

168 Aguas asturianas

Esta propuesta consta de dos intervenciones consecutivas. La primera, ya que en la actualidad el lugar elegido carece de medios de acceso, consiste en la adecuación del paraje natural para promover la visita de turistas durante todo el año. Para ello se disponen una serie de senderos que van vertebrando las diferentes perspectivas características de la zona, que culminanen el lago, el lugar central del proyecto. En segundo lugar, la propuesta de activación turística mediante la ocupación temporal del lago. Al tratarse de un lugar tan emblemático, se propone una intervención no dañina y efímera con el entorno. El lago pasa entonces de ser lugar desconocido, impenetrable y silencioso como es habitual, a punto de encuentro para que los visitantes disfruten y se liberen del estrés del día a día.

Se proponen tres áreas diferentes, una destinada a conciertos y festivales, otra a actividades acuáticas, y la tercera a una actividad más introspectiva del usuario. Estos usos pueden activarse simultáneamente o por separado, priorizando uno sobre otro. Así, puede ocuparse el lago durante los meses más calurosos, cuando el acceso es más sencillo, y desocuparse durante los meses de invierno.

Tamara García

Espacios temporales 170

En la Sierra del Áramo, a una hora de la AP-66, encontramos bosques que albergan pueblos fantasmas, embalses y lagos a los pies de las montañas. Este paisaje es majestuoso y complejo a la vez, y está colmado de pequeños detalles que lo hacen especial. El proyecto se desarrolla en tres escenarios: el bosque, el embalse y la mina. En el bosque las estructuras para pernoctar quedan expuestas a agentes como el viento y las diferencias de temperatura, que hacen que durante la noche se acentúen las sensaciones de misterio. Junto al embalse se propone una estructura esbelta consta de cinco alturas, donde la niebla, evocadora de las novelas románticas del siglo XIX, envuelve al lector. Finalmente, junto a las minas abandonadas de Texeo, se encuentran los lavaderos y barracones donde vivían los mineros. La memoria histórica del lugar hace de él un perfecto escenario para experimentar con dispositivos de luces y sombras. Entre los espacios donde se manipula la luz y el agua, el pequeño teatro de marionetas chinescas y la superficie de leds que crece hasta los lavaderos de la ruina, serpentean caminos y se alternan espacios de descanso.

Claudia Manenti y Valentina Occhini

Network City 172

Network City es un entrelazamiento de carreteras, caminos y personas. Su objetivo es la actualización de una nueva fábrica urbana cuya identidad se ha degradado a lo largo de décadas. Aunque su identidad es industrial, se fundamenta en un paisaje virgen donde se erige la monumental mina de carbón de La Camocha, una compleja intersección de rampas y caminos insertados en el terreno mediante raíles metálicos.

La mina era el lugar donde la metamorfosis del elemento natural, el carbón, agitó y transformó el subsuelo. Ahora, la mina es el lugar donde la actividad humana interactúa con la industria y el paisaje. Riadas de gente se mueven en los dos caminos de peregrinación, la ruta de Santiago y la de la Plata, de la que La Camocha es el inicio. El area se activa gracias a las conexiones estratégicas directas con las vías rodadas y con las ciudades de los alrededores, como es el caso de Gijón, puerto deportivo y centro cultural. Los espacios del proyecto se organizan para acomodar el flujo de personas, generado de forma secuencial en ciertos momentos del año. El proyecto, no obstante, no se limita a estas experiencias y se abre con el mismo entusiasmo hacia la reactivación del área desde dentro gracias a la dedicación de sus ciudadanos.

FUNCIONES Y LÍMITES DE LA ARQUITECTURA 174 TURÍSTICA

234
José Miguel Iribas
Sociólogo especializado en el diagnóstico territorial, urbanístico y turístico.

172 Casi 60 años desde la eclosión del turismo en España con las primeras oleadas de clientes extranjeros en la Costa Brava y Mallorca, la arquitectura asociada a la actividad se mantiene, desde la perspectiva profesional más exigente, como una especie de irresoluble y fantasmagórica entelequia, especialmente porque, siendo el turismo la segunda actividad económica más dispendiosa en el uso del territorio tras la agricultura, y, de forma indiscutible, la que ha generado un mayor parque de edificaciones, muchas de singular tamaño, no termina de cuajar como una disciplina caracterizada por un lenguaje autónomo, diferencial y reconocible. No ocurre lo mismo en otros campos de la arquitectura como la industrial o la ferroviaria, que tienen muchas más limitaciones conceptuales previas y tantas o más exigencias funcionales.

Así, aunque parezca haber una estilística arquitectónica asociable al turismo, éste ha dado la espalda a la arquitectura culta, de manera que, salvo contadas excepciones, no hay piezas de entidad suficiente para dar contenido a un número monográfico de una revista de arquitectura. A principios del presente siglo se intentó, pero la revista no llegó a cuajar por falta de material suficiente.

EL TIEMPO, MERCANCÍA BÁSICA DE LA ACTIVIDAD TURÍSTICA

La banalidad de la arquitectura turística tiene que ver, desde luego, con la debilidad cultural de ofertantes y demandantes, pero, sobre todo, con el incontrovertible hecho de que las propuestas turísticas de éxito tienen como base la generación de secuencias temporales de actividad y no la producción de espacio. Gran parte de los errores cometidos en los últimos años por la Administración española consistió en pensar que la magnificencia de los espacios producidos era argumento capaz de generar flujos recurrentes de visitantes. Craso error: la mercancía del turismo es el tiempo. Lo que el turista realmente desea y compra es que se le proporcione una sucesión interminable de actividades simultáneamente alternativas (salvo, obviamente, en el caso de las ofertas finalistas). En tales condiciones, el espacio tiene una condición instrumental: constituye básicamente el soporte del tiempo, de manera que suele carecer de valor sustantivo en la formación del producto y en la percepción final del turista[1].

Por espectaculares que sean los espacios turísticos, la secuencia de tiempo asociada a su mera contemplación es muy limitada porque, como decía el maestro Henri Lefebvre "la emoción del paisajes es, salvo para la mirada profesional, instantánea". Lo que explica, por un lado, el escaso peso que tiene, por ejemplo, la contemplación directa del Cañón del Colorado[2] en la distribución temporal de las visitas organizadas (pues ocupa apenas 20 minutos de las tres horas que dura la excursión); y por otro, la abundancia de establecimientos hosteleros en los alrededores de los grandes hitos geológicos frecuentados por turistas. Estos triunfantes bares y restaurantes no hacen sino prolongar en el tiempo la emoción del espacio, factor que constituye precisamente la razón de su éxito.

La inobservancia de este principio elemental ha conducido a catastróficos errores de concepto que han derivado en sonoros fracasos de público y rentabilidad. Quizá el más reiteradamente mencionado sea la Ciudad de las Artes y las Ciencias de Valencia, donde los enfáticos contenedores de Calatrava, aunque son o han sido capaces de atraer visitantes y curiosos, no consiguen desviarlos hacia los espacios lucrativos que albergan, y retenerlos en el tiempo para que consuman, debido a la flagrante ausencia de contenido. Puesto que la contemplación no profesional de los edificios apenas tiene durabilidad, esta Ciudad de más de 1.500 millones de euros se ha convertido en un absurdo y despilfarrador decorado cuyas cifras de visitantes están muy alejadas de las expectativas que generó su inacabable inversión.

LAS TIPOLOGÍAS BÁSICAS DE LA ARQUITECTURA TURÍSTICA

Existen, como no podía ser menos, edificios destinados al turismo que han dado lugar a tipologías específicas: los hoteles-fábrica, los hoteles-crucero, los edificios de apartamentos de gestión unitaria e industrial, los parques temáticos, las discotecas y la arquitectura naval para cruceros. Estas tipologías se caracterizan por ser ligeras[3] banalizaciones de sus equivalentes originales, evidenciadas en la profusión de estilemas psicológicamente reconfortantes que alejan de la mente del turista toda sombra de preocupación. En ese escenario de curvas ondulantes y ornamentos aparatosos, en esos no-lugares invariablemente pintados con colores pastel, que son inmunes a toda influencia del contexto (geográfico, territorial, cultural, social), toda preocupación que amenace por alterar el orden vacacional debe ser automáticamente descartada. De ahí los paralelismos entre la arquitectura tópicamente turística y el imaginario disneyano en su versión más cursi y acaramelada. Por tanto, el turismo se ha desentendido de la arquitectura culta y se ha confinado en la reiteración de fórmulas muy simples que responden invariablemente a la función (requerimientos de eficiencia de un proceso industrializado, como factor racionalizador de producción) y a la representación (configuración formal basada en estilemas uniformizadores fácilmente reconocibles por la clientela, que se asocian a la bonanza climática, la paz social y la ausencia de acontecimientos negativos que perturben la estancia, todo lo cual remite a la eficiencia del consumo, medida en términos de retorno satisfactorio de la inversión de tiempo-dinero realizada).

LOS PROBLEMAS DEL TURISMO RURAL

El nacimiento del turismo rural como oferta consistente, amplia y organizada nació en Francia en los primeros años de la postguerra mundial, formando parte principal de una estrategia del Ministerio de Ordenación Territorial que intentaba detener el éxodo de la población rural hacia las ciudades, especialmente hacia la periferia parisina. Determinados por el favorable diferencial que arrojaba la comparación entre los fondos necesarios para estimular la permanencia en el mundo rural y los gastos que suponía su instalación en el mundo suburbial (nuevas viviendas, infraestructuras, equipamientos y servicios), se emprendió una larga y exitosa acción propagandística que se sustentaba sobre tres ideas fundamentales: la exaltación de la figura del agricultor como depositario y guardián de la Francia republicana, que arranca con el humor paleto pero inteligente de Fernandel y, pasando por Astérix y Obélix, llega hasta la controvertida figura de José Bové, de parecido físico y similar talante a los del héroe galo de papel; la puesta en valor de los productos agrícolas como base de la (entonces) mejor cocina del mundo; y, para terminar, la convicción de la superior calidad de la ingesta de los productos agrarios in situ, en clara superioridad sobre la realizada en la ciudad.

En España, sin embargo, las propuestas de turismo rural no responden a programación alguna. Son decisiones que se toman individual y espontáneamente, lo que tampoco debería ser determinante para su fracaso, pues países como Suiza o Austria han desarrollado potentes ofertas rurales no planificadas desde sus gobiernos. España se diferencia en que el proceso ha tendido al escaso tamaño de los establecimientos y a la dispersión y aislamiento. Por otro lado, las condiciones estructurales de la oferta, especialmente en lo que concierne al comportamiento estacional y, como derivado de éste, a la ínfima tasa de ocupación anual (20%), son del todo insuficientes para abordar inversiones significativas que permitan la cualificación y la especialización. Para finalizar, el escaso rigor de la legislación sobre la calidad de los establecimientos y de los servicios prestados, incrementa el sesgo aventurero[4] del viaje turístico rural, pues impide estandarizar y homogeneizar la oferta de alojamiento y restauración. En tales condiciones se producen dos consecuencias que para el turismo tienen efectos muy negativos: la recurrencia excesiva de la clientela y la progresiva reducción de la masa de usuarios potenciales, que, junto con lo anterior, comprometen gravemente la rentabilidad de las inversiones.

Los resultados obtenidos por el turismo rural muestran con nitidez el fracaso relativo de esta modalidad turística. Estadísticamente insignificante en la formación de la renta turística global, tampoco ha logrado complementar satisfactoriamente las rentas rurales, que siguen en continuado descenso, pues el carácter escaso de la oferta y su origen individual, sin financiación pública que ayude a su emergencia, impide que los efectos tengan carácter estructural. Por último, mientras que en Francia, según se ha mencionado antes, existió una campaña de exaltación de su mundo rural, el retrato social de la España agro-ganadera se ha configurado en dos direcciones: las oscuras tragedias negras de la España profunda, y/o la ridiculización del paleto y de la cultura rural. Así, frente a la dignidad y solidez de los héroes rurales galos, en España representan al mundo rural personajes tan grotescos como Paco Martínez Soria, Pajares y Esteso.

Al tratarse de aventuras singulares que se desarrollan en parajes por lo general montañosos y abruptos, es prácticamente imposible generar una acumulación suficiente que permita la emergencia de las más elementales ofertas de tiempo, que debe ser configurado en todos sus extremos por los propios clientes: un esfuerzo titánico abocado al fracaso. Por otro lado, en estos lugares de tanta fragilidad paisajística, es difícil incorporar nuevas edificaciones sin que se produzcan rupturas significativas del paisaje, que se amplían en correlación directa con el volumen de las nuevas intervenciones, lo que contribuye a debilitar las alternativas de uso dinámico del tiempo. De esta forma, y como he manifestado reiteradamente en trabajos de investigación, artículos y conferencias, "la condición de éxito del turismo rural es que no tenga éxito", porque, de tenerlo, ello significa-ría la devastación de su argumento principal.

Como se ha dicho, el crecimiento experimentado en la oferta de turismo rural es muy escaso: hay urbanizaciones recientes realizadas en la costa mediterránea que tienen un tamaño superior al crecimiento de la oferta rural de todo el territorio peninsular. Y ya puse de relieve, hace algunos años, que la oferta de plazas hoteleras acumuladas en el Rincón de Loix de Benidorm, superaba en número y categoría media la oferta hotelera y rural (agregadas) de todas las provincias cantábricas en conjunto, incluidas sus capitales y, con ellas, su oferta de hotelería urbana, más orientada a los negocios que al turismo.

Siendo éstas las condiciones básicas en que se mueve el turismo rural, ni la arquitectura puede aportar soluciones eficaces a sus principales problemas, ni tampoco el turismo rural puede ser, por su insignificancia económica y su inevitable propensión hacia los costes reducidos, una solución eficaz al problema de baja actividad que sufre la profesión actualmente.

¿QUÉ HACER?: LAS LÍNEAS DE ACTIVIDAD PROFESIONAL

Si bien el turismo ha podido prescindir, sin menoscabo de su pujanza, de la arquitectura culta, es evidente que la planificación territorial y la ordenación urbana de la actividad son absolutamente decisivas: determinan el dinamismo de la oferta de alojamiento, y, a su través, de la estructura de la demanda y del modelo de uso del tiempo/espacio; promueven un reparto diferenciado de las rentas turísticas, tanto mayores cuanto más densa y dinámica sea la oferta; resuelven (con distinto grado de acierto) los requerimientos infraestructurales y funcionales propios de la actividad y definen su impacto medioambiental y económico; estimulan la acumulación y la densidad (es decir, la complejidad y el mestizaje) o, alternativamente, producen aburridos y extensos suburbios monofuncionales abundantemente clorófilos; generan espacios densos y concentrados para el disfrute de las masas subalternas o planean recintos aislados para el goce exclusivo de los elegidos. Y otros de menor enjundia pero igualmente interesantes.

En España, la planificación territorial del turismo se ha hecho generalmente a escala de la Comunidad Autónoma, una escala excesiva para poder entrar en detalle sobre el modo en que ha de producirse un reparto de roles entre los diferentes espacios que componen el territorio que sea coherente con las disponibilidades y complementario en sus propuestas. O, alternativamente, a escala municipal, que es un espacio de complejidad insuficiente para incorporar un programa completo de usos complementarios.

En cualquiera de sus escalas, la planificación territorial del turismo ha sido una actividad clandestina para los agentes del sector, e inútil para las Administraciones concernidas, porque siempre ha procedido de departamentos administrativos muy débiles y/o insuficientemente legitimados. Y se ha realizado con escaso tino, bien propiciando la reiteración de modelos elaborados sobre la estela de los destinos de éxito, pero sin comprender nunca las razones del mismo; bien consagrando los reiterativos e insustanciales lemas que la clase política española vincula al éxito de las propuestas turísticas: la baja densidad, la imperturbable clorofilia, la vocación rural o suburbana de las masas, o, como un concepto de inanidad absoluta, pues nada aporta: la calidad, mantra redentor que por querer ser referente de todo, no logra explicar ni definir nada.

Por su parte, la ordenación urbana de las ciudades turísticas, más que atenerse al modo en que deben resolver los problemas de la oferta y de la propia actividad, se han orientado a los menesteres propios de la planificación urbanística española: aprovechamientos, repartos y otros conceptos de tanto interés jurídico y práctico para garantizar la fluidez del tráfico inmobiliario entre los agentes urbanos, como de tan escaso valor como referentes de calidad de las ciudades.

Lo que termina siendo evidente es que las tesis sobre las que se edifica nuestra legislación urbanística, además de conspirar contra la ciudad y de haber producido espacios de pésima calidad urbanística (si nos centramos en sus efectos paisajísticos, medioambientales, sociales, económicos y convivenciales, que son, a la postre, los más decisivos), tienen otro efecto más pernicioso: con la legislación actual, ninguna de las más exitosas y rentables ciudades turísticas hubiera podido desarrollarse. Deriva que debe corregirse mediante un sistema de planificación integral en la que la arquitectura,
junto con otras disciplinas que posibiliten la 184
aprehensión de la realidad compleja, debe jugar un papel esencial.

1. Las investigaciones que en su día realizamos en el Seminario de Sociología Urbana, Rural y del Ocio bajo la dirección de Mario Gaviria así lo ponían de manifiesto.

2. La cita al Cañón del Colorado es pertinente porque se trata de un hito geológico cuya fruición es espectacular y evidente para todos los clientes potenciales. Su condición de espacio-espectáculo viene garantizada por su carácter abierto: para comprender su magnitud y asimilar su singularidad no hacen falta conocimientos científicos.

3. Se emplea el término ligero en el irónico sentido que atribuía J.A. Marina a lo ingenioso y liviano en su celebrado ensayo “Elogio y refutación del ingenio”.

4. Pese a la extendida convicción de que un buen viaje

turístico es el que aporta aventura y el exotismo, los estudios y las encuestas coinciden en señalar que los turistas prefieren experiencias muy controladas que eviten sorpresas desagradables, especialmente cuando los clientes son familias con niños, lo que es muy frecuente en el turismo rural.

233

BIOGRAPHIES

DAVID GOODMAN

Director del Grado en Arquitectura de la IE University. Obtuvo su Master en Arquitectura de la *Harvard University Graduate School of Design*, y completó licenciaturas con honores en Gobierno y en Historia de la Arquitectura y Urbanismo en la *Cornell University*. Es co-autor del libro *An Introduction to Architecture Theory: 1968 to the Present*, y su obra ha sido publicada en las revistas *a + t* and *Log*, en la antología *Chicago Architecture: Histories, Revisions, Alternatives*, y en el libro *Walter Netsch: A Critical Appreciation and Sourcebook*. Antes de cofundar el estudio *Roadwork Studio*, trabajó en el estudio de Rafael Moneo en Madrid y a David Woodhouse Architects y Nagle Hartray Architects en Chicago. Ha sido profesor de arquitectura en el *Illinois Institute of Technology* (IIT) en Chicago, en la *Harvard University Graduate School of Design*, y en el *Boston Architectural College*. El trabajo de *Roadwork Studio* ha sido destacado en la exposición *Burnham 2.0* en el Museo de Historia de Chicago, y la oficina recibió el segundo premio en el concurso nacional para el Centro Cívico de Reconquista en Argentina.

PABLO ORIOL

Pablo Oriol es arquitecto (2005). Ha sido comisario de actividades culturales para la Subdirección General de Arquitectura del Ministerio de Fomento, para la ETSAM y para el Instituto Cervantes entre 1999 y 2002. En 2003 fue socio fundador de Nolaster Oficina de Arquitectura en Madrid, en la que desarrolló su actividad profesional hasta 2007. A principios de 2005 estableció FRPO Rodríguez & Oriol Architecture Landscape junto a Fernando Rodríguez. Han sido distinguidos con el *Design Vanguard* 2012 y el premio *Europe 40 under 40* (2009). También han sido premiados en la IX Bienal de Arquitectura Española (2007), la 9ª Muestra de Arquitectos Jóvenes Españoles (2006), el *Bauwelt Preis* 2007 y los *Wallpaper Design Awards* 2007. Es, junto con Lina Toro y Fernando Rodríguez, Director de Proyecto Fin de Grado de Arquitectura en *IE University*, y Profesor Asociado de Proyectos Arquitectónicos en la ETSAM. De forma complementaria ha sido Profesor de *Design Thinking* en el *Launch Program del Iinternational MBA* de *IE Business School*, y participa en el proyecto de investigación "Beyond Tourism", escribiendo artículos y editando libros como "The Infrastructural Beach".

FERNANDO RODRÍGUEZ RAMÍREZ

Arquitecto (2003). Desde 2005 desarrolla su labor profesional junto a Pablo Oriol en FRPO Rodriguez & Oriol, obteniendo reconocimientos como los premios *Design Vanguard* 2012, *Europe 40 Under 40* (2009) y *Bauwelt Preis* (2007). Su trabajo ha sido además seleccionado en la IX Bienal de Arquitectura Española, la 9ª Muestra de Jóvenes Arquitectos Antonio Camuñas (2006) y los *Wallpaper Design Awards* (2007). Sus obras y proyectos han sido publicados y expuestos en publicaciones y exposiciones colectivas en varios países, formando parte recientemente de la muestra "Cut 'n'Paste" del MoMA de Nueva York. Es, junto con Lina Toro y Pablo Oriol, Director de Proyecto Fin de Grado de Arquitectura en *IE University*, y Profesor Asociado de Proyectos Arquitectónicos en la ETSAM. Actualmente escribe su tesis doctoral "El Entendimiento Infraestructural del Proyecto Arquitectónico" y publica artículos en Circo, Sociedad y Utopía, Quaderns y Pasajes Diseño. Ha editado los libros "Ma/SP Proyectos de Arquitectura", "Matterscapes" y "The Infrastructural Beach". Participa en los proyectos de investigación "Emergencia Creativa", "Beyond Tourism" y "TRLab".

LINA TORO

Arquitecta colombiana graduada con honores por la UPB de Medellín, acreditada por el RIBA (2001), y arquitecta española por la ETSA de Sevilla (2007). Ha trabajado en Medellín, Palma de Mallorca y Rotterdam. Es principal del Estudio Lina-Toro.arch y tercera parte del estudio Dosmasunoarquitectos. Desde 2003 ha sido premiada en 27 concursos nacionales e internacionales. Dentro de su obra construida y en proceso destacan las "102 viviendas en Carabanchel" EMVS, "67 viviendas en Colmenar Viejo" IVIMA y el "Centro de Servicios Sociales de Móstoles". Su obra está ampliamente publicada y expuesta. Es co-directora de la revista "Arquitectos" del CSCAE de España (2006-). Editó y comisarió el ciclo de exposiciones y monografías "Monoespacios", COAM (2004-2007). Es columnista de arquitectura en *Ivorypress* (2013-). Es profesora de proyectos la ETSA de Madrid en el Aula PFC (2008-), y pertenece al Grupo de Investigación "Prácticas Emergentes en Arquitectura" (2013-), dirigido por Juan Herreros. Es co-directora del PFG *IE University*, donde también es profesora de *Design Studio* (2013-).

RAFAEL ÍÑIGUEZ DE ONZOÑO

Arquitecto por la Escuela Técnica Superior de Arquitectura de Madrid (1992) en la que prepara su tesis doctoral. Actualmente es Profesor de *Construction Systems* y de *Technical Practices* en *IE University*, y del Máster en Dirección-Gestión patrimonial y *Facility Management* de la UEM desde su comienzo. Ha impartido clases de prácticas de Construcción en la Cátedra de Construcción de la ETSAM y Proyectos fin de carrera en la Escuela de Arquitectura de interiores. Desarrolla su actividad profesional en su Estudio con Proyectos de edificación para la Administración –fruto de Concursos- y el sector privado, en los ámbitos residencial, terciario, sanitario, comercial, Arquitectura de representación, Centros de datos, mobiliario, exposiciones… tanto en obra nueva como en rehabilitación, convencido de que el arquitecto constructor en la actualidad forma parte de un equipo multidisciplinar que le permite abordar los programas más complejos. Con el objetivo de conciliar categorías aparentemente contradictorias, como globalidad y realidad local ha trabajado en España y el extranjero, con edificios en Berlín, Guinea Ecuatorial y Astana. En su trayectoria también ha trabajado en Empresas constructoras y promotoras.

MANUEL PÉREZ ROMERO

Ph.D. en Arquitectura de la Universidad Politécnica de Madrid, B.Arch de la Universidad de Las Palmas de Gran Canaria. También estudió arquitectura en la Universidad Politécnica de

Torino, la Universidad Politécnica de Milano y la Universidad de Westminster. Es profesor de Proyectos en ETSAG en Alcalá de Henares desde 2001, y ha sido profesor de Proyectos de Diseño en ETSA Madrid. Es también profesor de Sistemas de Construcción, el Taller de Construcción y el Proyecto Final de Carrera a la Escuela de Arquitectura de la IE. Ha colaborado con Soriano & Asociados (Madrid) y el *Foreign Office Architects* (Londres). Fundó la asociación nodo17 architects (2002), y ha recibido premios en numerosos concursos nacionales e internacionales. Tiene más de 100 publicaciones en diferentes revistas y libros. Recientemente, la editorial coreana *Damdi Publishing Co.* ha publicado un monográfico "mook" sobre la obra de nodo17. Sus intereses se centran en dos escalas arquitectónicas diferentes y casi opuestas: la pequeña arquitectura basada en la técnica y la invención; y el urbanismo basado en la comprensión de una arquitectura lejos del equilibrio, orientada al tiempo y a la información.

JOSÉ MIGUEL IRIBAS

Sociólogo especializado en territorio, urbanismo y turismo. Formó parte del equipo ganador de la Beca March sobre urbanismo y arquitectura para 1972-1973, que realizó los primeros estudios urbanos sobre las nuevas ciudades turísticas españolas y obtuvo el 1º premio del I Concurso Nacional de Ensayo Turístico. Fue durante 7 años Jefe de Estudios del Ayuntamiento de Benidorm. Ha realizado más de 190 estudios y colaborado en 40 planes de ordenación urbana y en diversos Planes Especiales portuarios, y en la redacción de las Directrices de Ordenación Territorial de Asturias, Comunidad Valenciana, Extremadura y Galicia. Patrono de la Fundación Arquitectura y Sociedad y consejero asesor de la Fundación Metrópoli. Ha participado en diversos proyectos urbanos y turísticos, en España y en otros países (Argelia, Marruecos, Brasil, Taiwán, Italia, Francia, Rusia, Perú, Argentina, China y Corea). Ha realizado 60 estrategias y programas para proyectos de Jean Nouvel, Renzo Piano, Patxi Mangado, Jaime Lerner, Aicequip, Ben van Berkel, Rex Architects, Iñaki Ábalos, Juan Herreros y Benedetta Tagliabue y otros.

LINNA CHOI Y TARIK OUALALOU

Socios y cofundadores, de KILO, con sedes en París y Casablanca. Estudiaron en la Universidad de Harvard, Cambridge y la Universidad de Yale, New Haven (Linna) y en la *École d'Architecture Paris-Malaquais*, Paris y *Rhode Island School of Design*, Providence. Han sido finalistas en el *Grand Prix AFEX* 2014, ganadores del concurso *Young Arab Architects* (18 de junio 2012), y nominados para el Premio Aga Khan en 2009. Su obra ha aparecido en exposiciones en todo el mundo. Últimamente, en la Bienal de Venecia de 2014, *Pavillon du Maroc*, 2014; *Arab Contemporary, Louisiana Museum of Modern Art*, Copenhagen, Dinamarca, 2014; *Young Arab Architects*. CA 'ASI, Venecia (Bienal de Venecia) 2012. *L'Institut du Monde Arabe*, París, 2012. Han sido profesores invitados en Rice University, Rhode Island School of Design, Harvard University Graduate School of Design and l'Ecole d'Architecture Paris-Malaquais.

ELIA ZENGHELIS y ELENI GIGANTES

Elia Zenghelis es arquitecto y docente de arquitectura. Divide su tiempo entre Bruselas, Londes, Rotterdam y Atenas. Estudió, y más tarde impartió clases en la AA de Londres. Como uno de los fundadores originales de OMA, trabajó junto a Rem Koolhaas hasta el 1987, año en el que estableció el estudio Gigantes Zenghelis Architects en Atenas y Bruselas con Eleni Gigantes. Ha sido tutor de Fin de Carrera en el Instituto Berlage durante más de 10 años, y profesor en la Academia de Bellas Artes de Dusseldorf, profesor invitado en el EPFL de Lausanne, el ETH de Zurich, y en la Academia de Arquitectura de Mendrisio. También ha impartido clases en Princeton, UCLA, la Universidad de Columbia y otras escuelas de EEUU, América del Sur, España y Japón. Ha recibido el premio Annie Spink del RIBA por su contribución excepcional a la docencia de arquitectura. Sus trabajos actuales incluyen el *Flemish Administration Centre* en Lovaina recientemente concluido.

IZASKUN CHINCHILLA

Arquitecto por la E.T.S.A.M. desde 2001. Desde esa fecha dirige su propia firma Izaskun Chinchilla Arquitectos. Es *Senior Teaching Fellow* y *Senior Research Associate* en *Bartlett School.* Profesora de Proyectos en la *Ecole Spéciale d'Architecture* (París). Profesora Asociada de Proyectos Arquitectónicos en la Escuela Superior de Arquitectura de Madrid. Tiene una dilatada experiencia en docencia, *Head University Geneva*, Universidad de Alicante, Universidad San Pablo Ceu, IE, Instituto d'Arquitectura Avançada de Catalunya (Barcelona) y Universidad Europea de Madrid. Ha sido investigadora becada en Universidades Internacionales como *Columbia University* o *Princeton University*. Más de 200 revistas y publicaciones de arquitectura han hecho referencia a su obra. Sus propuestas han sido galardonadas en diferentes convocatorias. Ha intervenido como conferenciante o como comisaria en más de 150 foros especializados en universidades e instituciones en todo el mundo. Su obra ha sido expuesta en la 8a y 10a *Biennale di Venecia, New Trends in Architecture Europe-Asia* 2009, Innovación Abierta, *Fresh Madrid*, Jovénes Arquitectos Españoles, en la V Bienal de Arquitectura y Diseño de Sao Paulo. Su contribución a la arquitectura ha sido reconocida con una Mención Honorífica en el *Arc Vision Prize* 2013 que destaca la carrera de mujeres arquitectas en todo el mundo.

JUAN ELVIRA

Arquitecto por la ETSAM (1997) y fundador en el año 2000 de Murado y Elvira Arquitectos. Profesor Asociado de Proyectos Arquitectónicos en la ETSAM desde 2001 y *Design Critic* y profesor de *Urban Workshop* en la IE University desde 2013. Becado por La Caixa para realizar estudios de posgrado (1998), es Máster por la Universidad de Columbia de Nueva York (*Advanced Architectural Design,* 2000). Profesor invitado y conferenciante en diversas universidades nacionales e internacionales, como la NTNU (*Norges teknisk-naturvitenskapelige universitet*) de Trondheim, la Universidad Internacional de Cataluña o la Escuela de Arquitectura de Alicante, donde en 2001 condujo el proyecto de investigación 'Espacios Tácticos', que fue presentado en *Archilab'02* (Orleáns, Francia). Sus proyectos han sido premiados en diversos concursos nacionales e internacionales, y han sido expuestos, entre otros, en *Freshmadrid* y en la undécima *Mostra Internazionale de Architettura di Venezia.* Recientemente ha finalizado la construcción de una residencia de estudiantes y un eje verde urbano en Trondheim, nominados para el Premio Nacional de Arquitectura de Noruega (2012), y seleccionados en la Bienal de Arquitectura Española de 2013. Lleva a cabo una labor crítica y editorial que comenzó como director de la revista Oeste de Arquitectura, seguida por la publicación de numerosos ensayos en libros y revistas especializadas. Su tesis doctoral, 'Arquitectura Fantasma', es una investigación sobre la práctica cultural y tecnológica de la producción de efectos atmosféricos arquitectónicos.

MÓNICA GARCÍA

Mónica García es arquitecta por la Escuela Técnica Superior de Arquitectura de Valencia (1998). Se graduó en el Master en Arquitectura, MArch II, en la *Graduate School of Design, Harvard University* (2002). Obtuvo el Diploma de Estudios Avanzados en la Escuela Técnica Superior de Arquitectura de Madrid (2004). Desde 2002 es profesora del Departamento de Proyectos Arquitectónicos de la Escuela Técnica Superior de Arquitectura de Valencia. Ha sido profesora asociada en *Boston Arquitecture Center BAC* (2002), profesora asistente en la *Graduated School of Design, Harvard University* (2001-2002), así como profesora visitante en *L'École d'Architecture de Paris-La Villette* (2010-2011) y en *The Vienna University of Technology* (2011). Entre 1997 y 2000 colaboró con diferentes estudios de arquitectura en París: Ateliers 234, Olivier Chaslin Architecte y Architectures Jean Nouvel. En 2003 estableció su práctica profesional en Valencia. Junto a Frédéric Floquet es fundadora de Garcia-Floquet arquitectos, cuyo trabajo ha sido premiado en diversos concursos públicos nacionales e internacionales: Viviendas sociales en Nanterre (Francia), Inmueble de viviendas Rue Louis Favre en Ginebra, Cámara de Comercio en Valencia, Instituto Enseñanza Secundaria 9 d'Octubre en Carlet, Escuela Infantil Blasco Ibañez en Cheste. Su obra sobre vivienda colectiva fue seleccionada en la X Bienal de Arquitectura Española y Urbanismo, X BEAU, y finalista en la XI BEAU.

PEDRO IGLESIAS

Nace en 1958 en Madrid, donde cursa los estudios de Arquitectura en la Escuela de Madrid, y obtiene grado de doctor. Su tesis doctoral consigue el premio extraordinario de la Universidad Politécnica de Madrid y sirve de base para la redacción del libro "La Habitación del Enfermo" publicado por la Caja de Arquitectos en 2011. Trabaja en el estudio del Arquitecto José María García de Paredes durante los años 1983 y 1984 y posteriormente forma con Jose Luis Rodriguez-Noriega y Silvia Gámez Carrasco la sociedad Noriega, Iglesias, Gámez, Arquitectos S.L. con la lleva a cabo obras en edificios singulares como el Teatro Real de Madrid y el Hospital de San Pedro de Logroño. Ha obtenido diversos premios entre los que destacan los premios de Urbanismo Arquitectura y Obra Pública del Ayuntamiento de Madrid y la Medalla de plata de la bienal *MIAMI+BEACH School of Architecture Florida International University* con el Instituto Americano de Arquitectos (AIA). Desde 1985 mantiene su actividad como concertista de clave con una especialización en el repertorio barroco español.

LAURA MARTÍNEZ DE GUEREÑU

Arquitecta con premio extraordinario fin de carrera (1998) y doctora en Proyectos Arquitectónicos por la Universidad de Navarra (2006), se gradúa con premio extraordinario en el *Máster in Design Studies de Harvard University* (2004) para el que obtuvo una beca de la Fundación Rafael del Pino. Desde 2008 es profesora y coordinadora de ciclos de conferencias en *IE University*. Ha sido profesora en La Salle-Universitat Ramon Llull (2006-2008), *Visiting Fellow* en Harvard University (2004-2006) y profesora ayudante en la Universidad de Navarra (1998-2003). Su labor investigadora se ha centrado en una línea principal que explora temas de percepción, narrativas de proyecto y puntos de intersección entre la arquitectura, la tecnología y el arte. Ha publicado más de una veintena de artículos sobre arquitectos, artistas y pensadores de tradición moderna como Josef Albers, Mies van der Rohe, Romano Guardini o Le Corbusier. Es editora de 'Josef Albers. Una Antología' (1924-1978) (2014), 'Rafael Moneo. Portfolio Internacional'. 1985-2012 (2013) y 'Rafael Moneo. Apuntes sobre 21 obras' (2010), todas ellas con sus respectivas ediciones en inglés.

ANDREW VARELA

fundador del estudio OOAA, Inc. basado en Nueva York. Es arquitecto acreditado en los EE.UU. y en España. Andrew tiene un Master en Arquitectura por la *Harvard University Graduate School of Design*, un Master en Proyectos Arquitectónicos Avanzados de la ETSAM y una *B.A. de Brown University*. Su experiencia profesional se ha centrado en tipos de edificios específicos que incluyen, entre otros: instituciones culturales, tales como la expansión y renovación de la *Juilliard School of Music* y *Alice Tully Hall* del *Lincoln Center* de Nueva York; los edificios académicos, como la *Whitman School of Management* de la *Syracuse University*; los proyectos residenciales, como el *Sky House Tower* en Nueva York; los edificios comerciales, tales como la tienda insignia de *Abercrombie and Fitch* en Madrid; y los proyectos de infraestructura, como la línea de metro de la 2ª Avenida de Nueva York. Actualmente es profesor adjunto en el *New Jersey Institute of Technology* en Newark, donde es profesor de estudio. Es también miembro del jurado para el PFG en la *IE University* en Segovia, España.

UNCHARTED

The New Landscapes Of Tourism

Published by
IE University
Undergraduate Architecture Degree
Calle Cardenal Zúñiga, 12
40003 Segovia. España
&
Actar Publishers
355 Lexington Avenue, 8th Floor
New York, NY 10017, USA

Editors:
Juan Elvira
David Goodman
Pablo Oriol
Roger Paez i Blanch
Fernando Rodríguez
Lina Toro

Graphic design:
Juan Elvira & Clara Murado

Translation and copyediting:
Angela Kay Bunning

Distribution:
Actar D, New York
www.actar-d.com

New York
355 Lexington Avenue, 8th Floor
New York, NY 10017
T +1 212 966 2207
F +1 212 966 2214
salesnewyork@actar-d.com

Barcelona
Roca i Batlle 2
08023 Barcelona
salesbarcelona@actar-d.com
eurosales@actar-d.com

ISBN 978-1-940291-48-2
Cataloging-in-Publication data for this book is available from the Library of Congres, Washington D.C., USA.